Domestique

Domestique

The True Life Ups and Downs of a Tour Cyclist

Charly Wegelius and Tom Southam

EBURY
PRESS

7 9 10 8 6

First published in 2013 by Ebury Press, an imprint of Ebury Publishing
A Random House Group company

The Random House Group Limited Reg. No. 954009

Addresses for companies within the Random House Group can be found at
www.randomhouse.co.uk

A CIP catalogue record for this book is available from the British Library

The Random House Group Limited supports the Forest Stewardship
Council® (FSC®), the leading international forest-certification organisation.
Our books carrying the FSC label are printed on FSC®-certified paper. FSC is
the only forest-certification scheme supported by the leading environmental
organisations, including Greenpeace. Our paper procurement policy can be
found at www.randomhouse.co.uk/environment

Designed and set by seagulls.net

Printed and bound by CPI Group (UK) Ltd, Croydon, CR0 4YY

ISBN 9780091950934

To buy books by your favourite authors and register for offers visit
www.randomhouse.co.uk

Dulce bellum inexpertis

(War is sweet to those who do not fight)

GERARD DIDIER ERASMUS

Contents

Author's Note

Like most normal human beings I didn't set out in life thinking that one day I would be writing about it in a book. Some people might, but not me. Even when the possibility of writing a book came my way I didn't know at first if I was the person to do it. I didn't have anything to confess, but I had things to say. The book had to be right.

By July 2011, when this book first started to come to life, I had a clear idea of what I wanted to write about: life inside the professional peloton. However, the events of the past two years have made this vision very hard to stick to without devoting a disproportionate amount of space to a topic that played a very marginal part in my life.

As a professional cyclist whose career ran from 2000 to 2011 I lived through a turbulent time for the sport – full to bursting with scandals, drug raids, confessions, accusations, revelations and all the difficulties that came with a doping culture that was deeply embedded in the sport.

It is therefore a bitter-sweet taste to know that in 2013 there is enough interest in the sport that I love that a guy like me can write a book for an enthusiastic audience, yet at the same time have to be at pains to explain that the book – like my career – does not contain any exciting doping stories, nor does it attempt to.

It's not to say that a fair amount of doping wasn't going on around me, I'm sure. Anyone who feels the need can go and look up the names of the people I rode for and with and find numerous doping violations against their names. I am not trying to deny that. I have, however, chosen not to focus on those facts.

I have remained true to my vision of the book. This book, the one that I wanted to write, is focused on something else: an entire cycling career. Yes, doping makes an appearance or two, there is no way it couldn't, but I would like to feel that its small appearances in this book reflect just how minor a part it really played in my life as a cyclist. There was simply much more to be getting on with, so much more to the job and so much other stuff for me to be worrying about.

The role that I played, that of a *domestique*, a foot soldier in the sport, was often a thankless task that kept me perched precariously between the gutter and the stars for eleven long working years. It is this story alone that I feel I am qualified to tell, through the life experiences that I have had.

I can tell you that I have spared some people in telling this story in this form. Some of them I have no doubt unwittingly protected in small ways. If I have done so, their absence only serves to somehow repay some act of human decency that they themselves have shown to me. There are others who showed the opposite of decency to me, whom I have been forced to protect by the lawyers-who-know-what's-good-for-me, and to them I say: You got lucky, bastards.

Whatever the case, I can tell you in all honesty that I spared very little of myself in telling this story, and that, after all, is all I can really do.

Charly Wegelius, February 2013

Foreword

This book begins at almost the very moment I met Charly Wege-lius for the first time – the 1999 World Road Race Championships, in Verona.

I was fascinated by Charly when I first met him in Mike Taylor's room of the Hotel Antico Termine. I knew that on that very day Charly had signed his first professional contract, and when I looked at him all I could do was wonder, 'How did you do that?'

When I saw Charly in the flesh that day, I was seeing him the way that thousands of people have seen him from the roadside over the years: as an object of wonder, of athleticism and of profession-alism on the racing bike. My mind at the time – like his once had been – was obsessed with the idea of being a professional cyclist. I aspired to being a racer so much and, through growing up in the UK in the eighties, I had been so far removed from that world that professional cyclists seemed like gods to me.

Here was a man who saw cycling the same way I did, who came from where I came from, and who somehow had made it all work.

He had crossed the divide from where I was to where I dreamed of being. Four years my senior and with his professional contract in his back pocket, Charly Wegelius seemed like a man who had achieved the near impossible.

I followed Charly's footsteps into the professional peloton in my own ragged time, and over the years we became friends. Our paths diverged abruptly, however, when, after only three years in the peloton, I upped and walked away from the world of European professional cycling. I had found that it was nothing like I imagined it would be, and the shock of that realisation sent me reeling.

We remained friends, though, as Charly carried on with his increasingly successful racing career and I went off to learn how to write, and our paths crossed professionally again, but in a vastly different way: the opportunity eventually arose to write this story together. It was a story I knew well because, just like Kurt Vonnegut sitting next to Billy Pilgrim in the latrines in his masterpiece *Slaughterhouse Five*, at many times during the events in this book I too was right there.

I was there in Verona when Charly was the toast of British Cycling, and witnessed the awkwardness when he arrived at the Worlds in Plouay a year later. I was quite often there staying in his spare room when he came home to his inhospitable apartment and empty fridge while he rode for De Nardi, and I was right there, too, swapping turns when he made the biggest mistake he would make in his racing career.

I knew exactly what it was to feel average in that peloton, and to try so hard to be a decent human being in amongst all of the cutthroat realities of the sport.

And yet, at the same time, I wasn't entirely sure that his was the book that I wanted to write. The fact was, no matter how frankly he spoke of his life at the time we were both riders, I had never truly shaken the belief that Charly Wegelius had always had it all figured out.

It wasn't until I first sat down with Charly over a couple of mid-morning Negronis in December 2011 to discuss the book that I saw just how precarious life as a cyclist had been for Charly, too. I knew then this was the book I wanted to write, for I realised his was a story about cycling that hadn't been told.

This was a story that we both wanted the world to know – the story of the middle of the bunch, the story of the riders who go to work each day having sacrificed everything in their lives – girl-friends, jobs, wives and even their precious youth – to be there and to turn themselves inside out for little more than an average salary and the chance to do it all again the next day.

Charly lived the life he set out to – all the way to its conclusion, despite what it took to do it, and how many scars he picked up along the way. Charly lived a life the rest of us didn't, or couldn't, and getting him to pass on the story wasn't always easy for either of us, but it needed doing.

The purpose of this book, I thought, was in part to dispel the glorious myth that the professional cyclist is anything more than a normal person – albeit one with some physical talent. But, ironically, once I had seen the facts of Charly's life laid bare – the things that he dealt with to have the career that he did – I again marvelled at his achievement. It was a life that required the strength and determination of the most committed character to see it through. But it was also nothing like the life Charly had imagined either.

Through the experience that I've had of writing this book, and after knowing Charly for all these years, I have the answers as to why and how he got to where he did. But, even with all of that right in front of me, strewn through piles of papers, recorded interviews and the many hundreds of conversations we've had throughout the process of writing this book, there is a part of me that still thinks, 'How did you do that?'

Tom Southam
December 2012

Prologue

I live in fear, and that is what probably motivates me to do well a lot of the time – because, really, I'm just shitting myself.

The moment I knew, really *knew*, that I would become a professional cyclist, I was on the rollers warming up for the Under-23 World Time Trial Championships in Verona, October 1999.

There is always a big hubbub at those championships because the Under-23 category is packed with riders who are desperate to turn professional. The championships are the culmination of a lot of these guys' early lives, and, being young, the riders get very emotionally drawn in to the experience. It's an unavoidably tense event.

The competition to turn professional is fierce, and a time trial isn't like a road race where you can roll around in the protection of a group of teammates before the start. At time trials you all warm up individually on stationary trainers, within feet of the guys you have been competing with all year; guys you have consciously (or not) developed an intense dislike towards, without even knowing them. Everyone is jealous of everyone else.

I hate the mêlée: the press, the managers, the other riders and all the shit that goes with great expectations. But on that day, as I started my warm-up surrounded by my own crowd of helpers and observers, I saw two men in blue tops pushing their way through to me. Their sports jackets were printed with the multicoloured cube logo of Mapei, instantly recognisable to any cycling fan in the world as sponsors of the Mapei professional cycling team, the biggest and most iconic team in the sport at the time.

Alvaro Crespi and Serge Parsani, two of the directors of the team, were coming to find me to say hello. In amongst the jealous and curious glares from the other riders I was already proud enough just because it was *me* they were coming to see. Skinny little me had two of the managers of fucking *Mapei* stopping by for a chat. I was like a dog with two dicks.

It is hard to think and talk as you warm up, with the blood rushing into your legs and the loud drone of the rollers, set against the buzz of activity of the team staff and the booming commentary on the early starters coming out of the speakers around the circuit. But as they strolled over my mind was quickening with excitement. I already recognised the two of them from an earlier meeting, and in that moment I flashed back to the first time they had approached me – a team that I wouldn't have even dared to dream I would be riding for half-way through the year …

That fateful first meeting with Mapei had come on the way to the start of another time trial. It was half a world away at the Trans Canada stage race – a tiny pro event that happened once and was supposed to inspire the Canadian people into becoming a more unified country. As I went towards the start gate that day, Parsani stopped me in my tracks and said, 'Are you … ?'

He looked at my number, and then he looked at me, and I thought he was going to ask me, 'Are you off before my boy?' He fumbled, trying to speak English, which he couldn't, so I relieved by him telling him I could speak French, which put us both at ease. He asked again, in French this time, 'Are you Charly Wegelius?' I confirmed I was indeed Wegelius. He simply asked, 'We were wondering if you'd be interested in coming and riding for our team.'

I was dumbfounded. I thought that he had either got the wrong guy or that he was talking about some amateur team he was involved with. But he wasn't: he was talking about Mapei, and he was talking about me.

He asked for my phone number, and I went and rode the time trial in a complete fucking daze. I almost went off course; my mind was racing. I was blown away.

The trouble was that when Parsani asked me for a phone number I didn't know the number of the apartment I rented. I couldn't remember the number of my own mobile phone. Instead, the only number I could drag out of my brain was the same phone number I had memorised as a kid when I'd take ten pence out with me to call from a phone box if anything went wrong on one of my expeditions on my bike: I had given Parsani the phone number for my mother's house in York.

As I careered around the time trial course in a state so confused I was close to crashing, I realised this meant that I was going to have to go and stay at home when I returned from the race, for however long it took for them to call.

The offer had come so out of the blue that I was suddenly petrified that the manager might ring up and not be able to get through to me because I had popped out to the shops to buy a quarter of wine gums, or taken the dog for a walk, and I thought the interest that they had suddenly shown might just as rapidly disappear again.

But eventually, after a few agonising days waiting at home, the call came. Alvaro Crespi rang and invited me to undergo some testing for the team in Italy, and even just hearing his thick Italian accent excited me. I was a well-travelled guy by this point, but Italy was still foreign, still exotic. North-western France – where I'd lived as an amateur – was one thing in those days. Everyone went to France; it was foreign, but it wasn't exotic. Italy was completely different. It was further away, it was Mediterranean and intriguing, and it was also somewhere I knew very little about.

I took that call sat in the bay window that was covered in slobber from our dogs, who would stand there all day yelping at passers-by. Listening to this crackly Italian accent on my blue BT telephone was like listening in on an alternate reality. It was surreal. In an instant I had gone from being shown a complete lack of interest, even from small teams, to the biggest cycling team in the world courting me. I wanted to scream, 'You've got the wrong guy!'

I wanted to ask, 'Are you sure about this?'

If you were Belgian or French, the process to become a professional cyclist was much more gradual. Your team manager would probably take you to meet somebody at a race somewhere; you'd go out training with pros and you would know exactly what you had to do and where you would be heading. But in England you were completely isolated, you didn't really talk to people you went out to races with, and my teammates on the national team that year knew even less than me.

After the call, I went in for testing a week before the Worlds and stayed on the shores of Lake Como with my coach, Ken Matheson (then the head coach at the British Cycling Federation), for company. There I found myself at the doors of a world of wonder; the 'pinch me' moments were countless. I was overwhelmed by excitement when I first switched on an Italian TV and saw dozens and dozens of channels of Eurotrash shit. It was exotic, in the overblown way that Italy is exotic, from the warm autumn light that you get there in October to the man on the sales channel on TV, so worked up by the unbeatable value of the bargains he was advertising he would sound like he was having an asthma attack.

I went to the Mapei centre and saw their slick, branded professionalism; I sat in a real Italian traffic jam (exciting in itself if you've never heard that cacophony of horns) while the legendary trainer Max Testa casually spun stories to Ken and me about the days the Motorola professional team had been based right there in Como. It seemed like a door had opened for me to waltz right through. I just couldn't quite believe that it was being opened *for me*.

After going through the tribulations of testing with the team I felt much more confident when I saw Crespi and Parsani in Verona on the day of the World Championships, but still with nothing signed I couldn't be sure that this dream was going to become a reality. As I continued my warm-up that day in Verona, Crespi and Parsani watched my body heat up with the effort, my face reddening and breaking into a sweat as the time ticked down to the start. Finally, they decided it was the right moment. I got to hear the words I so needed to hear: 'Everything is OK for next year. We'll take you in the team. We'll come to sign you tomorrow at your hotel.'

Finally there was confirmation. I was really going to sign for a professional team, and the best one in the world to boot: my career as a professional cyclist was going to happen.

I nearly fell off the rollers.

I had spent practically the whole year riding as one of the best amateurs in Europe, but the lack of offers from teams had me feeling like I had almost failed. Suddenly, the best team in the world assured me it was taking me on. To the outside world it made complete sense, but I was in shock. The speed and surreal way in which events had passed left me feeling like it was all an elaborate hoax.

It was a feeling that I never shook, despite the enormous sense of pride I felt as I signed my first professional contract with such an esteemed team. That sense of achievement lasted only a moment. As the reality of the situation crystallised in my mind, I didn't start dancing on the floor, celebrating. I started shitting myself – already I didn't want to let my future team down by riding a bad time trial.

I returned home from the Worlds, contract in hand, and Paul Sherwen called me to congratulate me. Paul had played a hand in my early career and, of course, he told me it was really good that I had signed a contract. But he also said this would be like graduating from school to university. Sherwen told me that cycling was a hard sport that had been easy for me so far, and the truth was, I could only consider myself a real professional when I got a second contract. 'Loads of people get let in,' he said, 'but not many people get to stay.'

I went from living in fear of never signing a contract to living in fear of not getting a second contract. Paul's call set the tone for my whole career. I immediately started doing everything I could to start making myself useful, to be indispensable, to be remembered when it was new contract time.

I seemed to go through most of my career just thinking, 'If I can just save myself now ...' to the next lap, or to the next stage, to the next year; a constant negative motivation. People on the outside might think that cyclists are these sort of ultra-motivated beings who plan everything to the nth degree – this 'ultimate human performance' bullshit, but, in reality it's often just the really shitty stuff that motivates you, like the fact that you'd be ashamed to stop at the showers because you know what it will feel like on Monday morning when you know you haven't done a good job. A lot of what would end up pushing me was simply to have a good conscience.

Sherwen knew that I had no idea what I was getting in to when I had excitedly signed my first contract. The sport would reveal itself to me in its stark reality over the following years; it would be like seeing the carcass of an animal you've killed turned completely inside out.

· What it is to be a great cycling champion, I will never know. What I can tell you is what it is to race bicycles for a living. The job of a professional cyclist is extraordinary, but the professional peloton is full of quite ordinary men just like me, who find themselves at times exposed, and at times confused, by the profession that they work so hard to be a part of. I've never wanted to write a book about the struggle to become a professional cyclist; I want to write about the life you lead when you become one.

Becoming a professional cyclist was something I consciously decided I was going to do, and I had made the decision long before the two Mapei managers approached me in Canada. I was going to do it, and until I'd done it I'd have no peace.

CHAPTER 1
Something I Had to Do

'Monseiur Chaminaud … Charly Wegelius.'

Seeing a look of bemusement on the face of the middle-aged Frenchman who was propped up against the boot of a white Renault team car in front of me, I thrust my hand forward and tried again, this time thickening my well-practised French accent, distorting further the unusual sound of my Finnish surname.

'Char-lee Weg-he-lee-oos.'

After a brief moment, the look of recognition that I had hoped for finally spread across the face looking back at me, and a cold hand gripped mine and shook it in welcome. Despite the relief that flooded over me when Jean-François Chaminaud realised who I was, it was far from the welcome that I had expected. Behind the smile now being worn on the face of my sole contact at the French amateur team Vendée U, whose doorstep I had just arrived on, was a look that seemed to say with a hint of panic, 'Oh, fuck – you're actually *here*.'

In fairness the moment I arrived in France perhaps hadn't been the best one. As my mother and I had pulled up from our overnight trip on the ferry and arrived at the designated location, we had found that everyone in the team was already leaving for a training session. Even as I stepped excitedly out of my mother's red Ford Fiesta and saw the Gitane team bikes on the roof of the Vendée U team car, riders had begun filing out into the morning in ones and twos. Some had glanced at me warily; others simply weren't interested in the bespectacled blond teenager who had appeared and was waiting for someone to talk to him.

Being deliberately ignored by my teammates was something I would get used to in my amateur years in France, but right there and then it had felt like a strange kind of introduction. As far as I was concerned when I arrived at the accommodation at Le Domaine St Sauveur a few kilometres from La Roche Sur Yon in the Vendée to meet the Vendée U team I was in the right place at the right time, but, as it would soon become apparent, I was the only person there who thought that.

In 1996 professional cycling was a European sport, and being an aspiring young British cyclist meant only one thing: packing up your life in the UK and moving to continental Europe. It was a process that had been the same for generations: cycling was a minority sport in Britain and always had been – there was a sense then that it always would be too. If you were British, Australian or American the challenge of becoming a professional cyclist wasn't limited to what you could do on the road, but whether or not you could hack it 'over there'.

At the time, communication was still painfully slow between the UK and Europe. A few months prior to arriving in France I had been tenuously put in touch with the Vendée U trainer,

Jean-François Chaminaud, by the British journalist Kenny Pryde. For whatever reason, after a few handwritten letters backwards and forwards between us, Chaminaud agreed to take me on. I didn't think about it, but it was a strange thing for a team like Vendée U to agree to. I was 17 and still a junior category rider – not even old enough to take part in the same races as the members of the actual team. It was typical of who I was at the time, though, always wanting to be one step in front of where I needed to be, that I had set my sights on Vendée U, the best amateur team in France. And now here I was, only one day after finishing my A levels, ready to start life as a cyclist.

The absurdity of my situation wasn't the only thing that went over my head, either. Having never been part of any sort of organised team, other than my cycling club VC York, I had no idea of the complicated and often political structures within cycling teams. VC York had been delighted to help me get a racing licence and allow me to ride in one of their jerseys, but they were just a sports club with a committee that organised a road race and a club dinner once a year – that was it. I had been in no way prepared then, when I had gleefully taken up what I thought was a concrete offer to go out to join Vendée U, for the fact that one half of the team didn't talk to the other, and that Chaminaud, a marginal figure in the team hierarchy, hadn't told anyone else that I was coming. When I had eventually walked over and introduced myself, the riders, staff and the manager, Jean-René Bernaudeau, seemed to be taken completely by surprise by my arrival.

The team were in the middle of a training camp for the National Team Time Trial Championships, and they had no time or interest in delaying the day's session because of the unheralded arrival of skinny English kid. Clearly a little embarrassed, Chaminaud had a rushed conversation with Bernaudeau, seemingly formed almost entirely out of grunts. I was told to wait where I was, and that they would be back for me after the training session. By now Mum had gone to catch her boat, so I was left totally alone. I found myself a seat in the reception area of the house that the team was leaving, and I sat down and quietly waited.

My reaction was typical of who I was at the time. I had been told to wait by someone whom I considered could be influential to my cycling career, so I waited, and I thought nothing more of it. There were no questions in my mind, there was no part of me that wondered if I was doing the right thing, nor any doubt about what I was getting myself into. I was so determined I didn't even pause to think about the possibility of being homesick. I loved my mother and I knew that being away from home would be a challenge, but at the same time I knew that she had already done all that she could to help me towards my goal just by getting me there. Now there were other people to listen to, and the idea of entertaining emotions like missing home was a total waste of time to me. It was as if I had simply carved that part of my mind out with a scalpel and left it behind when I was packing my bags to go to France, reasoning that it was of no use.

I still can't put my finger on why I *had* to become a professional cyclist. I was quite smart at school; I didn't come from a penniless family; I didn't really need to try to make my living this way. Despite the fact that my parents had separated when I was only two, I was far too young to really know any different, and grew up as contented as only a child can be. I led what I considered to be a perfectly normal life. I grew up with my brother, Eddie, and my mother, Jane, in York but spent my summers and school holidays in Finland. Eddie and I travelled what felt like quite often between the two countries when we were both at a very young age. Being four years older, Eddie took the responsibility of looking after me very seriously when we were young. I was his kid brother, and he always made sure that we were both safe on our travels, and kept me out of trouble.

We both loved to go out to Finland. The whole country felt like a playground to us. The landscape of Finnish countryside was so uncluttered it felt like a world of opportunity. It was quiet and it was safe, we could walk as far as we could in any direction and we could be sure everyone we came across knew my father and who we were. My father, wanting us to be independent and actively look for things to do, allowed us a lot of freedom. Eddie and I were full of adventure, and left to our own devices we roamed like wild dogs, climbing trees in the woods, jumping in lakes, driving the tractors on the farm and messing around in the hay bales in the stables.

Then there were the times that my father would take it upon himself to try to educate us. Doing anything, even the most banal daily tasks, without trying your absolute best was totally out of the question for my father. He wanted us to push ourselves, to constantly want to better ourselves. It was here, perhaps more than anywhere, that my determination to succeed was forged. Summer swims in the Archipelago Sea became quests to find higher and higher rocks from which to jump into the icy water. Family bike rides became longer and longer, until I was riding over 100 km at nine years old.

On one such ride we were caught in a heavy summer rainstorm 20 km from home. The rain was belting down and it became so dark that we lined out into single file for safety, and I, being the youngest, took up position at the front. All I could think of was getting back to the house and having a warm shower. The bike weighed a ton and only had one gear and a back pedal brake, but I hammered on the pedals and started to pick up speed. I rode bent over the ill-fitting bike, feeling the freezing water coming up off the road and filling my trainers. I was squinting at the road ahead and thought of nothing but going as fast as I could to get home as quickly as possible. When I arrived there I was surprised to see that I was completely alone. I hadn't heard a crash so I thought nothing much of it, and carried on to the house. When my father and Eddie arrived home I was showered and warm. Eddie was incredulous. 'Where did you fuck off to?'

'I just rode. I wasn't trying to lose you. I wanted to get home.'

'Weren't you tired? We couldn't keep up. You just rode off.'

'Of course I was. I was knackered, and freezing. But I wanted to get back, so I rode hard. I thought you were right behind me.'

'Well, didn't you look?'

I realised that I hadn't. I'd thought that perhaps he would be annoyed that I'd left him behind. But Eddie wasn't upset that I could ride faster than him; he just didn't understand how someone could keep going without looking back to check on the others. Eddie might not have had the ruthless attitude of a performance athlete at his core, but I certainly did.

If Eddie was upset, my father, once he had got over the shock of being left behind by his young son, was no doubt impressed.

With my father everything, even affection and attention, was about performance. Because this was all I had ever known, I thought it was normal. Only the shocked expressions of family friends upon hearing of these feats gave me a clue at the time that it was a bit odd.

Like many kids, I took part in all sports at an early age, and through applying myself in this way I found that I was quite good at them. It was just a matter of time until I found a sport that I could dedicate myself to with real purpose. When I first discovered cycling, I instantly realised that I had found the sport for me. There was something different about it – exactly what, I was too young and too excitable to ever question – but unlike other sports, which I would rapidly lose interest in, it caught my attention from the very first moment.

It was 1990 when I really discovered cycling. My mother had taken me to watch a round of the Kellogg's professional city centre criteriums in York and I saw Malcolm Elliott there. He'd won the points jersey in the Tour of Spain. He looked like a fucking gladiator. He was tanned and his legs were so muscular they looked like they'd been carved out of mahogany. He looked so cool: he had a Teka headband and a posh-looking bird with him. He was shiny in every sense: his bike, his shoes, himself. He made cyclists look like something special. In a way, they didn't look like people; their bodies were like machines made to ride. I almost couldn't take my eyes off him; it was as if I was seeing the personification of every hero that I'd had. It wasn't just seeing an older kid who I thought was cool doing tricks on a BMX, it was as exciting as a movie star stepping out of a movie screen. The impression was lasting but the action in York was all too brief. I wanted more, and later in the summer I went to see the Kellogg's Tour, which went over White Horse Bank near where I lived. Robert Millar rode for Z and he had the mountain jersey, and I remember vividly the look in his eyes when he was going over that hill. I was exhilarated to see in their faces how *hard* the riders were all trying.

Cycle racing didn't really happen on a large scale in England, but seeing those flashy professional races and hearing about riders with foreign-sounding names who rode for exotic-seeming teams made me aspire to become a part of that world. Cycling didn't come from England like cricket or football; cycling was from another planet entirely. I became obsessed with everything this distant world of professional cycling seemed to promise. I quickly forgot about the one-week Kellogg's Tour of Britain and the one-hour city centre criteriums. My horizons switched to the biggest race of all: the Tour de France. It was the greatest thing I could imagine. I was totally consumed by it in the way only someone with as much free time as a child could be. I bought regional Michelin maps of the Alps and pored over them. I was young and a daydreamer, but already I knew I was resolving to make those dreams real; in looking at the Col de la Croix de Fer on a map it was as if I was grounding that place in reality. Bourg-d'Oisans, I realised, wasn't just something out of a Tolkien book: it was a place, and people lived there, went to school and worked there.

I'm sure maps of southern France are not what 11-year-old kids normally spend their pocket money on, but I was closing the gap between the unimaginably exotic world of professional cycling and my own life in York. By buying the maps and trying to plant these places in reality, I was taking the first steps to getting myself across that divide. My very first steps towards a cycling career, though, had to be taken at home.

'Mum, I need you to write a letter to my headmaster.'

It was late to be eating dinner on a school night, but my training ride that I had set out on had ended up being, as usual, a lot longer than I had promised when I left the house. It was nearly nine o'clock and my mother, who was serving up the portion of shepherd's pie that had been waiting for me, looked at me.

'Why is that, Charles?'

'I am wasting my time at school and I think I can use it better.'

'What do you mean by that?'

I had always been encouraged to think and express myself as an adult, and now at 15, and with growing confidence, I was beginning to express myself forthrightly. I presented my argument.

'I want to get out of wasting my time on Wednesday afternoons doing school sports and use the time to go cycling instead. The idea of going to school is to prepare me for my future, and I know I am not going to be playing rugby or football for a career, but I want to be a cyclist and so surely going training is as important as anything else. I wouldn't be missing any lessons, but I hate training in the dark: it's dangerous, and it means that by the time I get home I have no time to do homework ...'

My mother already knew that I wanted to be a cyclist. Until now there had never been any discussion about whether or not I would be allowed to follow a career path as a professional sportsman. My father had made a career as a professional show-jumper and although a career in professional sport of any kind was bound to be hard to achieve, and be precarious in nature, my mother, more than anyone, had always seemed to unquestionably believe in me. When I had first announced that I wanted to ride the Tour de France as a 10-year-old she had accepted my choice, and had gone to great lengths to get me started racing, driving me all around the country to get to races. She would sit, weekend in and weekend out, in car parks of village halls all across the country, with the *Sunday Times* and a Thermos flask of tea, waiting patiently for me to get on with whatever race I was doing. It was her way of supporting me. After each race she would leave it up to me whether or not to talk about how it had gone on the way home. Sometimes I would sit in moody silence all the way home and she never once got annoyed or pushed the issue. My race was my race and I did as well as I did, and she never questioned that. Likewise I had never once questioned that I would have to complete my compulsory education – it had always seemed a fair trade-off to me. I went to school and achieved satisfactory results, and I was allowed to spend my spare time either racing or training. Now, though – with this question in the air – I knew if I got my way I would finally be shifting the balance in favour of cycling at a crucial time in my education. Despite the fact that my GCSEs were looming, dedicating more time to cycling made total sense, in my mind at least. It was reasonable and it was practical, and it would give me an advantage over everyone else my age.

My mother looked at the clock on the wall before returning her gaze to me, and replying without even a hint of reluctance: 'Well, if you think that your time would be better spent going cycling, I will write a letter.'

It was exactly the answer I was gunning for. I knew then that I had the full blessing of my mother to pursue the real goal that I had set myself.

Two weeks later, after wolfing down a quick lunch and hurriedly dressing myself in my cycling kit in the school locker rooms, I picked up my bike from the bike sheds. As I clipped into the pedals and rolled towards the school gates I felt an almost unbelievable thrill. My headteacher at Bootham School had agreed to allow me to skip Wednesday afternoon PE and use the time instead to go cycling. As I passed through the gates and the sound of the school playground disappeared behind me, I felt a sense of freedom and achievement that was unparalleled in my life. I was leaving behind the ordinary life and making my way into the world I dreamed of.

It wasn't just the physical act of riding a bike that I was obsessed with. I was desperate to understand everything I could about the world of cycling. I absorbed every story I could find on how my predecessors had succeeded. I read every book and magazine I could on the subject. In a way, finding these stories was as much a part of the fun as anything else. There was no internet and no obvious way to go and get this information; professional cycling was drip fed to me through encounters, whisperings, handed-down books and stories.

Naturally I started to look around for people who I felt could help me with my objective. My mother's support getting me to races had been crucial, but by the time I reached the junior categories I knew I needed people with real knowledge of professional cycling to help me on my way.

I met Mike Taylor for the first time at the Junior Tour of Ireland the previous autumn before I had headed out to France. Mike had recently been appointed as the manager of the GB Junior team that I had been selected to ride the race for. I was instantly drawn to Mike; he had been taking teams to Europe seemingly since the dawn of time. He knew bike riders and he understood the sport; his insight was like no one else's I'd ever met. Mike wasn't for the faint-hearted; he was direct, and didn't take any shit at all. In one week in Ireland I felt like I had suddenly found a key figure in my future. I wanted to know how to become a professional, and I knew that Mike could help me with that. As soon as we returned from Ireland I was picking up the phone to Mike almost every day, hounding him with more and more questions. Soon, through his guidance, I recognised the path that I was going to take.

It became clear to me that the tried and tested method of becoming a professional cyclist was to go to Europe to see if you'd sink or swim. There were no schools or academies; it was just down to individual resolve and a lot of guesswork. It was the only option there was. Little had changed with the whole process since the sixties: to be accepted in the peloton British cyclists had to make themselves fit into a different country. It wasn't just a matter of moving out of home to go and find work. You had to completely uproot yourself, and be prepared to do whatever you were told by a French or Belgian manager – who had no real duty of care at all – to make yourself that bit better than anyone else. For me, and perhaps for others too, this formed part of the attraction of becoming a European pro – making it there was the ultimate accolade for a British cyclist, because it was so rare that anyone did, and it was so hard to do. By the time I arrived at that Vendée U camp in France there wasn't really very much that would have overwhelmed me. I knew this in my mind: I was a man on a fucking mission.

● ● ●

Things didn't get any easier for me to begin with, in France. After I waited patiently for their return the team eventually came back from their training and drove me to the house in Saint-Maurice-le-Girard. Here I found that once again my timing seemed to be fairly bad. On the drive to the house it was explained to me that the team house was looked after by a Polish guy who had at one stage been a rider, but who now worked in the sports shop across the road that was run by Bernaudeau. He lived there with his wife and the team's foreign riders: Aidan Duff, Piotr Wadecki (another Pole) and Janek Tombak, an Estonian. Aidan Duff, an Irish rider, was away at a race. I knew Aidan by reputation, and I had presumed that in him I would have at least one English-speaking ally. I wouldn't meet Aidan for another few days, though.

Clearly quite keen to get home to his dinner, Bernaudeau gave me a thirty-second tour of the house while rooted to the spot, pointing with one flailing arm at the various doorways you could see from where we stood in the hallway. After he poked his head into the kitchen and explained to the surprised gaggle of Eastern Europeans that I would now be living with them, he finally turned and looked at me and said, 'Make sure you shower before 1 p.m. After that – no hot water.' Adding, 'There will be lots of riders coming and going. Make sure you label your food if you don't want it eaten.'

With that Bernaudeau finished his tour and made for the front door. That was it. The house itself was basic; it had the air of a place lived in by old people, or even someone who was recently deceased, as if the occupants had only enough energy to clean the things that were close to them, and everything else was dusty and forgotten and a little bit out of place. Vendée U might have been the best team in France, but their accommodation was like a fucking terrorist cell.

I looked at my surroundings again, but I didn't even flinch. I knew there was no other option if I wanted to become a professional cyclist. It was a rite of passage.

In all honesty a part of me even considered myself lucky. The stories of my British predecessors in the sport prepared me to accept the shit things I had to do. I saw those hardships like a process of branding myself with legitimacy. Even when I was looking around at the shitty accommodation that was to be my new home, the only feelings I had were of guilt. I knew deep down, compared to my predecessors, I still had it 'easy' because I could always go out and buy a France Télécom phone card and call my mother if I really needed to.

• • •

My first few weeks in France were nothing like I had imagined they would be. Not because I was treated badly, but because I wasn't really treated like anything at all.

I had to pluck up the courage, but eventually it was time to do something. I went to the office where I knew Jean-René Bernaudeau would be sat, making calls and going through papers, and I knocked and walked in. Jean-René was not surprised to see me; in the few weeks that I'd been in France I had been an almost continual presence at the service course. Apart from when I was out training on my bike, there wasn't really anywhere else for me to be. My being a junior had caused a bigger problem than just the awkwardness of my arrival. The team had no idea how to get a licence for a junior rider, nor which races I could ride as a foreigner.

In short they didn't really know what to do with me. My first two weeks were spent training, hanging about and doing odd jobs like mowing the lawn. I realised that if I didn't do something about my situation nobody else would. I had decided to get proactive.

I unfolded my copy of the French Cycling Federation's magazine *France Cycliste* on the table and spoke in my GCSE French, *'Est ce que c'est possible de allez faire cette course?'*

Jean-René regarded me with a little surprise and gave me a very noncommittal Gallic shrug while he drew out a lengthy and speculative,

'Ouais ...'

It was the guarded kind of response that I was expecting. While it had been Chaminaud – the team trainer – who had invited me to come and ride with the team, I had little if anything at all to do with him after our initial meeting; instead I soon discovered that it was really Jean-René Bernaudeau who ran it all, and who was now stuck with me.

I explained to him, 'I went and bought myself a copy of *France Cycliste* and a map and I've looked up which races are close enough for me to get to. I looked and it is fine for me to race on my international licence, so I have sent entries in to all the races that I can do in the next month.'

He looked at me in disbelief and I could see a light bulb go on in his head: 'Shit! This guy really wants to race.' The first race was about an hour away from where we lived and, after I'd said my piece, I knew it was up to Jean-René.

'Well, you'd better take the van from the sports shop and drive yourself there. *Bon chance.*'

The loan of the van was a clear sign of approval, so on the day of the race I packed it and drove away. The race was a Nationale category race, which is for young riders and men who have jobs and do cycling for fun – a true amateur's race. Once the start flag dropped I went out, like I went out in every race I did at the time, attacking from the front and riding off when I wanted to. I won all the *primes*, as well as the race. After picking up my winnings I packed up and drove back to the team house satisfied with the win, but not thinking at all about the process I had been through to get myself to and from the race. It was what I *had* to do, after all. But everyone else in the team and the staff were astounded: 'Fuck me, you did that all on your own?' Winning to them was one thing, but it was my attitude that impressed them. Most riders in the team wouldn't dream of going to a race without a *soigneur* or a mechanic, or at the very least someone to drive them there. I had done the whole thing without any assistance at all.

It impressed people but I think it also compounded the inkling I had that everyone thought I was a little bit weird. I suppose I was: other cyclists my age were dedicated, but they still would have found time to have a life; to me it seemed that nothing else mattered. The fact was, for the first time in my life, I was doing nothing but cycling, and I was so into it – the thought that I had the whole day to do nothing but ride my bike was beyond exciting. But they came from a whole different world. In France cycling is a huge mainstream sport, and back then the young guys who showed talent were groomed like princes from the very first races they won. They were *vedettes*, these little superstars, and they were casual about the world of professional cycling because they had grown up with it.

I was the opposite: cycling was such an obscure sport in the UK that I was used to being treated as a freak. The two cycling cultures were so different that they nurtured completely different people.

The way that we looked after our bikes was a prime example. I washed my bike every single day after training with diesel, and did so until it was spotless. I made sure that my bike was race ready every single morning, every single fucking day. They were all watching this, the other riders and staff, and I was sure they were all laughing at me. The thing was, the riders at Vendée U had been given bikes all through their lives from various clubs and teams, whereas I had always raced on *my stuff* on parts and frames that I had saved up and bought with my own money. I still dismantled my race bike at the end of the season, cleaned all the parts in Brasso and wrapped them in newspaper so they stayed warm and dry for the winter. My attitude was that these things had to be looked after because they were hard to come by. But the guys in Vendée U didn't see it like that. When I was professional, years later, I adopted their attitude too. My race bike was a disgrace, it was always filthy and the tyres in my training wheels would be riddled with massive holes. But back in the early 1990s I stood out there each day washing my bike like a maniac, while my teammates laughed at me. I just didn't care.

● ● ●

That summer I kept winning, but at some stage in late July everything changed.

Carrying one of my kit bags for me as I wheeled my bike, Jean-René led me up the front path of a typical French suburban house and rang the doorbell. It was a warm summer's evening, and sprinklers were lazily watering the neat garden outside the front of the house. As I looked about the lawn the front door opened and a man a little older than Jean-René, whom I recognised from a few of the local races, ushered us into the house.

As soon as we walked in I was struck by how dark the place was: to keep the summer heat out all the blinds in the house had been kept shut and not yet opened for the evening air to refresh the house. The house itself was neat and tidy, and, despite the odd stillness created by the darkness, it felt like a home. We walked into the kitchen and sat down at the table. The man politely offered us a drink. He opened the fridge to pull out a cold French lager for Jean-René and a bottle of sparkling water for me. As he did so the nose-stinging scent of strong French cheese invaded my nostrils. It was the first time I had really been in a French home; I had lived in France with four foreigners; our own refrigerator only smelt of mould and off-milk, and there was nothing at all French about its contents. Here, though, I was hit by the reality that I was in a French home. I should have been contented with the small comforts that the smell of real food gave me, but instead my heart only sank further.

A few days earlier I had been told that I was going to be leaving the team house, as Jean-René had found some accommodation that he thought was more 'suitable' for me a few kilometres away in the town of La Roche-sur-Yon. Without my knowledge it had been arranged that I would go to stay at the home of one of the junior riders who rode for the cycling club from the town. La Roche was a club that was loosely attached to Vendée U, and they wore simi-lar jerseys, but they weren't what you'd call a cycling team by any standards; they were a club full of old men and schoolboys. The school holidays had begun and either Jean-René or the parents of the junior must have decided that it couldn't have been all that nice for a young guy to be living in the team house without people his own age. Perhaps they thought if I stayed with them I might even do some 'normal' activities instead of just riding or cleaning my bike. It was a really warm-hearted gesture, but I was so blinded by determination that instead of being pleased about the comforts of the family environment I was welcomed into I was absolutely gutted; I felt like I was back on school exchange.

In my singularly determined mind Vendée U was the only place I needed to be: Vendée U was the fast track to a cycling career. It was tough in the house; the older Polish couple had left shortly after I'd arrived, and with them had gone any semblance of discipline or cleanliness. At best each of us would clean our own plate and space on the table; anything else (like the shower or toilet) wouldn't get touched. The place might have been disgusting, but there were two things that made it worth wanting to be there. The first was the fact that, even though I wasn't doing any races with the team, just my being there was pushing open a crack in the door. The second was that I felt I had a real friend there.

As soon as I met Aidan we had hit it off. When he first came back to the house from a race to find I'd moved in he had no idea who I was or what I was doing there, but he didn't even seem the slightest bit surprised to see me. I introduced myself and there was no difficulty whatsoever, he just said hello and started chatting to me as if I'd been part of the team all season. That was Aidan; he just accepted whatever came along with a shrug and a smile, and carried right along with things.

Being sent to La Roche really made me feel like I'd fucked up, that I hadn't done well enough in the races, even though I'd won every race I'd ridden. From the moment that Jean-René stood up and left me still seated at that kitchen table I moped around the house like a surly teenager, beating myself up about the fact that I had been downgraded. I trained alone in the mornings and spent the afternoons lying on my bed reading *France Cycliste* over and over. Teenage boys are hardly masters of subtlety, and the family quickly seemed to real-ise that all wasn't well. After ten or so days the uncomfortable father knocked on my door one evening and came into the room.

'Charly. We have noticed that you don't really seem happy here, so I have spoken to Jean-René … If you really want you can go back to the team house …'

As soon as the words left his mouth I couldn't hide my delight. Without stopping to think about whether this family would feel embarrassed or if perhaps I should, I gleefully ran around the house collecting my things and started packing my bags. When I heard the team car pull up half an hour or so later I virtually ran out of the door to get back to the team house. As soon as I returned to that dirty old hovel full of Polish cyclists that I struggled to communi-cate with, frenzied with the constant upheaval of riders and team staff coming and going, I was happy as Larry. I was happier in that house full of lonely men than within the comforts of a family.

On my return to the house that summer I carried on winning almost at will, and, as any rider knows, when you are that driven, as long as you are winning it makes everything else in life seem OK. The winning was easy to me then, but I still had a lot to learn.

● ● ●

Before I went home at the end of that first year in 1996 I had one of my first real lessons in professional cycling. For the first time ever, I was put under pressure from someone other than myself.

After I had soundly beaten the local superstar, Sandy Casar, to win a round of the junior World Cup in Brittany, Jean-René decided to enter me for the GP des Nations – a prestigious professional time trial that is run at the end of the year, which had a junior race as a supporting event. The race was invitation only, put on by the same organisers as the Tour de France. But, for whatever reason, they didn't accept my entry for the race. Jean-René was furious. When Jean-René had a cause he was a force of nature: nothing would stop him. He called me into the office and told me, 'Sit down. I will sort this out.'

He rang the Tour organisers there and then and, although I desperately wanted to ride, as I listened I felt like I should tell him that it really didn't matter that much, that the world wouldn't actually end if I didn't ride. I heard the whole thing: he insisted that I would be good, telling them with all the bluster of an insulted Frenchman, 'You've *got* to take this guy. I *promise* you he will do well.'

Before this incident the only pressure I'd felt I had piled on to myself. Now the stakes had changed: I – skinny little Charly Wegelius from VC York – was responsible for Jean-René Bernaudeau's word. The fact that this man – who had a successful career as a pro, and had managed the Castorama professional team – was relying on me made me quake in my team issue blue and yellow Carnac *claquettes*. Even at that age I understood what I was undertaking. I would find out later that pressure, and the ability to deal with it, was one of the key parts of being a professional bike rider.

After pushing so hard for me to get a start, Jean-René really got behind me. To him, it became a point of honour that I performed, so he put everything he could at my disposal. I was sent to the race with a team car, with three bikes, four disc wheels and the team masseur, Jacques Duchain. Jacques had been around professional cycling for years, and had worked with various French professional teams. He was really good, the best the team had, and he was there just for me.

The race was at the Lac de Madine near Nancy in the north-east of France. I travelled up with Jacques the day before, and watched in amazement as he meticulously planned out my schedule. His presence calmed me, but not enough to rid me of my internal stress. My sleep, usually peaceful and easy, was for one of the first times in my life truly fitful and agitated.

On the morning of the TT my nerves increased. All I wanted to do was to get up on the ramp and get the race underway; until I could get going every second was agony.

As I took to the start ramp and I was held up by the marshal, I tried to block everything out. I focused intently on the countdown; I watched the starter as he looked down at his stopwatch, and as he thrust his hairy hand out in front of me dropping his fingers one by one, '*Cinq … quatre … trois… deux … un … TOP!!*'

I was so eager to get going that I pushed hard on the pedals and my wheel slipped sideways slightly on the surface of the wooden start ramp made wet by the thick morning mist. My heart fluttered momentarily but as I hit the tarmac at the bottom of the ramp still upright I stood up and stamped on the pedals. I went straight up to maximal effort as quickly as I could. As I rounded the first sets of barriers that led out to the open circuit I began hyperventilating. I panted like a dog that was too stupid to stop chasing the rabbit. As I charged out of the centre of town into the countryside I heard the squealing of the team-car tyres behind and I could feel Jacques' eyes on me. The course undulated but the air was still. All my thoughts focused on the image in my head of Jean-René making that phone call: '*He will perform, I promise you.*' My lungs burned but I was so desperate to do well that I became angry with myself for suffering. I thrashed myself, I went harder and harder – and even then it wasn't enough. I kept asking myself for more; when I was at my limit I taunted myself that I had to give more. The 35 km passed in a blurry rush. I focused as far as I could see ahead of me and I willed every fibre in my body to get myself towards that point as quickly as I could.

I shot across the finish line to the excited voice of the announcer, but with the first gasping breath that I took as I crossed the line I instantly wished that I could be allowed to start again. I was sure it wasn't enough. I swung the bike into the race car park and looked for Jacques. As the pain of the effort eased out of my body, I saw the Vendée U car hastily parked at an angle in a space 50 metres away. Jacques hopped out of the driver's seat and started gesticulating excitedly at me. Suddenly I saw that it had been worth it. I pulled up at the car and Jacques grabbed me by the shoulders, 'Fantastic, Charly, fantastic!' He couldn't hide his delight; I had smashed the best time. I fulfilled Jean-René's promise to a T. I won, beating the second-place rider by a minute and twenty seconds, a massive margin over that distance.

In the car on the way home Jacques was still beside himself. It was as if he had just discovered something very special. More than just winning I think he had seen something in my ride that he recognised could take me a long way. Jacques was a part of the tradition of cycling, the kind of *soigneur* who had a wealth of knowledge acquired through pure dedication to his *métier*. He knew cycling and how to nurture talent. As we drove home, he tempered his excitement as he spoke very carefully to me, 'Charly, this is the beginning of something. You have the talent, but you must not get too excited. If you want to be a professional there is a long way to go and you have to remain calm. It is a hard job, you have to *faire le métier*, you have to work a lot, and hard, and you have to keep your head, but this is a nice beginning. A very nice beginning ...'

The GP des Nations was my last race of 1996, and the end of my first experience of racing on the Continent. Before I left to go back home to England, Jean-René told me that the following season I was invited back, and that I would receive a monthly salary of 4,000 francs. The fact that I was going to go straight into one of the best amateur teams in France didn't seem like a success, it just felt natural. Money, like everything else, was a means to an end. Four thousand francs was a lot of money to me at that time, but in my mind it simply meant that, combined with the prize money I had won throughout the year, I knew I had enough to get me through a winter without working, and I could dedicate my time to the serious business of preparing for my first full senior season. Despite being fully able to concentrate on working on my cycling career, and already becoming a full-time rider at 18, nothing would have been enough to prepare me for my first season as a senior rider.

• • •

In April 1997 I stood on the start line of the Trophée des Grimpeurs and looked around me. Only a few months ago I had still been a junior rider, albeit a very good one; now I looked about and saw that I was surrounded by some of the top French professionals of the day, including triple Tour de France King of the Mountains Richard Virenque and his Festina teammates. I was petrified. In the Nationale races the previous year I had been so superior to the competition that I had been able to do whatever I wanted, and I loved that. In one race I had looked behind me into the eyes of the one grown man left holding my wheel, and almost laughed when he had begged me to 'please slow down', because he wanted to finish second. I had been sadistic and cruel, but now I was no longer in the little kids' playground, and I was about to feel what getting hurt was really like.

By virtue of their status as one of the best amateur teams in France, Vendée U got into a lot of professional races that accepted amateurs in those days, and the Trophée des Grimpeurs was one such race. It might not be well known, but it was a tough bike race, and I was still only 18. As we rolled out of the start line and the race took off, I dived into the wheels hoping that maybe the speed wouldn't be exaggerated too quickly and I could hide in the bunch for as long as possible. No chance. The race was only 96 km on a circuit outside of Paris that literally went up and down one hill. Once we started I felt like I was slipping into quicksand; riders kept passing by me, and try as I might I just couldn't match the speed. I couldn't even make myself hold my position in the bunch. I looked on desperately as rider after rider passed by me. Even before we hit the climb for the first time, the fucking pace was phenomenal; I had never known anything like it. I didn't even last a lap. When I pulled out I felt totally ashamed of myself. I was so embarrassed with my performance that I braced myself to get shouted at when Jean-René next saw me. I thought he would be angry or disappointed, and that the team would see that I wasn't as good as they had thought I was. Amazingly, though, no one seemed to be bothered by my woeful performance – at least outwardly. My results the previous year had convinced Bernaudeau that I had talent, and perhaps he believed in me even more than I did, or perhaps the expectations that I had of myself were unrealistically high. Perhaps I wasn't doing *that* badly. Either way, Jean-René continued to select me for the first team, and I kept going to all of the biggest races that the team rode.

After the Grimpeurs, we went to the Tour de Vaucluse in Provence, and the demands and suffering were multiplied again. In a stage race you are compelled to stay there suffering through to the next day, because there *is* a next day. I was consistently the last to finish. As soon as the action started I would be in the convoy, slowly dropping back through the cars and out of the race. I was completely gobsmacked. I was going to breakfast and then going back to sleep in the short gap between breakfast and going to the race because I was just so fucked.

It wasn't just the racing that was hard to cope with at the time. To my teammates, who were in most cases much older than me, I was another foreigner who was vying to take their spot, and I deserved no quarter. On one stage at the Tour de Vaucluse I found myself caught out in the wind when the bunch had lined out and, as I fought desperately to try to get into the line, even my own teammate Walter Bénéteau wouldn't let me in. I was incredulous;

he only had to ease slightly to save me from being bounced all the way out the back of the race for good, and he just looked at me and shook his head before pushing me back out. That really disappointed me then, and still does now. I don't think it was a language barrier, or a culture barrier, or a sense of humour barrier. I wanted to become a professional, and my teammates all wanted to become professionals too, and there just aren't that many places, so in our own way we were all fighting tooth and nail for it. These kinds of rivalries are what make or break so many riders. They force you to either give up or dig in deeper.

In this environment my only saving grace was Aidan. Aidan had been out in France for two seasons before I got there. He already had a little experience of what I was going through, and his understanding meant that we got along like a house on fire.

Money was tight and the two of us decided that we would make ours go a long way. We competed with each other, inventing more and more ways to save every penny. It was an extension of the world that we saw ourselves as being part of: amateur bike riders were supposed to be broke, so we made ourselves live like it. We laughed about it, and we laughed at ourselves doing it, but whenever he put the car out of gear and cruised down a hill to save fuel, or drove us out to the supermarket at 8 p.m. to buy the stale bread because it was cheaper, he'd look at me with a grin and say, 'We're doing this so we can drink champagne later.' It became an obsession in its own right; even getting the free cookies at a Campanile hotel was an enormous triumph. We got so used to finding ways to save money we would often return from hotels with ludicrous hauls of 'swag', our suitcases stuffed with toilet rolls, soaps, packets of sugar

– anything we could claim would save us money at the supermarket (and could be seen to outdo the efforts of the other).

While the adventures with Aidan were a nice distraction, that was all they were. I knew that deep down, after taking so many kickings and never seemingly once getting to ride races that I could realistically have thought of winning, by mid-1998, my second senior year at the team, things had to change. I was becoming increasingly frustrated in France. Determination and youth are a combination that allows misery to go unnoticed at times and you don't know how you really feel until one day you make a snap decision to change everything.

I almost caught myself trembling as I rang Jean-René's doorbell. I forced myself to stand up straight before I pressed it, and as soon as I did I felt the surge of adrenaline that told me there was no going back. When you make a difficult phone call there is always a fraction of a second in that first ring when your heart races and you think, 'I can still hang up.' But as soon as I rang that bell I knew I couldn't run away from Jean-René's front door. I was going through with it now, no matter what.

As the door unlatched my heart pounded in my chest. Jean-René was a little surprised to see me at 9 o'clock in the morning: 'Charly?'

'Jean-René, I've come to tell you that I'm leaving the team. I'm heading back to the UK as soon as I have organised a flight. I appreciate everything you've done, but it is time for me to leave.'

He looked genuinely stunned.

'And l'Avenir?'

The Tour de l'Avenir in September was one of the biggest and most important races of the team's season and it was only three weeks away. My mind had been made up, though, and I knew there was absolutely no way I could either turn back or carry on with the team. It had taken so much for me to arrive at that moment that I was determined to go through with the decision I had made.

'I won't be riding it for Vendée U. I am leaving, I'm sorry, but this is the best thing for my career.'

It was done. Jean-René accepted my decision, but I knew that his pride was hurt. Riders didn't leave Vendée U of their own accord. It was the best amateur team in France, and Jean-René had a great deal of respect in the circles he moved in. He was a man who could make a young rider's dream to turn professional a reality, and he was treated as such by everyone around him. My decision to leave must have seemed quite insolent to him, but it made sense to me.

It hadn't been an easy decision to come to; the flipside of the blinkered determination that allowed me to ignore all the shit was that I couldn't see I had to take a step back to go forwards. Something had to give, and eventually, on returning from a training camp in the Pyrenees the previous day, it had. Back at the house that evening it transpired that something (I'm still not sure what) had happened while we were away, and someone had broken into my room when they had found it locked. It was a small thing, perhaps insignificant, but I took that invasion of my privacy very seriously and it became the trigger I needed. I had been so angry when I discovered what had happened that a tirade started spewing out, and I feel eternally grateful to Aidan for taking the part he did. Aidan had long since seen my frustrations, when I couldn't see them clearly for myself. And seizing the opportunity he encouraged me: 'You can't go back now, you have to leave.' It was exactly what I needed.

I had gone to France because I thought that it was the only option I had to turn professional. I was part of a tradition of British bike riders making it through the shit in France, sleeping on a bed held up by bricks, in a house full of cockroaches, getting fucked over time and time again by the people and the system around me. All of that I could deal with. My trouble was that the racing in France didn't suit me at all, and I wasn't getting any opportunities to win. I felt that since I had made the step up from junior I had been doing nothing more than failing. I had won eleven races in that first year in France and since then I had barely scored a result. For the first time in my career my confidence had begun to falter. I soon started to doubt everything around me. When I thought about it I saw that I was spending my time grinding away against 35-year-old amateurs in Mavic Cup races, or riding French Cup races with the pros. The latter was way too hard for me, and the former, the typical French races, were on flattish, rolling roads, and were only really suited to riders who could slog away all day or filled themselves full of cortisone and rode everywhere in the 11. There was never any debate about what kind of rider I could develop into; at 60kg with a thin figure and a light frame it was obvious that I was built for climbing. While I could still ride relatively quickly on the flat, because I was strong, my physique was a huge handicap in those flat, windy races.

As I started to think more and more about the reality of becoming a professional, I started to see this as a problem. You need race wins to become a professional, pure and simple. I was getting no results, and Vendée U raced tactically as if they were a pro team, so I was always covering the early moves and getting nowhere near

the action. I'd started to think I was shit, but Jean-René understood about racing, he recognised that I had talent, but he didn't
know that I couldn't see that. I became more disillusioned with
what I was doing. I was finishing the races, and that was it. I felt
like no one in the world was paying any attention. In reality I was
becoming a much better rider, but I couldn't see the progress, and
Jean-René never opened his mouth to explain this to me.

By the time I had vented all of my frustrations, and Aidan had
helped coax the real issues out of me, I could see quite clearly what
I had to do, and what was going wrong. From that moment I
couldn't bear to stay another day. My mind was made up. I sold my
car to Aidan that night, and readied myself to go and tell Jean-René
face to face that I was leaving for good.

CHAPTER 2
Ambition Bites Hard

When I returned to the UK in late 1998 I knew I had a lot of thinking to do. I returned to my mother's house in York, and made as many phone calls as I could to find out what options might be available to me for the 1999 season. I had just turned my back on the best amateur team in France, so I was uncomfortable at the thought of returning to the same system in another French team. I had taken the bold step to leave behind what wasn't working. Now I had to find out what would.

In no time at all, though, I had a phone call that would offer me a new direction entirely.

'Charly, it's Ken. How are things looking?'

Ken was my coach and normally rang to discuss training, so, as always, I gave him a brief run-down of my physical condition: 'I'm still quite tired actually, Ken. No sickness or anything, but you know how it is looking at team options.'

'That is actually what I am calling about. How would you feel about coming in to the Velodrome in Manchester to talk to John and me about the World Class programme? I think that there could be something that really suits you here.'

Ken Matheson had been my coach since I was 16, and while our working relationship had drifted somewhat while I had been in France, due to the distance and the fact that I had to follow the training programme set out by the team, we were still close. Along with Mike Taylor, who I still called as regularly as I could (without spending too much money on phone cards), Ken was one of the few people that I would traipse out to a phone box to call when I needed advice during my time in France. Ken had recently been appointed director of the newly formed World Class Performance Programme Under-23 men's squad, and he had seen the perfect opportunity for us to be able to work together again.

I had ridden the previous year's Under-23 World Road Race Championships in Valkenburg, Holland, for GB, and so I already knew that there was funding due to come into the national cycling team, and that plans were being made to create a platform for aspiring British riders, but I hadn't thought for one second that programme would be of any use to me. Until this point there had never been any sort of assistance, financial or otherwise, from the British Cycling Federation for British cyclists abroad. I had received a small bursary from the Dave Rayner Fund, a charity set up in memory of a British cyclist who died in tragic circumstances, that selected a handful of young British cyclists each year to help financially, but the world of professional cycling was a real mystery to our national federation, just like it was to a majority of British cyclists. It wasn't simply a matter of a lack of funding; it was a lack of knowledge, a lack of contacts and no real understanding of the professional cycling world. At the time our national system was so bad that it had handicapped its riders for generations, leaving young cyclists at the mercy of the unpredictable world of amateur racing in Europe. Unbeknownst to me that had all just changed, and the World Class Performance Plan, or the WCPP as it came to be known, was about to change things for me too.

A few days later I arrived in the windowless chilly depths of the WCPP office in the bowels of the Manchester Velodrome and sat down in front of Ken and John Herety, the national team manager. I knew Ken so well that the formal setting and tone of the meeting felt slightly awkward.

It was John who spoke first: 'I know that you might have an idea what this is about. Basically, our funding has been confirmed and Peter Keen has developed the idea of a programme for British Cycling. Our aim is to create a system that will back riders financially as well as providing equipment and a race programme that will allow British riders to be competitive at World and European Championships.

'You have been identified as a rider who has the talent to win medals at major championships, and we would like to offer you a place on the programme for 1999 … Of course, what this means for you is that by performing at these races for us you are going to put yourself in the ideal position to attract a pro team.'

The deal was laid out for me. I would be paid a salary of £12,000 and I would be based in the UK and travel to races in Europe where we would race as the GB national team, but to my calculating mind there was only really one detail that mattered. I knew that John and Ken both knew what I wanted, more than money or medals, was a professional contract. Everything else was simply a means of getting me there.

Despite how good it sounded, I had some thinking to do. Ken and John were both enthusiastic and kept on about the benefits of the new programme. It was true the WCPP had been given a lot of money, but I still had the feeling that they didn't really know what they were doing. Even though there was a new logo, letter-heads and people who would fax race programmes through, this was still the British Cycling Federation, and part of me just didn't believe it was possible to be based in the UK and manage to turn professional with a European team. Deep down I still believed that a professional cyclist was forged in a certain way; living and racing in Europe had simply been the *only* way that had existed up until then. It was a tough decision.

'Can I have a little more time to think about it?'

Both Ken and John seemed a little perplexed. They had just offered me what many other British cyclists would have considered a golden ticket. And yet I hadn't bitten their hand off.

Over the next few days I mulled the decision over. The problem was that continental Europe was still the only recognisable route into the professional world. Teams like Vendée U, or their equiv-alents in Italy and Spain, churned out two or three professional riders a year. To my knowledge only one British rider in history had managed to turn pro without going through the European amateur system, and that was Chris Boardman. He was the exception that proved the rule, however; his chosen niche discipline of the time trial meant that he managed to avoid really ever being a part of European cycling.

I knew that the WCPP didn't have history on its side, but I did recognise that it would give me back the opportunity to work closely with Ken. Ken had been my coach from my first races as a junior. He, more than anyone else, knew how my body reacted, and his training ideology fitted perfectly with my physical capabilities. The idea of working with him again was a big draw. The other major credit was that the WCPP programme would be completely Under-23 rider orientated, and would allow me to race Under-23 World Cup races. After two years of riding semi-pro events, going back to age-restricted events seemed like going back and riding as a junior again. But by being at these races I would be competing with the best Under-23 riders in the world; I would be putting myself in the shop window for professional teams.

A certain ruthlessness eventually swung the decision to go to the fledgling programme instead of heading back to Europe. I knew the general standard of the other riders being considered for the programme; I knew that I was the sole hope for success on the road. I realised that the whole programme would have to be tailored to suit me. For it to succeed, I had to succeed. The programme was designed to put me in the best condition to perform. They needed me, and I needed them.

While the races may have been considerably easier for me, the Under-23 system also had its pitfalls. The age limit put a false sell-by date on riders, something which had already been playing on my mind in France. By considering a place on an Under-23 team the idea now came charging right up to the forefront. The idea was prevalent amongst us young riders that if you were 23 years and 15 days you couldn't turn pro any more; subsequently I realised this was all bollocks. Riders all mature at different ages, and there is no age limit on turning pro. I, like everyone else, was just in a rush. Even before I went to sign the agreement with the WCPP I was an intense young man, and once I did make the decision to join the programme it felt like the clock was ticking. In 1999 I had two years left in the Under-23 category, but in my mind *this* had to be the year.

But things couldn't have got off to a worse start than they did.

* * *

I woke fitfully in the night, in pain and in the unmistakably starchy white cotton sheets of a hospital bed. I was never awake enough to form a conscious thought, but I could hear talking. Very close to me was the sound of two Irish accents.

' … young boys messing around in the woods like that …'

'Well, if he is going to go … I just hope he hurries up, I could really do with getting home.'

I awoke the next day to a great deal of pain, and the realisation of what had happened caught up with me. It was November, and I had agreed to ride with the WCPP, but before I began training for the 1999 season I took a holiday in Ireland to see Aidan. The morning I arrived Aidan's neighbour, Killian (or 'Killer' to his friends), had lent us his quad bike to go messing around in the woodland. It was great fun, but being the young, testosterone-fuelled boys that we were, we inevitably got a bit too cocky and pushed it too far. With me riding pillion and Aidan putting the quad through its paces, we hit a turn at high speed and, finding it tighter than Aidan had anticipated, we cut sharply part way through the bend. The quad rolled and threw Aidan clear off, but I somehow stayed on it and was dragged underneath, taking the whole weight of the bike on top of me as it turned over. I had crashed plenty of times on my road bike before, but as soon as I sat up I knew it was bad. In panic my first thought was, 'I am alive,' and then my brain started to focus again and I took in what I was looking at. I stared in horror as I saw my foot was twisted right around, pointing in the wrong direction.

My mind went into shock. Aidan, realising he had to take charge, scrabbled to call for an ambulance. Aidan was one of the few people I knew at the time with a mobile phone, but we were in the middle of a wood in Ireland in 1998 – as far as phone coverage was concerned we might as well have been in the middle of the fucking Atlantic. Our only option was to tip the quad back over and drive out. The ride back to the flatbed truck that we'd used to transport the quad was pure agony. Every tree root and bump on the trail sent stabbing pains from my ankle through my whole body. When we reached the flatbed Aidan finally had a signal to call for an ambulance, but we had no idea where the fuck we were. Aidan hurriedly tried to describe the route that he had taken, but he realised that it was of no use. I heard him talking but it was slowly dawning on me that something was seriously wrong. I was bent double with stomach pain, and I couldn't even look at my foot that was dangling at the end of my leg. I could feel everything draining out of me.

Aidan decided that waiting for an ambulance was out of the question, but in the panic and confusion we had lost the keys and were locked out of the van. He smashed the window of the cab, and hotwired his own truck before lifting me into the passenger seat and starting to drive. I began drifting in and out of consciousness. Desperate not to pass out, all I could do was to focus on the terrible and seemingly unending pain that was surging through me. As soon as we arrived at the hospital it was too much; I scrawled on the consent form that was put under my nose and the doctors finally put me under.

Until I awoke in the night that was all I could remember. While I had been out, the doctors had operated to remove my spleen and reset my ankle. I had slowly been bleeding to death from the inside, and the time it had taken us to get to the hospital had put me in real danger. By the morning I was stable, but the pain was still agonising. My stomach had to be held together with staples, and an allergic reaction to the anaesthetic I was given made me vomit constantly. The pain I felt when I awoke and began dry retching remains the most intense agony I have ever felt in my life. All I could do to fight the pain was to keep asking for more morphine. I slipped into the groggy semi-comatose state, drifting in and out of a painful consciousness, while Celine Dion sang 'That's Just the Way It Is' on a seemingly endless repeat on the hospital radio. Even now when I hear that song I get chills.

My first visitor was Pat McQuaid. He had heard about the accident from Mike Taylor, and came straight in to see me. Pat was the organiser of the Junior Tour of Ireland at the time and his visit was a real boost to my mental state. I was eventually moved to a bigger hospital in Dublin, where I had another operation, this time to put two pins in my ankle. I had been frightened by the severity of the accident in the previous hospital, but when the doctor came to visit me after the second operation my fears only worsened.

'Well, it went very well. You will have a good range of movement ... but you won't be winning any yellow jerseys.'

The doctor's comment shocked me to my core. And as he swept out of the room and on with his rounds I was filled with dread. I repeated his words out loud, 'You won't be winning any yellow jerseys.' What sort of a comment was that? In my panic I became angry. Had he just thrown a mention of the yellow jersey in there to try to relate to me? What, though, if he knew what he was talking about and he knew I wouldn't quite be the same again? There didn't seem to be any doubt that I could be a 'normal' person again, but I didn't want that; I wanted to be a professional athlete in one of the hardest sports in the world. What if my cycling career had been taken away from me before it began? I was so angry that I wanted to chase him down the corridor and ask him what the hell he meant, but even the thought of moving sent shockwaves of pain through my body.

I was stuck there immobile for two weeks before I could return to York. Horizontal in that hospital bed, I actually saw the very real possibility of my dream of becoming a professional cyclist being taken away from me. It didn't feel like *just* a setback; it was more serious than that: not being able to race would have meant I was unable to do what I loved, what I needed. I was so meticulous in my life that everything I did was geared towards this one overarching goal, and now, after a moment of stupidity, it felt like it could all be over. My mood swung from determined optimism to absolute dejection. Not knowing was the worst punishment of all. In that Irish hospital bed I developed a callousness that would drive me through the next twelve months; a ruthlessness that even I hadn't anticipated. Coming back from France had been a kind of defeat, and now this accident would cost me at the very least precious time.

If I felt I didn't have much time before … there was even less now, and I was determined to make it work.

Less than a month later I walked to my bike on crutches to get back in the saddle for the first time (much to the confusion of my neighbours who must have wondered what on earth I was doing, hobbling around the driveway before jumping on to a racing bicycle). It was as clear as day to me that as soon as I had enough movement to pedal I needed to be riding my bike. I needed to know. I didn't care if I had to walk on crutches for the next year as long as I could get on my bike and train. My first ride lasted a little under 45 minutes. I was content when I came home because after weeks I had finally ridden, but I was still frustrated that I wasn't able to stand up out of the saddle. I had tried but had simply collapsed back down into the seat because my ankle was still so weak from the injury.

No matter the weakness I knew that I could do it, I just had to work harder. My sense of determination only doubled. I hobbled into the house on my crutches and made my way up the stairs and into the bathroom. I stripped my cycling kit down to my waist and took a pair of electric clippers from the bathroom cupboard. This I knew was the moment; from now on there was nothing else. Any little thing – even having to brush or style my hair – was an unnecessary waste of time and energy. I switched on the electric clippers and felt the vibration against my skull as I set the blades to my head and began to shave. My blond hair fell in lumps to the floor, and stuck to the sweat on my back and neck. When I finished I ran my hand over my prickly white scalp and looked into the mirror. I saw my face, suddenly made to look harder without the softening framing effect of my hair. I grinned a brutal sadistic grin to myself. I looked as pragmatic and ruthless on the outside as I felt on the inside.

Over the following winter months I didn't do anything apart from ride my bike. To avoid the winter weather I rented an apartment in Spain with Tim Matheson, Ken's son – also an amateur cyclist. We holed up in Benidorm, in out-of-season accommodation, and lived like assassins: we did nothing but eat, sleep and train. The only other human beings we saw in January on the Costa Blanca were old-aged pensioners or other cyclists. There were no distractions, and no consideration for normality; there was only cycling. In my head everything had become clear. I knew that the push to turn professional was going to require absolute focus, as well as making every single sacrifice that I could. I completely ignored anything that wouldn't help me or was superfluous to the cause. I shrugged off the remnants of my ankle injury, telling myself that if I could pedal, that was all that mattered. I was living at my limit.

Ambition had total control of me. As a cyclist, or any kind of an athlete, you get the idea into your head that to have peace with yourself each night you must go to bed exhausted from training. My compulsion with improvement didn't just stop at what I could do on the bike. I had to feel that I had done absolutely everything in my day correctly so as to be able to get the best out of myself on the bike. I had to have trained properly, eaten properly, stretched properly and recovered properly too. It was an issue of conscience; if I lost and I had done everything, then I could accept it. But if I lost and there was one little box I hadn't ticked, I couldn't forgive myself.

I obsessed over every minute detail of my life; there was nothing I wouldn't do to try to improve. The trouble was that, without much frame of reference in the UK at the time, learning the trade of cycling came by way of osmosis. Tips flew around like Chinese whispers. People fed me the most ridiculous ideas, but if it came from a convincing source I'd do it.

I followed titbits of illogical advice religiously, advice that with just a pinch of common sense I could've torn to pieces. But it wasn't logic, it was pure emotion dressed up as science. I remember reading that riders had tea in their bottles in races (which they do) but I had only seen my mother drinking tea with milk in, so I made milky tea for my bottle and ended up with the most atrocious stomach ache. I would find myself riding around the Yorkshire countryside with thermal jackets on because I had seen that some of the pros had worn hats and legwarmers in 30-degree heat, but I had no fucking idea why I was doing it (and perhaps they themselves were doing it for misguided reasons). I would never drink a cold Coca-Cola because apparently it gave you diarrhoea, nor would I eat the middle of bread because it was said to expand and bloat your stomach. All these little 'tasks' or tests, whatever they were, became the checkpoints of my life. I absolutely had to pass them, and I couldn't let even one person get in the way of me ticking them off each night.

I did everything I could, and sure enough it all started to add up: as soon as the racing season got underway I knew that amongst this kind of competition I was incredibly strong. The single biggest difference that I noticed when I started racing with the WCPP was the standard of racing. Suddenly, compared to what I had spent the previous two years doing, the Under-23 World Cups felt like they were easy. The benefit of all the times that I had been put in races way out of my depth in France was that compared to the Trophée des Grimpeurs, the Espoir Triptyque des Monts et Châteaux was a walk in the park, and I had gone from getting my head soundly kicked in to being the one doing the damage. I still received little or no support from most of my WCPP teammates – the other riders were either well out of their depth, or track riders who were drafted in to a few races on the road for training – but my determination to succeed was bolstered by the confidence of early success, and the big results duly came. I won two stages in the Thüringen–Rundfahrt, an Under-23 World Cup in Germany; I was third in the Under-23 Liège–Bastogne–Liège; I won the Under-23 National Road Race; and was second in the European Time Trial Championships.

My whole life was tailored towards winning these races and getting these kinds of results, and yet when I won them I still didn't even allow myself to celebrate. Victory wasn't something special that I felt I should sit back and enjoy; success was the natural conclusion to my hard work. My focus was so intense and my approach was so exhaustive that I didn't have room for that kind of emotion; I took satisfaction in winning, and nothing more. I didn't keep a single magazine cutting or race number; there was no room for sentimentality. A win was simply another box ticked in what was turning out to be an almost infinite list of boxes I had to tick to be content.

The success continued through the summer, but it didn't take my nervous mind long to start worrying about when the big moment that I was working so hard towards would actually happen. I had plenty of results now, but no pro team managers were coming up to me at races and asking about what plans I had for the following year, or even showing the faintest bit of interest. I had invested so much that the thought of not getting a contract almost made me physically ill. The nearest it felt that I came to a break with a pro team during the year was a brief moment in a pub in Edinburgh after the Tour of Britain (the PruTour as it was then known). Someone introduced me to Brian Holm, who was then the manager of the second division AcceptCard team, and Brian said, 'So you wanna be a pro?' and I shyly replied, 'Yeah,' and that was it. After a slight pause he went off chatting to someone else. It was the last night of the race and it was quite late by then, and I convinced myself that Brian had walked away from me because I was showing that I was unprofessional by being there. I beat myself up for weeks afterwards, wondering how I could have been so stupid. I was so young and determined that I had no idea that Brian was just having a good time, and that talking to an intense young amateur cyclist about professional cycling was probably the last thing he wanted to do.

Then, in September, with only a month of the season left, there came a small step in the right direction. I accepted an offer to ride as a *stagiaire* for the Linda McCartney team at the Trans Canada stage race. The McCartney team were a British-based third division professional team, and even though they talked up their plans for the future very convincingly it wasn't anywhere near the kind of ride that I had been aspiring to, or that I thought my results deserved.

But Trans Canada was a tough test for me; it wasn't just that the weather was grim – it pissed it with rain all week – but the stages were all along straight Canadian roads that meant every day ended in a sprint, which didn't suit me at all. The thing that killed me was the fact that my body found the whole thing so traumatic. I was so in tune with my own body, but I just wasn't yet used to long-haul racing trips, which meant that going over to the other side of the Atlantic to race was a big deal for me. Everything that had been regular seemed to become irregular, and I was waking up in my hotel room at all hours, lying there wide awake only to start to drift off again by the time we were due to wake up. It was a feeling that I would get used to in the years to come, but at the time it felt like I had been picked up by my ankles and tipped upside down.

To add to everything, I had to become an honorary vegetarian for the race. Linda McCartney sold vegetarian meals and the company was trying to promote the fact that you could perform as a professional athlete and be meat-free. I am sure that it was a good idea on paper to have a cycling team that promoted the vegetarian diet (perhaps less so in Europe where the idea of it still causes consternation among chefs and pitied looks from waiting staff) but it was absolutely ridiculous to expect me to suddenly make such a drastic change to my diet and try to perform to the same level. It was just too much for my body to try to take on. The ride with McCartney had seemed like a glimmer of light at the end of the tunnel, but by the time the race neared its conclusion that light seemed nothing more than the briefiest flicker of optimism.

And then, as I rolled to the start of the time trial on the last stage, my world changed for ever. The tall and sympathetic figure of Serge Parsani stopped me in my tracks as I made my way to the start ramp and asked for my phone number. Parsani was managing the Mapei team at the race, and they had been there for a full ten days, the same amount of time that I had been there, and yet until then he hadn't said a word. For the life of me I couldn't fathom why all of a sudden contact had come from the biggest team in the world. I was beside myself. The intensity of excitement was so strong that I wasn't sure if I felt joy or relief, or a mixture of both. I wanted to laugh, to cry, to kiss someone and throw a TV out of a hotel-room window! My head was propelled into the clouds. From the moment I left the conversation with Parsani until I finally put pen to paper with Mapei three weeks later, I felt like my feet didn't touch the ground.

After being contacted at home by Mapei when I returned from Canada, I was called in to the Mapei offices for testing. Before we left to go to Italy Ken pulled out a huge file of my blood test results: 'Just in case they need to see them.' At first I was surprised; growing up with no exposure to erythropoietin (EPO) had meant that I lived in a completely different world to almost all of the Italian amateurs that Mapei were used to dealing with. It had never even occurred to me that professional teams would want to look at my blood before they signed me, to check what they were buying.

I had first started finding out about my blood values when I was still a junior. With his interest in sports science, Ken had periodically tested my blood to make sure I wasn't getting too run down by the training he was giving me. I had extremely high values then, long before the UCI (International Cycling Union) had introduced the 50 per cent rule and the system of UCI 'health checks' that could prevent a rider from racing. At the time of my first tests these were just a bunch of figures that I knew nothing about; all I had wanted to know was if my blood was good, or bad. As far as I was concerned, if having 'high' values meant I was healthy, then I was happy.

Once I had done the tests and we sat in the Mapei centre awaiting the results I realised the importance of it all, and I became slightly panicked. I started thinking that they would instantly see my high haematocrit and refuse to sign me because I was a danger. I kicked myself for not having paid more attention to something that was so vital. But without any exposure to drugs there was no reason that I should have known. When the results came through my haematocrit was sky high as normal, and Ken – being well prepared – had started to explain the reading, assuring Aldo Sassi that I was 100 per cent clean. To both of our amazement Sassi wasn't fazed at all: he had seen the high score, but he had also looked thoroughly through the numerous other test results that they took and said, 'No, it's OK. We can tell.' It turned out that the haematocrit test was the most basic kind of blood analysis test that could be done, and that Mapei were smart enough to look not only at the haematocrit level (the cheapest and easiest thing to analyse) but other values that were a more accurate pointer to whether or not someone was taking EPO. The doctors there looked at reticulocytes (which gave a count of the number of immature blood cells being produced), a clear sign if the levels were too high that they were being manipulated in an unnatural way. These methods were available to the UCI too, but, for whatever reason, they were happy to go with a basic form of detection and to draw a line in the sand that could potentially cost innocent athletes their livelihoods. I was so relieved. All I cared about then was that Mapei were still interested in signing me, but I knew I was going to have to start paying attention. Over my career, though, haematocrit would become something that I wasn't allowed to forget about.

After the testing I was finally due to sign my contract with the team at the GB team hotel after the World Under-23 Road Race Championships in Verona. When I arrived at that World Championships with a professional contract on the cards, I was the pride of the WCPP. There was one more event to go, however, the biggest race of the year – the World Road Race Championship itself – and, just like at the 1996 Junior GP des Nations, I was the centre of attention again. This time it wasn't just Jacques Duchain looking after me, and Bernaudeau's word at stake; now it was a whole national cycling team.

The pressure had grown – I could feel it building up inside. In the few days before I rode the GP des Nations in 1996 I had a huge spot appear on the end of my nose. Maybe it was stress, maybe just coincidence, but just before that World Championships another colossal zit appeared in *exactly* the same place. I was so convinced in all the odd things I had been believing in that I told myself the spot must be a sign that I was in great form, and was about to do something special. As such, despite being all too aware of its glaring obviousness on the end of my nose, I refused to burst it. I left it there full of pus. As it turned out, the spot was just a spot, and it wasn't a sign of form at all. It did, however, get its moment of glory – despite my poor performance in the race – when it ended up captured in full colour on the cover of *Cycling Weekly*, as the news of my contract went out.

The Under-23 race was held on the Friday, and, after signing my contract on the Saturday, at Mapei's request I stayed to watch the professional race as a guest on their gigantic team bus on the Sunday, the last day of the championships. After a day spent on their swanky team bus, stealing glances at the coloured Mapei logo tiles on the floor and feeling like I was about to get kicked out by security at any moment, I drove with the team to the apartments so I could see the accommodation they would be providing for me the next year.

If a day inside the Mapei bus had been surreal, nothing prepared me for the apartments.

As we had driven along the shores of Lago di Comabbio to the complex, Patrick Lefevere, one of the team managers who had driven myself and two of the team's American riders, Chann McRae and Fred Rodriguez, up to the apartments talked in modest – almost embarrassed – tones about the accommodation. But as the car entered through the electric gate and pulled up inside a cobbled courtyard I couldn't believe my eyes.

The 'apartments' were 110 square metre luxury condos that sat right on the shores of the lake. As Patrick disappeared to collect the keys to my apartment from the complex manager, I looked about me and saw to my delight that the complex had a swimming pool, and a huge garden overlooking a picture-perfect view of Monte Rosa. It was stunning, but the best was yet to come.

Patrick returned, keys in hand, and looked about the place trying to work out which of the apartments would be mine. His eyes fixed on one that matched the number on the key ring in his hand.

'Ah, this way.'

He hurriedly led me across the courtyard to one of the condos closest to the lake, and opened the door before ushering me in. The apartment might as well have sparkled: it looked like a home in a commercial for cleaning products. It was kitted out head to toe with brand-new furnishings. I walked into the pristine kitchen and, out of curiosity, opened a drawer and saw that it was full to the brim with every imaginable piece of cutlery I could ever need, and some that I hadn't even known existed. It was a ready-made home, and it was there for me. I was flabbergasted.

As I walked about in disbelief, still stood by the entrance Patrick continued to downplay the apartment, coyly remarking, 'You may have to share with another rider to begin with, while we work everything out. I hope that's OK?'

I nearly burst out laughing. Only two years previously I'd been living in a house seemingly held together with grime, sleeping on a bed held up by bricks. Patrick could have told me I was sharing that apartment with five riders and I still would have thought I had landed on my feet.

I spent the night there before travelling home the next day. As I went to bed, my head was spinning. I'd had such a sensory over-load in those three weeks; it was my first time in Italy and it felt like everything I could have imagined it to be, and more. I lay there and thought to myself that this is my home now. I wasn't just visiting; this is where I was going to *live*. It was incredible; it was like waking up in a dream. It took me so long to fall asleep, and when I did eventually wake in the night again to pee, I switched the light on in the bathroom and looked about the place, I was so happy to see that it was all still there.

Things got better still the next morning when I went to the Mapei office for some blood tests. The secretary there told me that the only available seat on the flight back to Britain was in business class. When I heard those words I hoped that the delighted laugh that I heard in my head wasn't actually audible, but by now I felt I couldn't really tell what was real anyway. I sat in the lounge at Malpensa airport sipping champagne, still dressed in my cheap Gap trousers and Great Britain cycling team T-shirt I'd been wearing all season, and tried, somehow, to take it all in.

When I arrived back in the UK, Mike Taylor picked me up at Manchester airport. All through my years in France and my year with the WCPP I had continued to seek advice from Mike, calling regularly and always making a point of visiting when I did come back to visit the UK. He and his wife Pat had become family to me. They had been my first port of call whenever I was struggling, and the first people that I wanted to share news of success with. To celebrate my contract they had organised a party in my honour at their house in Chapel-en-le-Frith. They squeezed eighty people into their house and entertained them all. It was a rare occasion indeed that a British rider managed to turn professional, and it felt like everyone I knew in the sport was there, an extended family all linked through cycling, and of course through Mike and Pat. Ken of course was there; Dave Millar – who had met Mike at the same Tour of Ireland as me, but had already been a professional for two seasons – was over from France, Graham Jones, another of Mike's 'boys', plus a whole cast of local riders that I had ridden with over the years. It felt incredible; it was a kind of deliverance from one world into another. Mike and Pat were incredibly generous people who loved the sport and never asked for a thing in return. Coming back to them a professional and feeling the genuine warmth of that celebration was a special feeling.

I had a few months at home to prepare for my first season as a pro, and after a short break it was soon time to think about getting back on my bike again. In December I was ready to train to be a professional, but I still didn't quite feel like one. Just before I had left Italy Mapei had given me a bag full of clothing to train in during the winter. If you looked at it totally pragmatically, it was such an odd thing: Mapei were a cement company who made glue and flooring, probably some of the most mundane things you could think of. But such was the culture in cycling that for someone like me who was a fan, who still read *Cycling Weekly* cover to cover, having that kit plastered with the famous logo was ludicrously exciting. I looked at it in its various plastic packets, and I took it out and tried it on, but it still took me until the first day of the New Year before I could go out and ride in it, before I felt worthy of it. Until I was officially on the Mapei professional cycling team books on 1 January 2000 I still felt like the amateur I had been all this time. I was ashamed to wear the kit; it felt like it would some-how have been wrong, like I was pretending, so instead I spent the winter training all in black. When January came around, though, a package arrived: it was my Mapei business cards. They read: Charly Wegelius – *Ciclista Professionista*.

CHAPTER 3
Per Vincere!

The Zì' Martino hotel was what travel guides would describe as a 'family hotel'. Every building that made up the hotel could be, and probably was at one point, private housing. The hotel was in a place called Castagneto Carducci on the Tuscan coast, and it had been the destination of choice for the American Motorola team for their early-season training camps throughout the nineties. When I sat down to dinner in the hotel's homely dining hall – a long low-ceilinged room, with a warm fire that seemed to be permanently lit – there were framed pictures of the Motorola cycling team adorning the walls: pictures of Phil Anderson and Steve Bauer smiling and posing with the hotel's portly owner and his tired-looking Alsatian, as well as one of the whole Motorola team stood outside the very same hotel, with the very same staff who were busily serving me now. As an English speaker, I had grown up idolising the likes of Phil Anderson and Frankie Andreu, and staring for hours at pictures of those guys in places just like the one I was now in, doing exactly what I was now doing. No matter how hard I had worked for it, and how much I thought I deserved it, being a professional cyclist was going to take some getting used to.

In early January 2000 I had spent a week at the team houses in Varano Borghi, before heading down to Tuscany to join up with the rest of the 'young riders' group for the first time. That year the Mapei team had thirty-nine riders; it was effectively two teams within a team. There was the established order that was made up of many of the best riders of the time: Johan Museeuw, Michele Bartoli, Stefano Garzelli and so on. Then there was a young rider group that I was part of. The formation of our little squad was totally new to cycling at the time; we were seen as the new generation, one that would be successful through pondered, logical work and *not* drugs. The whole project was dear to the heart of Mapei's owner, Giorgio Squinzi, a passionate cycling fan and a man of science and rationality.

The young riders team was in many ways way ahead of its time: Mapei had a genuine ambition to clean up the sport and at that first camp the management had outlined what the project was. Cycling was going through a very difficult period at the time. The Festina affair had blown the lid off the widespread and flagrant doping culture that had gone on for so long; now there was pressure to catch riders, but there was also an entire generation of riders who had raced for years under a system (and a governing body) that had turned a blind eye to doping. The concept of our team was based on the idea that to renew cycling they had to invest in a group of young riders who Mapei could back properly, and allow to develop without the pressures of financial and job security that would potentially be put on them by other teams.

Mapei knew that the doping culture existed, but fixing it wouldn't come through drugs raids in the Giro d'Italia, or throwing the rulebook at stupid individuals who got caught. They wanted to make doping an unacceptable part of their team, and they made a team that was so good that being a part of that was enough for riders. We were overpaid, we were looked after better than any other cycling team on the planet, and we were reassured that as long as we toed the line we would be looked after. It might have been a naïve approach to rid cycling of doping, but it was ahead of its time because it was positive instead of simply prohibitive. It was how Giorgio Squinzi wanted it to run. Cycling wasn't just about money for Squinzi; he was a genuine fan of the sport, and he believed that positive reinforcement against doping was the way to combat it. It was a way of doing things that struck me as very just. There were plenty of riders who might have pushed the boundaries as amateurs, and got better results than the guys in the team, but Mapei kept a close eye on the riders that they wanted to sign, and tested them before they did – anything that appeared suspicious meant they simply wouldn't offer a rider a contract. It was a powerful statement to all young riders, and it felt good to look about the room at that camp and know that the people really flaunting the rules weren't there.

The camp also served to give our group – made up entirely of neo-pros – ten days to start to get to know each other and the staff, without the potentially imposing presence of the team's big stars. Roberto Damiani was the man who would be looking after our squad, our team manager. I had met Roberto a few times before the camp, but when we arrived there and the serious work began there could be no mistaking that Damiani was a man who wanted to do great things. His presence was unavoidable; he was authoritarian and highly disciplined, and he wanted us to get the best out of ourselves, and he took every opportunity to remind us why we were there.

The first time I experienced this first hand I was part way down the corridor of the hotel that led to the dining room on the second evening of the camp.

'Charly … where are you going?'

I heard the voice from over my shoulder, and I stopped and turned to see Damiani walking in rapid paces towards me. I wasn't sure what I was supposed to say to this, so I responded, 'Going to dinner.'

'Why are you going to dinner, Charly?'

I was completely flummoxed by this second question, thinking it was blindingly obvious why I was going to dinner. I hesitated before suggesting, 'To refuel?'

'No. You are going to dinner, Charly, *per vincere*! To win! Everything that you do, Charly, you must do to win. That is why we are here, that is why we are bike riders: to win. *Allora*, whenever I ask you why you are here I want you to respond: "*Per vincere!*" And I want you to think of that in everything you do. So, why are you going to dinner, Charly?'

'*Per vincere!*'

'*Bravo, ottimo!*'

And with that Damiani walked off happily. It may have seemed funny but he wasn't joking. Whenever he saw a rider anywhere at the hotel during that camp he would go through the exact same routine, and no matter what anybody was doing he always wanted the same answer: *per vincere!* It made us laugh to hear it, and to say it after a while, but there was no escaping the fact that he was deadly serious about it. He was a man who I imagined woke in the morning and used his first thought to think about how to win bike races. I noticed at that first camp that even when he sat down to dinner his fists would remain tightly closed on the table, as if he couldn't let himself relax even a little, in case he missed an opportunity to improve us.

With all the changes that were happening in my life and my desire to train well that winter, I'd barely had time to start to study Italian by the time the first camp came around. It was a mistake that made for a pretty tough week. I shared a room with a guy called Nicola Chesini, who didn't speak a word of English and spoke with such a weird Brescia dialect that I think I'd have had trouble understanding him even if I knew Italian. Chesini was actually quite rare for an Italian, as he seemed to make no effort at all to be friendly, and perhaps that explains why he lasted only a year on the team. Turning pro may have been a big deal for Chesini and the other Italians in the team, but they were in Italy, amongst Italians in an Italian hotel eating Italian food. It was nothing like what I was experiencing. I felt like I'd been thrown out of a spaceship. I didn't understand anything that was happening on the television; I didn't understand a word anyone was saying at the dinner table. I would sit there in the evening at the table, fucked from the training, working out how to ask for more pasta or less sauce. By 8 p.m. each night I was completely exhausted from the effort of it all.

My only chance for real social interaction was through Damiani, who spoke French, and a Belgian rider, Kevin Hulsmans, a really nice guy who made a real effort to talk to me in English. I committed myself to learning the Italian language and trying to understand the culture as quickly as I could. Without the vocab I would be marginalised, and might as well not be there at all. Being part of a pro team was a less cutthroat experience than an amateur team, where everybody is desperate to make the next step and only a few can. In a pro team everyone has 'made it' in a sense, but it was still a fight to survive, and that meant socially as well as on the bike. By that stage Lance Armstrong had 'only' won one Tour de France, and the Europeans were still reeling in shock that he refused to speak French in press conferences. It would be years before the language of the peloton would slowly shift to English. For a rider like me at the time it was crucial to fit in and ingratiate myself with my hosts. I had to work out how the Italian psyche worked, and quickly. Italians, I realised, are quick to interpret shyness as being a form of arrogance or a sign of an antisocial character. Being social is so fundamental in Italian culture that perhaps unknowingly Italians could often have very little empathy for those who did things differently.

László Bodrogi was one such rider who suffered in this culture. László was Hungarian and he came to the team with some really impressive results but he just didn't fit in, and perhaps never got the best out of himself as a result. László was a bit different, I have to admit. I lived with him in my first few months in the Mapei apartments and he would do all sorts of odd things like line his socks up on the washing line in colour order, insisting that all objects had to always be at right angles, even down to the knives and forks on a dinner table (I took great delight, of course, in rearranging these things as soon as he left the room, just to see how frustrated he got when he came back in). He didn't seem to enjoy socialising, often spending time between races playing his PlayStation instead. He wasn't a bad guy, but he was immediately put in a box because he was deemed odd. Cycling, in Italy in particular, had a schoolyard mentality, and if you didn't fit in you were either picked on or cast aside.

Perhaps not understanding the language in the first camp allowed me to observe the behaviour more objectively – whatever, but after that first week I felt like I started to understand Italians a little. Not so much that I could claim to entirely come around to their way of thinking – that would be something I would grapple with through-out the years I spent there – but for the time being I knew what I had to do. I pushed myself to be a gregarious person, to fit in. I had spent years being known as someone who was determined and dedicated, so it was a massive relief to feel I could actually be socia-ble too. I was always someone who enjoyed joking around with people, but my determination through my amateur days meant I had repressed that. I hadn't interacted with my WCPP teammates because I saw it as a waste of energy. In Italy my survival depended on my being a part of the team and a new side of me came out as a way of integrating myself. I threw myself into learning Italian with gusto in the first months in Italy, and although I made mistakes, as anybody would, I was happy to laugh at myself when I did. The Italians really loved that because they aren't very good at laughing at themselves so it endeared me to a lot of people really quickly.

I had no idea at the time, because I was so blinded by the desire to make myself a part of that world, but in promoting the parts of my personality that best suited my environment and going from the ultra-serious rider who barely spoke to a gregarious figure of fun I was changing myself to suit the situation, to please others.

My ability to quickly 'fit in' became one of the qualities that made me most suitable to the job of a *domestique*, but, ironically, by the time I came to finish my career it would be one of the things that I would grow to dislike most about myself. It was like falling in love and moving in with someone; when I arrived in the world of professional cycling I was so head over heels about my situation that I ignored any of those little annoyances, but in the long-term relationship I was embarking on the little lies I was telling myself were bound to come up again.

● ● ●

Those first months around the busy schedule of training camps and team engagements were spent trying to adapt to life as a professional. Another significant change in this period was with my training. Aldo Sassi had taken over my training from my former coach Ken Matheson as soon as I had signed for the team. I had first met Sassi the previous October, and had been instantly impressed with how smart the man was. He had the air of a nutty professor: the day-to-day things in life were little more than an inconvenience that took time away from what he loved to do – namely, think about new ways to make cyclists improve. I took to him instantly because I recognised that he was someone who shared my approach to being prepared to be innovative to go faster. He was also a kind man, who I believed always really cared about me as a person, and he would go on to have an immeasurable influence on my career. At the beginning of our relationship, though, I had found that the training methods he was recommending were very different to those that I was used to, and I was already out of step with most of my teammates. Italy was right at the forefront of developing training techniques, and they had been the dominant nation in the sport for years. There were things I learnt in my first year as a pro that others had been doing since they were 15; things I didn't even know existed, like motor pacing or strength training. Ken had been brilliant for me, and he had developed my fundamental comprehension of how my body worked, and how to train, but in Sassi I found the man who could show me how to finish the job, refine me and take me to the next level.

Despite this big change, when we eventually got to our first races it seemed I had adapted well. The impact of becoming a professional didn't even compare with the shock I had in that first year as an amateur in France. I was operational from the beginning; I started to work out what to do in the races and did everything I was told. I felt like someone in their first week of a new job, running around the office amid glares of disdain from the old hands, doing as much as I could and thinking, 'This is so easy, I could still do so much more.' Initially I rode the programme of a lower-level professional, not dissimilar to the better races I had ridden with Vendée U, but in April, only four months into my professional career, that all changed.

'How do you feel about riding Flèche?'

Damiani's head was leant back as he looked at me through the open car window and passed another *bidon* out to me. I couldn't believe what I was hearing. I stopped pedalling and just looked at him wide-eyed for a moment. The faintest beginnings of a grin broke out on his usually stern and concentrated face.

It was the third stage of the French stage race the Circuit de la Sarthe, and there were only a handful of days until the Belgian Classic Flèche Wallone. As one of the most important races on the professional calendar that spring, Flèche wasn't on the young riders' programme, and was an infinitely more important race than any of us in the young team expected to be riding at that point. As Damiani handed over the last of the *bidons* he explained, 'One of the Classics squad is sick, so they need one of you to fill in. I suggested that you do it.'

It was a hugely important moment for me and I knew it, and I think Damiani enjoyed it a little bit too. I was struck by a thought: the team needed to fill *one* single space with a young rider and they had chosen *me*. It was only April and I had no results to speak of, but in a short time I must have done something to impress them. I rode back to the bunch with my pockets full of *bidons* and I felt like a kid who had just drunk his first pint of beer: I felt like a man.

At Flèche I shared a room with Axel Merckx, and even being in a room with the son of the greatest cyclist on earth was quite a big deal for me. Axel was so relaxed and so 'normal', but when I looked at him there was a tiny part of me that was still a cycling fan; I still thought, 'Your dad was the greatest cyclist ever to live, and you are just there!' When I thought like that the whole situation became surreal again. Axel's world and my world had at one time been unimaginably far apart, and now they were intertwined. Things got more surreal still while I was lying there on my bed the afternoon before the race. Axel had gone down the corridor for his massage and the phone rang. A man's voice asked if Axel was there, and I said, 'No, he went for a massage.' The voice replied, 'Never mind, good luck for tomorrow – tell him his dad called.' I said, 'Yeah, no problem,' and put the phone down, before I suddenly realised: Fuck me, that was Eddy Merckx!

It was quite something going to Flèche as part of the strongest Classics team of a generation. I was so excited to be there, yet my first sensation once the race began was one of mild surprise. I had seen the final hours of the race on TV so many times that I had imagined it would be hilly from the off, a race perfectly suited to a climber like me. Eventually, after a blustery and uncomfortably flat start, we came through the finish for the first of three passes of the Mur de Huy. Racing up through the deep crowds on the steep corners, I finally felt a part of the great race as I'd imagined it. It felt like the real thing. I was a part of a scene I'd seen a thousand times, and among the faces shouting on the side of the road I glimpsed the proud face of Mike Taylor, who had come to watch. But the moment didn't last: as soon as we went over the iconic climb we were back on the flat, lined out in another crosswind and fighting for survival. Being there as the bunch raced up a famous climb like the Mur de Huy might have given me a brief spine-tingling moment, but there was a lot more to those races than I knew, and they were a lot harder than I had ever imagined.

I had been allowed to be a part of the 'big team' for that race because even though Mapei was divided between the young riders group and the older guys, there was no definitive line like there would be later on, when the UCI limited the numbers of riders in a team, and the team had to register two separate squads (one in the first division, and one in the third). In that first year riders were often mixed up between teams, and I raced with a lot with riders such as Andrea Noè, Davide Bramati, Paolo Lanfranchi and Paolo Fornaciari. They were undoubtedly the loudest and most vocal group in the peloton. Both Noè and Bramati had deep, booming voices that seemed to travel for miles. No matter where you were in the peloton, if either of those two spoke up you'd be sure as shit to hear them. In fact the whole group of riders were loud off the bike too; on a flight to one race other passengers actually asked to be downgraded to Economy to get themselves moved further away from the din that lot were making. They were all good strong riders, riding high on ten years of Italian dominance in the sport and being the core *domestiques* of the biggest team of the time. In me they found someone who, for whatever reason, they decided they would teach the job to.

It was never something that was announced, or spoken, and there were plenty of other guys that they could have chosen to help: Gerhard Trampush, for example, an Austrian guy who was the same age as me, and probably a better rider too, but they completely ignored him. I think that they could see that he wanted to be a winner, but they saw me as someone who was going to fill their role. If Trampush wanted to win ten races, then good for him, they couldn't teach him how to do that, because they didn't really know how – they had barely won any races between them. But they could teach me how to be a *domestique* – that was a job they knew. They didn't have to do it, and even by doing so they threatened their own careers, but there was something there that made them want to teach me, and they did it in the way that they themselves had been taught.

The job of a *domestique* was something that I knew of, but I too, like many, had never really understood its intricacies. Physically the *domestique*'s role is to use his energy to protect that of his team leaders, with the aim of delivering him to the crucial moment of a race with as much energy left as possible. This meant knowing when and how to protect a rider from the wind, fetching food, clothing and information from the car, and, most importantly, placing a rider at the correct spot for the key part of a race. But there were other more complicated things to learn, like how to manipulate, or force, the shape of a race to change it in the favour of his leader. There were dozens of ways a *domestique* could be put to work to do this: infiltrating breakaways and driving hard to wear down the opposition, or by infiltrating the break but being passive and thus discouraging breakaways and slowing the race down. Sometimes it would be important to go with a break, and sit and wait for an attack from his leader from behind, so that there would be a fresh helper waiting up the road. The options, I started to learn, were endless. But the key thing I had to learn was that a *domestique* has to be almost as strong as his leader, and must also be smart and aware of what he is doing. Often it was the job of the *domestique* to make split-second, race-defining decisions on all of these things without direction from the team leader or the manager. Being able to make those kinds of calls in my career would be what could define me as a *domestique*, and to do that well would mean that I had a lot of learning to do.

Their method of teaching me was nothing like the kindly apprenticeship I had hoped for. It was more like getting the job pummelled into me. That group was on to me constantly: 'Why are you doing that? Don't do that! Stop doing that! Ride here! Ride there! Why's your saddle like that? Don't wear that jacket today.' They were boisterous and rough. At times I felt harassed, but it was their way of teaching me. They made my life tough at times: I was the butt of every joke, and I always got all the shit jobs, like going for water at the most terrible times. The 'method' that these riders used to toughen me up almost took me to the point of cracking. There were times in races when the pressure was off that I dreaded going back through the bunch past their group, where they rode near the back, knowing that as soon as they saw me they would want to know where I was going and what I was doing, and then I would here the yells, *'Ecco, Charly! Ma dove vai? Dove vai, Charly?'* Then they would all start laughing about something or nothing at all. At times it could be difficult, but, sure enough, what they taught me kept me in a job for the next ten years.

There were exceptions in the senior group, who helped me out in different ways, and they were the riders who kept me sane. Stefano Zanini was a rider I got on really well with from the off. He was a bit different to the others because he was a winner, he won big races and he was paid to do so. He was big guy, born for the Classics, but he was also a quiet guy, who stood out from many Italians with his blond hair and generous smile. He never really said much but through the first couple of years I started to notice that he was often there next to me, and it was a kind of assurance for me. He became like a big brother. He took the time to help to integrate me into the training groups in the area around where we lived, as well as, remarkably, helping me to integrate socially with his friends. 'Zaza' grew to be one of the most important and longstanding friends throughout my career.

I found it incredible that some of my teammates, like Zaza and Daniele Nardello – another cheery face in the local training group – went so far out of their way to introduce me to people. They were always ringing me, even though I would never think to make the effort to get in touch myself. It was all the more strange for me as only the year previously I had been so ruthless to my own team-mates at the WCPP that I had barely given them the time of day. I had seen their level as cyclists, and thought that I didn't have time to help them along because you couldn't do that if you wanted to be successful at racing yourself. And yet here were men who had actually made it to the top of the sport, ringing me up and taking me out to meet their friends. It was a real wake-up call.

* * *

Though some of the riders had made up their minds, the team management didn't instantly pigeonhole me as a *domestique*. But the few times that I fell into a leadership role, as happened occasionally in 2000 and 2001, I felt the weight of responsibility that comes with being a professional, and I realised very quickly that I didn't like it one bit.

In the Peace Race, in early June 2000, I found myself in the break on the hardest stage. The Peace Race ran through several former Eastern Bloc countries and that particular day we were due to finish the stage in Poland. It was pissing with rain, and the roads were dirty and covered in a thick black film that gave everyone the appearance of having just emerged from a mineshaft. The conditions and the riders' willingness to race had meant the stage had been hard from the start. It was a slog match and it was grim. After 100 kilometres or so I was on the back of the group consoling Antonio Rizzi, who was in tears, crying because he said he couldn't take it any more, because he was the only Italian in the Mapei team at the race and it meant he had no one to talk to – a real issue for an Italian. He wouldn't stop blubbing and I could feel that my being there probably wasn't helping anyone, so I said, 'Oh, you stay there then,' and looked for a wheel to take me back up the bunch into the action. When I found a wheel it turned out it was a good one. Andreas Klöden dragged me all the way up the outside of the bunch and straight past it. Before I knew what was happening we had a gap with riders coming across to us. I put my head down and the next time I looked around into the murk we were clear.

There were six of us in the group: a couple of Poles, Denis Lunghi from Colpack, Juan Manuel Gárate from Lampre, and Klöden. It was a good group, proper riders. We built up a decent lead before the finale and entered the finish town of Kudowa Zdroj all together. The final kilometre is one of those strange distances that can seem to be over all too soon, or can seem to be far too long. This particular final kilometre felt like one of the longest I can recall riding. As we went under the red kite we dropped down a descent into the streets of the town and took a sweeping left-hand bend that dragged up to the finish line. As we shot down the hill towards the bend it felt like the moment was going too quickly, my mind speeding, thinking about what I had to do. I was sure by the time we came out of the bend we must have covered at least 750m. The crowds were big and I was trying to keep an eye on the other riders in the group, as well the distance to the finish that was now in sight. Everyone was playing a game of bluff, the calm before the rush. I looked at the others, and I looked to the finish line, and I went. I stamped on the pedals and launched my sprint against the gradient. I sprinted as hard as I could, with every ounce of muscle I had. I could feel the distance between me and the riders behind me, and then I flicked my head up to see how much closer I was to the line. What I saw was heartbreaking. The finish line had stayed impossibly distant; the gradient of the road had been a tease all along, making me feel that I was much closer than I had been. I felt my legs buckle and my determination turn to embarrassment. In no time I felt the rush of the rest of the riders as they gathered pace and shot straight past me. In an instant they were going for the win and I was left behind. The line still seemed to get no closer at all. The incline reared up as if in some kind of cyclist's nightmare, and my legs slowed to what felt like a crawl. The last stretch took for ever: in 200m I lost a massive four seconds to the winner. I had made a complete mess of it.

It was humiliating for a neo-pro, and it felt especially so for me. I hadn't asked to be there in the break, and a part of me had thought I would get a pat on the back at least for being in the winning move for the first time as a professional. The loss hurt, but Damiani's reaction when I saw him after the finish was devastating.

'If I didn't know you better I would have thought that you'd sold it.'

He didn't yell, but his remark cut right through me. I'd gone too early, and I fucked it up and I felt bad enough about that, but what he said crushed me. He seemed genuinely surprised that anyone could really be *that* bad without taking money to deliberately lose. By that stage of the year the team had already won over thirty races – Mapei was a team that expected to win. In a smaller team being in the break fighting for the win would have been some sort of achievement at least, but with all of the bonuses of being in a team the size of Mapei came a clear picture of the serious side of the sport. This was real business. When I had been an amateur with the WCPP, whatever I did was great because I was their best rider and they would have been fucked without me. Now, when I sat down in a foreign hotel room the night before a race for a team meeting, I was part of a machine, with nine other cyclists in the room who were all ambitious, who needed to earn money. There was a huge bus parked outside that'd been driven half-way across Europe to get there, and we had ten staff members to help us; there was even a girl sat in an office in Milan whose sole job was just to buy our plane tickets to get us to the race. The existence of that whole system came down to whether or not we could win. If I put my hand up in that meeting, and I fucked up and fell short, then I would get blamed for it. It was an uncomfortable kind of pressure, it was serious, and I hated it.

I felt I was surrounded on all sides by winners; even in our young team, riders had been picking up wins left, right and centre from the very first races we took part in at the start of the year. My failure to do so in Poland only added to doubts I had that I wasn't quite like the others. Riders like Luca Paolini, Crescenzo D'Amore and Rinaldo Nocentini were widely considered as future stars of the sport. Between them they had won countless major amateur events, as well as medals at junior and Under-23 World Championships, and now they were already winning as professionals. I knew I had been good at stages of my career, but I still didn't see myself in the same league as my teammates. Once I had moved out of the junior categories winning had become increasingly difficult, and I couldn't help but reflect on that. I began to worry about how hard it would be to win and keep winning at the level I was now at. The proof was in the pudding, I suppose; a charismatic guy like Paolini would have shrugged off a result like mine in Poland and just got on with it, assured that his time would come again. I, on the other hand, saw things differently.

If I didn't want to deal with the pressure of being a winner and shoulder the responsibility of a professional team, then I was going to have to think about what I could do in my career to make myself useful enough to keep myself in a job. If I wanted to be a *domestique* then I knew that I had to be good at that. I knew enough already to understand that being a *domestique* would be a hard career choice in its own right, but the pressure of having to win felt so acutely uncomfortable to me that the decision was already made in my mind. I still wanted to do everything I could *per vincere* but I didn't want it to be me that had to do the winning.

• • •

If ever I had needed confirmation that the role of the *domestique* was perfect for me, it came at the Tour de l'Avenir in September 2000. That remains one of my fondest memories of my time in the professional peloton. The l'Avenir was a major focus for Mapei; it was, to all intents and purposes, a young riders' Tour de France. The race was restricted to riders under 25, and it was only ten days instead of twenty-one, but it was organised by the same people, the money came from the same sponsors and, most importantly, the leader's yellow jersey was exactly the same as the one worn in the Tour de France. Until that point, despite all its success, the Mapei team had never worn the yellow jersey at the Tour. For this reason, Damiani wanted to bring it back to Milan as a way of showing the owners that the young riders in their new system could do the job that the older team, using the old techniques, could not.

We prepared for the race as seriously as we would have for the Tour de France itself. A month or so before the event, a long-list of riders was drawn up and the group was taken to altitude on top of the Stelvio Pass in the Alps for a training camp at the start of August. We took an entire staff of doctors, masseurs, mechanics – everything was taken care of with the utmost attention to detail. When we had arrived at the camp I didn't hold out too much hope of finding a place in the team, considering how many others had won races or performed exceptionally well that year. Yet after those two weeks at altitude I was told that I had made the team. Selection, as always, was music to my ears.

The race started well. Luca Paolini won the first stage for us, and it was a big deal. From the first training camps at the start of the year Luca had been the leader of our group; he always had the ability to lift his teammates' morale with his performances and attitude. It was as if he knew he had to set the ball rolling for us, and he did. The next day László Bodrogi took the yellow jersey by winning the time trial. The only trouble was that one of our number, Crescenzo D'Amore, had been forced to pull out through illness on the first day, which left us with only five riders to defend the jersey. When he lost the yellow to Bodrogi, Paolini still had the green points jersey, so we were trying to save him for that competition, meaning it was down to the four of us to defend the jersey for eight days.

Once we had the lead with Bodrogi other teams naturally expected us to control the race in a traditional sense, but with so few resources we knew we had to get inventive. In that situation a team normally locks down into defensive mode. The leader's team is expected to take up the responsibility of riding on the front each day, and trying to keep the race together for the smoothest ride possible to the finish. Damiani had other ideas, however, and we threw the rule-book out of the window. We tried all sorts of different tactics: splitting the race at unexpected times, attacking *en masse*, and a few times we even put Bodrogi in his yellow jersey into breaks, forcing the others to chase. It was alternative thinking, and the other teams could never work out what we were up to.

But this could only go on for so long. We were being so successful that the other teams wanted to see us lose. On the seventh stage it all came to a head. A big break went down the road but, amazingly, when the order from Damiani came down the radio, it wasn't to chase, but to sit up. It was the moment when we should have been panicked, the race lead was going down the road, and we were letting it go. The bunch ended up at standstill. The gap quickly grew, and Damiani kept on repeating on the radio: '*Stai tranquillo, ragazzi.*' His voice was so calm we were utterly convinced that he knew what he was doing. Riders in the bunch were confused. They didn't know what to expect: we should have been chasing, but it seemed to them that we had just made a humiliating mistake. Other directors started driving up to Damiani in the convoy and asking him what the hell he was doing. It wasn't just us who wanted the break to be reined in, other teams weren't there either, but the game of bluff that Damiani was playing was so ballsy they didn't know whether to believe it or not. I dropped back for water, and stuck my head through the open car window. Damiani told me in conspiratorial tones that Eddy Ratti and I were to keep ourselves ready. Damiani knew our capabilities better than anyone and, as I made my way back through the bunch, he kept on reassuring us over the radio, saying, 'Don't panic, keep eating and drinking.' By the time the lead reached 15 minutes the tension got too much for the other riders, and they started coming up to us in the bunch, asking what was going on. We were holding all the aces, but no one had any idea when we would be playing them.

Then we hit one of those classic stretches of French road: it was dead straight and rolling for mile after mile. The order came bursting through our radio earpieces, 'Hit them hard … now!' Eddy and I were ready for the call and we jumped across to the left-hand gutter and started riding as hard as we could, both of us giving a faster, stronger turn than the other had just done. We went flat out. I could hear the yells and panicky shouts of the riders in the bunch behind; we had caught the race off guard and now suddenly we were riding like it was the last kilometre. We were going so quickly that the pace felt impossible to maintain. I started to suffer. My mind was still fresh and determined, though, and I told myself that until Eddy got dropped I couldn't let go. We were causing chaos behind us, and pushing each other to the limits. The official motorbike kept showing the gap as it started to fall. It was just the two of us against the three guys in the break. As the gap tumbled, I just wanted to give more and more. With less than 10km to go the break crumbled and we swept them up and put the race right back into our hands. It felt incredible.

That evening at dinner as I chatted to Eddy, and was once again astounded by just how slowly the man I called 'the hamster' could eat his spaghetti, he confessed between thoroughly masticated mouthfuls that the only thing that was driving him to keep going so hard was the thought that he couldn't stop until I did. It was amazing what we had done. It was the truest sense of a team: the sum of our achievement had become greater than its parts. As we sat at dinner and grinned at each other it felt so special to be a part of that team experience. The following day brought more of the same, although this time it was me who became greater than my parts. On the final climb of the tough stage to Le Grand-Bornand, I found myself catching Bodrogi after he had lost contact with the leaders. His hopes of winning the race were disappearing. I was on my knees from the effort on the previous stage but I knew it was our last chance. The climb was really fast big-ring stuff that meant there was a lot of benefit to be had from sitting on the wheel. I pushed out the hardest rhythm I could and kept upping the pace. Soon the leaders were in sight and I managed, with what I thought were my last scraps of energy, to get him back to the group before I blew completely with 2km to go and was dropped. Damiani pulled along-side me in the car and looked at me, he said, '*Ancora una volta, solo una volta.*' I was so fucked I didn't think I could get back to help, but I was determined to do the best possible job I could for everyone there; I wanted to do my bit. I still don't know where I found the energy, but I rode back up to Bodrogi in the group, and he gestured that there were riders who had attacked and were in front. I got to the front of the group and buried myself into my pain. I dragged the group as hard as I could until, with 600m to go, I just exploded. I was so over the limit that I literally stopped at the 400m sign to hold on to the barriers. I had ridden myself to a standstill. Bodrogi ended up losing the jersey that day by four seconds. I was devastated.

Later that evening as I lay on my bed there was a knock at the door of my hotel room. Without moving I yelled for whomever it was to come in. When the door opened I was a little shocked to see the face of Álvaro Crespi, the general manager of the team, along with Damiani. Crespi was visiting the race, and had spent the day in the team car with Damiani. The paranoid, worried side of me immediately thought that they were upset that we had lost the jersey. I sat up to attention on my bed and steeled myself for a serious bollocking.

Crespi took a seat on the bed next to mine and said, 'Charly, are you happy in this team?'

'Of course,' I said, still fearing the worst.

At that he reached into his pocket, pulled out an envelope and handed it to me.

'For your hard work today.'

I opened it and I saw to my disbelief that it was a cash bonus of 5 million lire. It turned out that Crespi was delighted with what he'd seen from me that day. He then proceeded to rip up my two-year neo-pro contract, and made a new one with a raise. I couldn't believe it. I had won no races, and nobody in the public knew what I was doing, but all of a sudden I realised the importance of my job, and what it meant to the people that mattered.

After they left I fell back on to my bed in amazement. Suddenly I saw that I didn't need to win as a professional because I had found another way to get all the gratification that I wanted. It wasn't just about money, it was the feeling of those important people, who had power over me, coming in and giving me a pat on the back and acknowledging what I had done. I loved it.

CHAPTER 4

The Vuelta:
A Distribution of Resources

The moment that I found out my ambition of riding a Grand Tour was about to become a reality, I was lying on a hotel bed in France with seeping wounds all over the left side of my body.

I had that morning abandoned the Tour du Poitou et Charentes, a grotty four-day stage race in the Vendée. It was a race that I knew quite well, having been taken along to watch by Jean-René Bernaudeau when I was still a junior. But unlike when I was an impressionable 17-year-old, by 2002, in my third year as a professional, I was no longer happy just to be there. The style of racing and the terrain at Poitou–Charentes didn't suit me at all. I had struggled my way through the first day of crosswinds and rain, and my morale dropped down into my shoes by the start of stage two in Saintes, where I was expecting more of the same. I knew the roads in the area well and I dreaded what was coming: less than half an hour later, sure enough, I was tucked up behind another rider, millimetres from the gutter, as the bunch was being torn apart in the crosswinds. Whoever it was in front of me started to lose the wheel and put his hand back to offer me a sling. In desperation I grabbed it, but he lost balance. I went straight over the top of him and went skidding on my arse across the tarmac, tearing up the left side of my body. My race was over – there was no way I was getting back on the bike. Lying there, bleeding on the floor, I wished that I could just finish up the season there and then. As it would turn out, I had much further to go.

That night, as I lay on my hotel bed, half naked and swathed in sticky bandages like a leprosy victim, Eric Vanderaerden, one of our Belgian managers, strolled into my room to ask how I was. I gave my standard response that I was doing OK. Eric, like many Belgians I knew, could be quite direct when he spoke English, but what he said next felt like a one-inch punch from Bruce Lee: 'Good, because you're going to the Vuelta.' I couldn't believe it. The entire left-hand side of my body was a freshly torn wound and I was being told that I had seven days to get my head around riding a three-week stage race. Racing a Grand Tour was something that I desperately wanted to do, but I didn't want to go into it like this.

I had imagined that I would be given at least a month's warning before I was thrown into riding a Grand Tour. It had always seemed like such a momentous task that I had perhaps naïvely assumed proper preparation time would be granted; I thought that was what being a professional was about. This was like telling a 400m runner at the Olympics that they were doing the marathon the next day. I was shell-shocked. When I picked up the phone and called Sassi he confirmed my selection. My participation in the biggest event of my life so far had come down to one simple factor – there was no one else. Sassi told me, '*Senti*, Charly. I know that it is short notice … It is far from ideal, but there is no one else who can go. We can't be sending someone who is going to get off in three days because they have a contract in their back pocket. This will be good for you, I am sure.'

Mapei was stopping sponsorship at the end of the season and the team was full of unmotivated riders who had already signed contracts for the following season, meaning that no one was really all that keen on three more weeks of suffering. I was working hard to find my own contract, but that was a drama that I knew I couldn't let interfere with the challenge ahead. Óscar Freire, Mapei's reigning World Champion, wanted to ride in preparation for his World Championship defence, but due to the proximity of the Vuelta to the Worlds he would be abandoning after ten days, leaving whoever was left to steer the Mapei ship to the finish. I was the ideal rider to call on in this situation: I was dependable because I was so desperate to please. The team knew I would go to the Vuelta (or anywhere) no matter how short the notice, and they also knew with a well-calculated certainty that I would be desperate to finish my first Grand Tour.

This kind of incident wasn't an isolated one in my career. I had already worked out in my three years as a pro that a lot of being a professional cyclist was down to a rider's ability to just *manage*: to be able to go to races when you were tired, and to be able to keep yourself in a good enough condition to perform; that you'd often be starting races with far from ideal preparation, perhaps already tired, sick or injured. No matter how nicely a year would look laid out on a spreadsheet at training camp in January, a professional cycling season was a series of blows that knocked you down; blows that you had to keep getting up and coming back from. Without doubt throughout the year the phone would ring just when I least expected it, and I'd know by the overtly friendly tone of the manager's voice what was going to come. 'I need you to be at this race. There is no pressure – I just want you to ride.' This was always a glaring half-truth on the manager's part: of course, I could never 'just ride'. I always knew I'd be judged if I rode badly, not least by my own relentless high standards.

The Vuelta is a classic example of a race full of riders who have been cornered this way. Since switching its place on the calendar from May to September, the race has suffered from the weariest and most unmotivated peloton that the cycling year could gather together. The Vuelta field was like the crew of a pirate ship. It was cobbled together with unmotivated riders who'd been press-ganged into racing, riders who'd been injured earlier in the year, and a decent smattering of desperadoes and mercenaries to boot.

There was no middle ground; either riders didn't want to be there, or they were desperate to perform. The rate of rider abandons was staggering as teams sent troupes of exhausted riders to compete with Spaniards who wanted to plunder the race as quickly and violently as they could. For the riders like me who had been forced to face this fierce armada against their will, this was a frantic and often dangerous place to be. And, indeed, in this situation many riders reacted differently to me: they would turn up when they were forced to, but then fake an injury or just abandon in the first few days. Dario Pieri, a man who liked his food and the good life considerably more than riding his bike, turned up to that 2002 Vuelta with just a rucksack on his back and no suitcase or luggage.

He did the team time trial prologue and then stopped on the first stage after 1km. It was all quite amusing to us, but it was probably less amusing to the Alessio team that paid his wages. Abandoning was simply never an option for a rider like me. My job security relied on an absolute toeing of the line, and doing what no one else would do. Showing resistance wasn't an option. I was going to the Vuelta, ill prepared and injured, whether I liked it or not.

      • • •

One week later I lay on yet another hotel bed, this time in Valencia, in a new pair of pyjamas waiting for the doctor to come and re-dress my wounds. In the few days that I had at home after Poitou et Charentes, hobbling along to the shops to buy a new set of pyjamas had been a high priority. In the scant time that I had it was the most important bit of preparation I could think of doing. I knew I would be staying in at least twenty different beds; my environment would be changing nightly and I knew that I had to try whatever I could to make each of those alien beds a little bit more accommodating. Lounging about a hotel room in a tracksuit is comfortable, but for real comfort the only way to go is to wear pyjamas at all times that you are not outside of the room. New pyjamas were hardly the most rock 'n' roll accessory, but they were vital to me. From that race on I brought a new pair for every Grand Tour I rode; it became my one ritual and, while it hardly made the difference between winning and losing, it did go a long way to keeping my mental health in check.

It was unbearably hot when I arrived in Valencia. Most of the Spanish guys were used to the heat, but their reactions to it went from the sublime to the ridiculous. In our team we had two Spaniards: Óscar Freire and Pedro Horrillo. They were both good guys who I got along well with; Pedro had been a philosophy student before he was a cyclist and Óscar continued to fascinate me, as I wondered how any man could be so relaxed and yet achieve so much. I think their time in foreign teams had helped tone down some of the eccentricities that the Spanish guys normally displayed. Three years living in Italy had thankfully taught me that the habit of deliberately over-dressing on the bike to stop myself getting sick or injured (or whatever it was said to do) was nonsense, and that as soon as the hot weather arrived the sensible thing to do was to try to stay cool. But the Spanish still did the opposite: they have an obsession with wrapping up in the heat that borders on absolute insanity. It was so hot that year that the day before the Vuelta began, on our last pre-race ride, Óscar stopped a few kilometres short of the hotel to strip down to his bib shorts and get into the sea for a swim to cool down (much to the delight of the occupants of the gay beach that he had unwittingly chosen to stop at). If Óscar's impulsive dip was a little amusing – the sight of the World Champion stripping off his rainbow jersey mid-ride to swim in front of a delighted male audience was the stuff of tabloid dreams – it was at least, I suppose, a normal human reaction in those conditions. When we returned to the hotel to find one of the Spanish teams riding the rollers with woolly hats and legwarmers on it was simply ludicrous. I still have no idea what the hell they were up to, and if it was supposed to freak the non-Spanish riders out it certainly succeeded.

Whatever the locals were up to, I didn't allow myself to worry about it. In the days preceding the race my entire mind was fixated on getting to grips with the magnitude of the Vuelta. The longest race I had embarked on up until that point was twelve days. Knowing how hard that was … then adding another nine stages on top seemed unfathomable. I wasn't just worried; I was petrified. I tried everything I could to break the race down into sizeable chunks in my head. I played mental games; I counted out the time-trial stages, and tried to assess which would be the easier 'flat' or transitional stages and removed them too. I tried to persuade myself that it was in fact a three-day stage race, followed by a couple of training days, and then another eight-day stage race straight after. No matter how much I managed to delude myself that the Vuelta wouldn't be that much harder than what I was used to I'd soon remember the reality of the situation and trepidation would resume its normal place in my psyche.

Things actually seemed to start well when, before the first stage, Vittorio Algeri, a close friend of Gianluigi Stanga's and the *directeur sportif* of the Vini Caldirola team, came and found me and thrust a letter in a Colpack-stamped envelope into my hand: 'This is something to keep you *tranquillo*.'

I had negotiated a verbal contract with Stanga before I'd left for the race so I opened it immediately and found it was a letter of intent, stating that I had agreed to a contract for the following season. I felt so relieved. The letter was my guarantee of a future, or so I thought. No matter how hard that Vuelta would get, I knew that I was safe because I had that letter. I put all thoughts of my team situation to the back of my mind.

* * *

The sound of a tinny drum machine tapping out a pop rhythm and the opening strains of a Latin-tinged Europop number sent a frozen chill down my spine. I opened my eyes again and heard it kick in; the voice of a female singer came blasting out over the music:

Que el ritmo no pare, no pare no
Que el ritmo no pare
Que el ritmo no pare, no pare no
Que el ritmo no pare

Acércate un poquito, acércate un poquito
Dame un besito nene que esto esta muy rico
Por qué yo quiero que, que
El amor sincero vuelva ya ya ya

In the start village of the Vuelta the organisers played the race official theme song, seemingly incessantly. Every time I heard the opening bars of that jangly saccharine pop song my heart filled with dread. It was a jaunty song that for the spectators who came down to the stage starts would have been harmless fun; to me it was the chimes of a Eurotrash death march. As the singer piped up again, belting out another chorus of laughable sexual innuendo around bike racing, I cowered in the back seat of the team car in my kit, ready but not wanting to go to the start.

Once the race had finally got under way with the team time trial, my focus switched solely to my survival. On the first stage I lost a massive 7 minutes; on the second stage I was dead last – 5 minutes 30 seconds behind the winner. By the finish of stage five I had already lost over half an hour to the race leaders. The anticipation of pain is the worst kind of torture imaginable, and after only a few days of the Vuelta I was finding each start village a terrifying place, not to mention the roads that led out of it.

The starts were particularly terrifying because some genius in the organisation had decided to experiment with shorter stages.

The concept behind it was that, because almost no one watched a long stage in its entirety, the organisers could pack more action into a shorter space of time (plus there were a few vague notions kicked around about the shorter distances playing a role in the battle against doping). The problem was that with a shorter distance the riders fought twice as hard to make a difference. Riders were no doubt also still doping left, right and centre, but now they were in a rush to make good their advantage as soon as they could. There was no gentle warm-up to the stage, no time to roll your legs out and get a little bit of blood flowing again to allow you to feel even the slightest bit recovered. As soon as the flag had been dropped (to the sound of the fucking Vuelta theme song) the race was flat out, and the speed was incredible: by the time we left the neutral zone the bunch was already doing 60 km/h. If you are suffering in a stage race, every kilometre that you can manage to stay in the group without too much effort is a bonus. When races start so quickly it can feel like you are caught in a rip tide. In amongst the speeding peloton even my best efforts left me feeling almost motionless. The harder that I thrashed away, the more my legs seemed to turn to stone. The average speed of one of the stages in the first week was a staggering 51.6 km/h, and the only reason it wasn't faster was because there was a bloody great 6 km climb near the finish that brought the speed down a bit! At times it felt like madness; on one occasion we were doing 77 km/h on a flat road and I looked down at my 53.11 and wished I had bigger gears because I simply couldn't pedal it fast enough.

The Vuelta was characterised by these high speeds: the fastest road stage of all time was clocked only a year later in the 2003 edition; that day the race winner *averaged* an astonishing 55 km/h. It would be naïve to say that the Spanish were just motivated; the rumours were widespread in the peloton of how lackadaisical Spanish authorities were when it came to doping. I saw this for myself when I went for a doping test during the race. I sealed the sample bottle lid and, as I always used to do, turned it upside down to check that it wasn't leaking. This time it was, so the doctor said, 'Well, that's null and void then. Off you go.' He simply cancelled the test instead of making me wait there to piss again! This kind of attitude would have been practically criminal in any other country. So it was evident that there was a different attitude to doping in Spain, but I refused to let myself be fixated by this knowledge. Once you started worrying about who was taking what you only had two choices: to admit you're beaten, or to dope yourself. I was racing the Vuelta clean and I was determined to do so because that was what the people who were helping to build my career expected of me, and that was all I cared about. I told myself that if riders wanted to dope they could always do it: I was sure Belgians took EPO, the French took EPO, and plenty of Americans were taking EPO too, and for lots of races other than the Vuelta. The way I saw it my problem wasn't drugs or the Spanish attitudes to doping, my problem was just how fucking fast the riders in front of me were going.

* * *

At times in that first Vuelta it felt like the organisers had put every possible obstacle in my way. That year, on top of the shorter stages, the organisers were making some quite radical changes in order to boost viewing figures for their struggling race. For example, they moved the weekday stage starts to 2 p.m. so that the finish would be on at prime time in the evening, which was a big change in routine for those of us who were used to racing in the mornings in Italy and France. The Spanish were OK with it because they went to bed so late they could sleep in until the very last minute, but I awoke early in the morning, only to have to hang around killing time until we could go to the start. Then, on the weekend, the organisers started the stages at 9 a.m. so the television audience would get the best part of the race for peak viewing on Saturday afternoon. It was like racing in another time zone entirely.

The flat stages had been fast, but the mountain stages were brutal. We raced the Angliru for the first time that year, a gruelling 12 km climb in Asturias, with a 10 per cent average gradient and sections as steep as 20 or 25 per cent. It was so hard most of us considered it a gimmick that had no place in a bike race. Compact gears were yet to be adopted by road riders, so the lowest possible gear that was available was 39.27. The climb was so steep that if I rode sitting down I would lift my front wheel off the floor when I pulled back on the bars, and if I rode out of the saddle my back wheel would spin around hopelessly, costing me yet more energy. It was savage; Dave Millar was so appalled by it he ended up abandoning the race 150 m before the line. The press was delirious about it, but for many of us the Angliru was only the tip of the iceberg. I was dropped long before it on a climb that was just as hard, and although Dave's outburst at the summit was dramatic (and the kind of thing only a rider with his talent could get away with) he was just doing what a lot of us wanted to do.

Besides the high speeds of the first week and the severity of the mountains the Vuelta also had a strange emptiness to it. The race quickly passed into the middle of the country, and it troubled me for some reason to discover that there was nothing there. Spain seemed to empty out in the middle. The Vuelta still had all the parts for a big bike race – a gigantic noisy start village adorned in advertising for household products, for example – but in the middle of the country it felt like nobody was watching. The towns appeared straight out of a John Wayne movie, with tumbleweed rolling about the place. We would set off and go charging down the road with all noise and drama going on and we'd pass through villages that were fast asleep. I would imagine people sat there in their houses in total silence sitting up after we'd passed and saying, 'Did you hear that?' before listening to the sound of the wind again, and going back to their silent business. The hotels were basic, and when we were crawling back to our temporary home after the race each night I knew exactly what I would be facing on my plate that evening: *pollo*. On eighteen out of the twenty-one days we were fed chicken with asparagus and half a boiled egg for dinner. It was exactly the same every day. Night after night I felt like weeping into my watery salad when the same awful food was dropped on to my table – at a time of day I'd normally expect to be asleep.

The harder things were off the bike, the more attention I had to pay in the race to make sure that I could survive. My desire to finish the race was so strong that on many days it even slowed me down. Even when my legs were strong enough for me to feel encouraged, my desire to make it all the way to Madrid kept me in defensive mode. I thought to myself, 'Why would I try to get in a break today, when tomorrow I could be suffering again? It's safer to stay where I am, and save something.' Whether I liked it or not, my philosophy for that first Grand Tour became my byword for the rest of my career: a calculated distribution of resources. As I saw it, I had a certain amount of energy and that had to get me to Madrid; if every day I could save one tiny amount of energy that would be able to help me through the following day, it was a bonus. I was so tired, each night I would look at the route for the following stage in the race book and work out exactly where and how I could distribute my resources. On some stages I knew that I would have to hang on to get as close as possible to the finish; on others I knew that finding the *gruppetto* – the group of sprinters, non-climbers, as well as the weak and the exhausted who huddle together to try to battle through the climbs – as quickly as I could was my best option for survival. Throughout the race I started to feel like I was so focused on my own goal of survival that I wasn't even really there. I was oblivious to everything else. I kept up to date with what was actually happening in the race by reading *La Marca* each morning, and often I was genuinely surprised to see the results. I was so far from being in the action that I had no idea what was going on in the actual race.

● ● ●

'Go on, you're doing well!'

'*Venga, venga!*'

'Keep going. You're nearly there.'

I heard these encouragements from fans throughout the race each day, but they sounded like nothing more than pieties to me at that Vuelta. I wasn't doing well and I knew it. Being so far out of the back of the race was new to me. Deep down it felt like humiliation. It made me harden my attitude to the fans by the side of the road;

no matter their intention I couldn't help but feel that their encouragement was more like rocks of pity being lumped in my face.

There is no manual for surviving a three-week tour, but I learnt a lot about survival in that race. Cycling was still a craft – if a brutish one at times – and in these desperate times I gleaned knowledge and wisdom from those around me. It was Davide Bramati who taught me the knack of letting go at just the right time. His theory was that if you are not riding for the general classification, then you didn't *need* to finish in the bunch on the flat stages. When we were strung out at 65 km/h. on the run in, and I was hanging on by the skin of my teeth, he would just ride alongside and say, 'Charly, let go.'

Getting inside the time cut can be no easy feat, and making sure you got into the right *grupetto* wasn't about what you knew, it was *who* you knew. Life in the *grupetto* was something completely new to me. The term many cyclists and fans use to describe the *grupetto* is the 'laughing group', which is a cruel irony, as no one there is laughing.

In each generation there are certain riders who are practically walking mathematicians when it comes to calculating time cuts and average speeds. The German sprinter Erik Zabel was one such rider. At the Vuelta Zabel knew at the start of the stage when they would be able to let go of the front bunch; he would plan it the night before with the race book. You could see each day which rider was preparing themselves for the *grupetto*, because they would swarm around Zabel all day, and as soon as he decided it was time to let go there would be a collective sigh of relief from what felt like half the bunch. There was a world of organisation that I had to learn to be good in the *grupetto*; I had to be sure that I didn't end up in a group that was too small, or that was made up of riders who were unlikely to make the time cut. I had to know that I had taken on enough food and liquid before I was left behind by the team car for the day, and that crucially I had at least one friendly face that I really knew I could rely on for a little help, if I needed it. Not being a regular, I was well out of my depth in 2002.

Over the course of the race, though, I became quite expert at seeing who was smart in the group and who wasn't, and it wasn't only when I was getting dropped that I realised I could save myself any undue stress or effort. There were riders, for example, who would never get caught out pissing at the wrong time, and I worked out who they were. When I saw one of them stop for a piss I would know that it would be a good time to stop myself. Even the energy wasted by chasing to get back on to the bunch when they were riding at a hard tempo instead of a slightly easier one was crucial. There were other guys who it was worth keeping an eye on, too, who had an informed sense for what was coming: old dogs, so to speak. There wouldn't be a cloud in the sky, but if I saw one of those riders with a rain jacket in his pocket I knew the smart thing to do was to go and get mine straight away. Experience in those long races is invaluable, and there was always a lot of sense behind what they were up to. In Spain we could find that we'd pass over one mountain and suddenly it would start pissing with rain, and the old pro would already be prepared with his rain jacket because he had known that in those particular mountains showers always come at a certain time in the afternoon.

The other crucial factor for survival in a three-week tour was the way you conduct yourself in the group. Being with the same group of riders day in and day out for three weeks makes for a prison-yard mentality: there was a process of building up favours around the place, making the right friends quickly through whatever few little things I could do. I stopped throwing away unwanted food from my *musette*, as it was much better to give it to someone else … someone who might be in a position to help me out on another day. In this particular prison yard I quickly found I was at a major advantage: I spoke French and Italian fluently and had picked up enough Spanish that I could talk to everyone in the group, and so I worked hard at being on good terms with everybody. It was essential to talk to as many people as possible. I didn't ever really say a lot, just a hello or a quick word as I passed by in the bunch, but it was enough. The Vuelta is such a Spanish affair that if you go there and never talk to the Spanish riders then you never get the information that helps you plan the distribution of your resources. You need to know that the race might be going down a really dangerous road in three days' time, or that the wind will be really strong in a certain region, or that one of the Spanish teams will be getting ready for their big attack later in the week. If the first week of the Vuelta had taught me a lesson in speed, the second and third weeks taught me how to hang on.

On the 13th stage I crossed the line at the very back of the peloton. The ride from Burgos to Santander had been a relatively quiet one in the bunch, and the group drifted in almost nine minutes behind the break, which had taken off after only the second kilometre of the stage. The stage might have been relaxed, but once I was over the line I made a rush towards the team bus. I was desperate for news of the stage result; our race radios had gone out of range when the break's advantage had got too large and we hadn't been able to listen in to the action in the front. We knew that Davide Bramati had been on the break and was one of six riders who had fought out the finish. I dropped my bike by the side of the bus and clambered up the steps. As soon as I arrived inside, though, I knew that things had not gone well. 'Brama' was sat with his head in his hands, quietly cursing, and no one else said a word. Even Elio Aggiano, a man who could barely go ten seconds without cracking an obscene joke, was silent. I quietly asked Dario Cioni what had happened; Bramati had made a huge effort to get across to the four leaders inside the last 500 m and had immediately attacked, only to be caught and beaten by Giovanni Lombardi of Mario Cipollini's Aqua & Sapone team.

It was devastating. Aqua & Sapone had already taken three stages through Cipollini, and we had done nothing at all of note. Second place was so close, but it was worth nothing in cycling. With it being Mapei's last ever Grand Tour we had wanted to do something, but once Óscar had abandoned we knew that our chances of doing anything were impossibly slim. Bramati, though, had refused to lie down and die. He'd talked incessantly about that stage, because he knew it was the best chance for a breakaway to succeed and for him to salvage something for the team – for all of us. Bramati hadn't needed to try to win a stage; he already had a big contract with a new team for the next year, and so he could easily have just ridden around. He wasn't even a race winner – he was a *domestique* and it wasn't his job to win – but he was proud. We were the biggest team in the world; it was embarrassing for us to be seen to be going through the motions. It struck me then that

Mapei had indeed been something special, and I'd been privileged to be part of a team that inspired riders to race for more than just their pay cheque.

The setting for the climactic final stage was unspeakably grand: 60,000 people awaited our arrival in the Bernabéu stadium, and yet to me it felt like an insult, rather than a celebration. As the final days of that Vuelta approached, it seemed that, through either simple exhaustion or a desire to move on, everybody was increasingly desperate to leave the sinking Mapei ship. Our sole highlight in the race was Bramati's second place, but the rest of us had just been battling through, a state of affairs that hardly served to raise the morale amongst the riders or the staff. By the time we reached the last stage, a time trial that finished in the Bernabéu in Madrid, the team had completely fallen apart.

The team staff were so eager to get home that the team bus left early for Milan, leaving us to get changed in a crappy Fiat Doblò, and to warm up on the pavement like juniors. It should have been a big moment for me but I was absolutely finished, totally used up. I eventually finished the time trial 5 minutes down on the winner, Aitor González, and ended my first three-week stage race in a lowly 109th place out of the 132 finishers.

I flew home to Milan after the time trial, harbouring a huge feeling of anti-climax. I had built up the idea of doing a three-week tour so much in my mind that when I finally reached the end I didn't really know what to do. I felt like the world should have stopped, or at least paused while I was there, but it hadn't. What was more I had done nothing in the race but survive – there was no hero's welcome for a good performance; it felt more like I'd come home from three weeks of doing the nightshift than anything special. At home, I caught up with the news I'd missed, and the bills that were waiting to be paid, and the rest of the time I just slept. Finishing your first Grand Tour is a rite of passage amongst professional cyclists. It is confirmation that you are a *real* professional. I was desperate for a deep sense of satisfaction somewhere inside me, but after being so daunted by the task itself, when I was finally home I found myself lying there in my bed in the middle of the afternoon like a grumpy teenager thinking, 'Fuck me, how am I ever going to do that again?'

Getting home from that Vuelta was made doubly hard by the circumstances that now came careering into focus on my return to reality: the fact was that in finishing that 2002 Vuelta I had just completed one of the last races the great Mapei team would ever take part in.

CHAPTER 5

The Post Office

Back in June of 2002, during the Tour of Switzerland, those of us Mapei riders at the race had gathered together in a soulless, nondescript hotel room for a team meeting. It wasn't unusual at Mapei for there to be a meeting called on the evening of a stage race like this, but, as staff started to file into the room after the riders, it struck me something was up. 'This must be serious,' I thought to myself. Serge Parsani stood up and called for quiet. The room turned silent and looked to him as he leant back slightly on the desk in the corner.

'Mapei have announced that they will be stopping their sponsorship of the team at the end of the season. We are looking at various options, but it looks like the team will be disbanding.'

No one spoke a word. It was like a bomb had gone off. People were in utter shock. After a moment of quiet a sense of panic filled the room and at first whispers and then chatter and questions started up. In no time at all we were in a rowdy classroom that a teacher had lost control of. There were so many of us in the team, riders and staff alike, who like me had been fixated on keeping our jobs. All we had been thinking from the moment we arrived at Mapei was, 'If I keep my bosses here happy, then everything will be OK.'

There were forty-two riders employed by the Mapei professional cycling team in 2002. We were the cream of the world's élite. The announcement may have been made in June, but we knew straight away that the sheer size of Mapei's investment, and the costs of the organisation, meant the likelihood of another sponsor stepping in was almost non-existent.

After the years of dominance there were a lot of people who were very satisfied when Mapei announced it was disbanding, and many of those people put it down to the fact we'd spent too much money. Mapei had been generous to its riders, sometimes overly so. It had led to all sorts of stories of excess: rumours circulated that our riders would apparently ring up the team travel agent to get them to buy entirely new plane tickets because they wanted to arrive home twenty minutes earlier from races. Despite the absurdity and the waste (I could well believe that these instances may have occurred) they weren't the reason why the team stopped.

The truth was that over three years the team had unwound. In our history we had won 653 races, but it was always supposed to be about more than that; the sponsor and the management had big ideas and a real passion for the sport, they really wanted to change things and create a new generation of riders who raced free from doping. The team was perhaps too far ahead of its time, as well as ahead of the general public in their attitudes towards the sport. In that last season Mapei paid an advertising agency to do a poll amongst people in the street, asking which cycling team was doing the most to fight doping. Inexplicably, the majority answered Mercatone Uno, the team of disgraced former Tour de France winner Marco Pantani. Perhaps people thought that because the team had sanctioned Pantani they were fighting doping – but in reality that couldn't have been further from the truth. These were minor things, but they began to add up for Mapei.

The same month, June 2002, the team was dealt a much more serious blow when Stefano Garzelli was expelled from the Giro for testing positive for an outdated steroid masking agent, Probenecid. The whole affair was rather odd, and as riders we received very little information other than what we picked up in the press. But whatever had gone on, with the negative publicity that followed, it seemed that Squinzi had just had enough: he decided it was time to pull the plug on sponsorship.

Over the ensuing weeks and months, following the definitive announcement that Mapei would be pulling out at the end of the year, there were countless meetings and discussions in hotel rooms, at races and in the back of the team bus, about what we were going to do. A cycling team of Mapei's size closing its doors was going to create more than just a ripple in the riders market – more like a deluge of people looking for work. A lot of the team really wanted to stay together, so the organisation initially thought that it was doing the right thing by trying to find sponsors to take over the whole infrastructure and keep everyone together. In the long run this proved a waste of energy. By spending so much time trying to find a sponsor to take on a gigantic team full of expensive stars like Garzelli and Paolo Bettini, they didn't seem to realise that for a fraction of the price they could have kept the wonder team of the younger riders. They would have had the *crème de la crème* of future cycling: Fabian Cancellara, Filippo Pozzato, Bernhard Eisel, Michael Rogers, Evgeni Petrov – the list of talent they had and the riders they had to let go was eye watering, with hindsight.

It dawned on me slowly that I was one of the riders in the worst position of all. I had worked so hard to be a useful part of the system at Mapei that I hadn't realised that in the outside world people didn't really understand the value of my performances. Mapei had made sure that I had raced clean, and in the climate of 2002 this was no small thing: I was managing to perform in the midst of a peloton full of riders chemically enhancing themselves. However, that was only going to be of value to team managers who saw things in a certain way, and at the time those types of managers were very thin on the ground. Prospective team managers wanted to see results, and that was it. I knew that if I went into a meeting and tried telling most managers that everything I had done had been done clean, at best that would have raised an eyebrow while they thought, 'Well, what the fuck are you telling me for?' At worst they could have seen me as 'unprofessional' for trying to race clean in the first place.

Typically, my salvation came by way of chance. Seeing an opportunity to pick up some quality riders at a bargain price, Gianluigi Stanga called Aldo Sassi that August and asked what crumbs were left over from the Mapei table. Sassi immediately called me into his office and said that Stanga was looking for young, strong riders. He explained that it wasn't a big team, but it was well organised and got into all the top Italian races. Stanga had been in charge of high-profile teams for quite a few years, the last of which, Polti, had just lost its sponsor, so he ended up with Colpack – a much smaller sponsor who could only fund a second division team.

I went to the team service course in Bergamo just before I left for my first Vuelta and spoke to Stanga and the other general manager, Antonio Bevilacqua. Stanga's appearance was not too dissimilar to any other 50-something Italian businessman, but he had an impressive, deep voice and an imposing personality. It wasn't just his size that I made a note of; he was adept at using his whole demeanour to gain the upper hand. After he had welcomed me into his office above the garage that held the team's bikes, I sat down opposite him. The office was classically Italian: immaculately clean, marble him, a sturdy wooden desk and a smattering of beautifully designed furniture. A signed and framed rainbow jersey that had once belonged to the double World Champion Gianni Bugno hung on the wall behind the desk.

Stanga boomed at me in his Bergamasco dialect, 'We have signed Serhiy Honchar from Fassa Bortolo and we need to build a team around him for the Giro. You come highly recommended from Aldo. He tells me that you are a quality rider.'

It was strange that Stanga was speaking dialect in a business meeting, and despite the fact that I could speak it I kept my responses in classic Italian. I was sure that it was some sort of negotiation trick, so I stuck to what I knew.

'That works well for me. Obviously I have had a few years at Mapei to learn the trade and I've been very happy in that role.'

'Well, for now I think we can offer you one year. Our budget isn't huge; this isn't Mapei … We can offer you 30,000 Euro.'

Stanga was part businessman and part politician. €30,000 was just above the *minimum* salary he could legally pay me. He was direct about it and I was in no position to bargain. It was less than I had been earning at Mapei, and less even than I would have expected to be offered after three years at one of the best teams in the world, but I knew it was more than likely my only chance to be a professional cyclist next year. We made a verbal agreement that Stanga would draw up the contracts and I would sign when I returned from the upcoming Tour of Spain, and left it at that. After the brief meeting concluded and I left the office, Stanga's voice echoed behind me: 'Call me when you get back from the Vuelta.'

As I made my way down the stairs to the courtyard where my car was parked my relief was still underpinned by a deep hollow feeling. It had gone well, but I knew that leaving there without anything written on paper was far from an ideal situation to be in at that stage of the year. But I had no other choice.

• • •

Once the Vuelta had started, and I'd been delivered the letter of intent by Algeri, I didn't have the mental energy to think or worry about anything else, and while I was engrossed in getting my arse through the race, Stanga, looking to increase his budget, signed a deal to merge with the existing De Nardi-Pasta Montegrappa team. The team changed from Colpack to De Nardi-Colpack, a subtle difference on the outside, but one that had catastrophic repercussions for me. With the merger, the team was obliged to take on a number of riders already contracted to the De Nardi team. There was suddenly no space for me, and I had no idea.

News of the merger wasn't released immediately, so I was totally unaware of the situation when I called Stanga soon after I'd dragged myself home from Spain, and asked to arrange a meeting.

When he answered, it suddenly seemed as though in three weeks he had forgotten all about me. Acting a little surprised, he enquired, 'You don't have another team, do you?'

I could not believe my ears; he said it so casually it was as if he assumed I would have reserve teams lined up! It was suddenly all off: my little letter I'd been carrying around Spain like a party membership was worthless. There were three weeks of the season left and I was high and dry.

I was crestfallen. This was not meant to be happening. My only option was to take another trip to Aldo Sassi's office in the hope there was something he could do. Despite being so exhausted from the Vuelta – the effort of even getting dressed was physically distressing – I hopped into my car and headed to the Mapei centre. Aldo welcomed me into his office immediately; he must have known I was desperate. I explained the situation, and showed him the letter. Aldo went straight into action and called Johnny Carera (an agent and lawyer) to pull in a favour. There I was – the dependent employee – once again sat in an office listening to my fate as a cyclist being debated by others, as Aldo spoke down the receiver telling Carera, 'Listen, Johnny, even though he's not your rider you have to fix this.'

And just like Bernaudeau previously, I witnessed the influence of a respected name in the world of cycling. Johnny agreed to help me out, and the next day I drove to an anonymous McDonald's in Cormano, near Milan, and met him. Over a coffee I showed him the letter. He looked at it briefly before folding it away in his jacket pocket, saying, 'OK, I'll take care of it.'

After three days of pacing around my apartment my phone eventually rang. It was Stanga.

'So, when are you going to come and sign the contract?'

When I eventually put pen to paper a few days later, officially becoming part of the new De Nardi-Colpack team, I noticed Stanga had knocked €5,000 from my original price. It felt like it was his way of letting me know he called the shots. It was typical for a rider like me to get treated like that: even to a small team €5,000 was nothing, but to me it *was* a noteworthy amount of money – not enough that I would complain or go back to the lawyers, but enough to wind me, like the jab in a boxing match designed to let you know that your opponent is still there. It was enough for Stanga: he never again referred to the situation and he certainly never held a grudge. The fact that I went on to prove to be his best mountain *domestique* never seemed to provoke any irony in him either. That's how it seemed to be in that world: 'If I have to flick you, I will, without a second thought, but if things work out OK, then … no hard feelings.' I took it on the chin, like I knew I would have to while my back was against the wall. I would accept these little defeats now, because when I first put pen to paper with Stanga for my reduced fee I promised myself that within two years I would be back at a bigger team. It was that or I would have to stop cycling completely. It was either up, or out.

By the time all this stress had been sorted out and the deal with Stanga was set in stone, it was already mid-October, and I returned wearied to the Mapei apartments to start getting my life on track for the following season. Stanga had offered me a flat in Bergamo when I signed my contract, but I didn't want to go there because I was paranoid about going back to an amateur-type lifestyle again, with other riders constantly coming and going from the place. I

Stood alongside Chris Boardman after winning the junior Grand Prix des Nations at 18 years old. One of eleven wins I took in my first year in France.

I needed them and they needed me. Racing for the Great Britain team as an Under-23, at the World Championships at Valkenburg in 1998 (right) and in the PruTour of Great Britain in 1999 (below), aged 20 and 21 respectively.

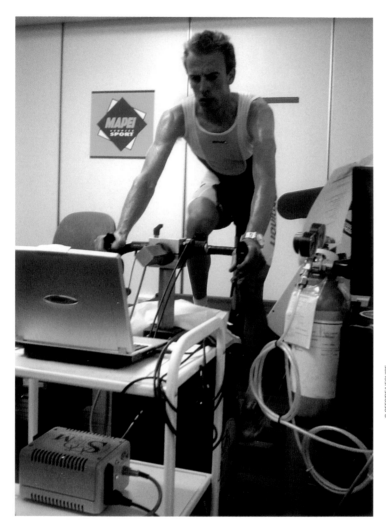

Mapei was a team and an organisation that was ahead of its time. Their approach was cutting edge but more than anything they wanted the best for the sport.

Tour of Denmark 2000. Mapei may have been the super team at the time, but changing, washing and basic medical attention was still done out of the back of a car. How times change.

Riders like Andrea Noe (right) took it upon themselves to teach me the only job that they knew: that of the *domestique*.

By the time I returned to the GB team for the 2000 World Road Race Championships (below) I already felt like a stranger in a team that I had been an integral part of only twelve months earlier.

If Mapei had been DHL then De Nardi was the Post Office. Everything worked, and we had nothing to complain about, but everything was stripped down to the absolute bare minimum.

I started my first Giro a little over seven months after my first Vuelta, and things couldn't have been more different. Unlike in Spain, where I had solely been surviving, in Italy I was able to be a part of the racing.

Riding on the front of the Maglia Rosa group on the Mortirolo in the 2004 Giro. It was the moment I had waited my entire career for. All the other things that I felt complicated racing for me disappeared: I could just ride.

Tom Southam leads the peloton at
the 2005 World Championships,
where I made a mistake that would
impact both our careers.

Representing Great Britain at the
Athens Olympics in 2004 should
have been a big moment for me,
instead the whole thing felt like more
of a tourist trip. (And overleaf)

Stefano Zanini, or 'Zaza', was like a big brother to me in Italy.
He always knew when I needed some advice, an invitation to dinner,
or, on one occasion, throwing against a wall for a stern talking to.

wanted my own life. I didn't have much to hold on to in Varese – a few friends that I had met through other Mapei riders – but it was all I had, and I wasn't about to give that all up.

When I started to enquire about apartments in Varese that month, I had a shock. I realised that it wasn't just in Mapei that I had been taken care of. From the day that my mother had dropped me off in France, my dedication and my obsessive approach to cycling had somehow kept me protected from a lot of things in the outside world. For a young athlete complete dedication is encouraged, while other people take it upon themselves to take care of the other details of life. I was only 24, and I had no idea how to deal with rental contracts and all the other kinds of bureaucracy that came along with being independent. It was a harsh awakening. It is something that can be a big issue for many young bike riders, as most are young men who are kept in a closeted world as they grow up, and when they arrive at a professional level they are suddenly exposed to all sorts of new and tricky situations. What made it harder for me was that Italy is so full of dishonest people that I had to learn to be wary. Instead of relaxing or taking a holiday my whole off-season was spent totally at sea, trying to work out the logistics of my newly independent life in a foreign country.

The only way to survive in Italy, it seemed, was to get by through personal connections. Knowing the right person can change everything, and in Stefano Zanini it turned out I knew exactly the right man. 'Zaza' had always been helpful in the past; he'd previously helped me find a car, and then came out with me when I went to buy it to make sure that I wasn't getting ripped off. We got on well, and knowing my situation he'd quietly gone about making a few enquiries. A couple of quiet words from Zaza and suddenly the whole Italian system started moving in my favour. Sure enough, he found me an apartment in the very same unit that he lived in with his family in Olgiate Olona, just a few kilometres from Varese. A friend of Zaza's had a spare apartment under his own and he didn't mind the idea of renting because he could do with a bit of extra money. He didn't, however, want to be stuck with someone who he couldn't chuck out at a moment's notice, so they gave me a very casual rental contract and explained to me that if someone in their family suddenly needed the apartment I would be out on my ear without a word of warning. I was getting desperate, and the apartment was furnished and ready to go, so I took it without hesitation. It was a bloody lifesaver.

* * *

After getting my own place, I trained hard through what was left of the grey Italian winter in order to prepare myself for the change I was about to undergo. I continued to work with Aldo Sassi, and my training remained much the same. The first gentle rides in December slowly built up to long steady rides through the mountains surrounding Varese, with our star-studded training group remaining tightly knit. The influence of Mapei was still evident in the number of pros who now lived in the area and I trained most days with a very select group: Mick Rogers, Daniele Nardello, Ivan Basso, Dario Andriotto, Andrea Peron, Zaza and others. It made me feel quite special to be a professional there, and after my difficulties getting into the team I felt relieved to be racing for Stanga.

I noticed a distinction between his team and the other smaller Italian teams of the time. Stanga was a serious team manager and, although he hadn't found a big sponsor for that year, the structure of his team was still very professional, so I knew we'd be guaranteed places at the biggest Italian races like the Giro. Even though we didn't have any really big stars signed, if Honchar could perform, all the riders in the team were decent enough to at least support him cohesively and give the impression that the team had a focus and some ambition, instead of just being a bunch of chancers wearing the same colour jersey. Furthermore, Stanga had a good image, and that was very important. It was the small details that could be easily missed: the jersey, for example, wasn't splattered with various cousins' businesses and hydraulics companies. This perhaps wasn't a sign of how good things were to be with Stanga – rather, how badly other teams were run: some were more like second-hand car dealerships than professional sports teams.

In fact, although Italy was the best cycling nation in the world, Italian teams were still remarkably shakily run. Stanga, however, was well respected in UCI and, more impressively than anything else, he actually paid his riders pensions. This was a sure sign that he was above board, unlike many other team managers at the time, who were out to make money for themselves any way they could.

I had been shocked by this kind of thing at first when, in my first year as a pro, an amateur rider with an immaculately styled quiff approached me in our training bunch in Varese, and asked, 'How much did you pay?'

'I beg your pardon? Pay for what?'

'To turn pro. The standard is about 40,000 Euros, but you must have paid a lot to get in to Mapei?'

It turned out it was quite well known in the Italian amateur ranks that you had to *pay* to turn professional. It was a simple arrangement: the rider brought a sponsor with them who put roughly €40,000 in to the team to cover the rider's salary plus a bit more to sweeten the deal, and the sponsor's name would appear on the side of the bus. (Sometimes the individual's 'sponsorship' *was* the donation of the bus, as was the case at another high-profile Italian team of the time.) It was desperate madness, which proved how hard I had worked and how well I had done to get a contract that paid me, instead of the other way around.

So many teams were run by other kinds of dubious means. It was chaotic. It was quite standard procedure for riders to sign contracts for the minimum wage and then have to give half of it back to the team in a bag of cash. Italian cycling teams could also be good places to launder money – not difficult in the pretty much unregulated world of cycling finance, a world where teams were willing to cut as many corners as they could to operate on the minimum expenditure.

The Italian cycling world was like the Italian economy: the guys at the very top were OK, but life amongst the working class was shambolic, segregated and insecure. The knock-on effect of this kind of unscrupulous behaviour was that, as far as I could see, it actually encouraged the doping culture. It was the complete reverse of the philosophy that Mapei had been trying to employ: the pressures were so enormous, and the foundations so shaky, it seemed to make it a difficult decision for a lot of riders *not* to dope.

For me it was like getting thrown out of your mother's womb into the big wide world where, suddenly, the fact that I had my pension paid was seen as a big bonus, not a given. It was madness. The only thing that kept my head above water was the fact that

Stanga, despite often seeming to want to do things on the cheap, was a fair man. In my experience, if there was nothing in writing then he was likely to find a way to tighten the screw on the deal if he could – that was just business to him – but once it was on paper you could be guaranteed to receive every cent he said he would pay. If I'm honest, anything less would have broken me.

● ● ●

If Mapei had been DHL, De Nardi was the Post Office. Technically De Nardi did everything right – everything was functional, everything was working – but it was trimmed down to the absolute bare minimum with no concession to anything bar keeping the costs down.

Even our very first training camp was something of a cost-cutting exercise: the team gathered together to train in early January like everyone else, but instead of flying somewhere warm (and expensive) we all had to hop in our own cars and drive down to Cesenatico, near Rimini, on the Adriatic coast. Rimini is the workingman's holiday destination in Italy, and for one month of the year, in August, when the factories close down, the place is heaving with nightclub-goers and sun-worshippers trying to get the most out of their holiday. In winter the place was completely deserted, and had that awful eerie sadness of an out-of-season holiday town. Almost everywhere was closed at that time of year, but Stanga had managed to convince one of the many privately run hotels to open its doors just for us (at a discounted rate, of course). The hotel and location served its purpose of allowing us to train together for two weeks, but as with everything in my new team it couldn't help but seem just a little bit crap, after Mapei.

I was sharing with Serhiy Honchar, our soft-spoken Ukrainian team leader. Honchar was a different kind of leader to what I was used to at Mapei. He never gave any orders, or felt the need to show he was a leader in any way other than on the bike, and even, on the bike his philosophy seemed to be: 'Look, I am quite strong, and if you can help me we might do well.' On the first day, as we'd walked into the hotel room, I had immediately gone for the smaller fold-out bed as he was the senior rider – but to my amazement he asked if I was sure that I wanted that bed because he didn't care where he slept. Given that the previous year Andrea Tafi had tried ordering me to hand-wash his shorts for him after a stage of the Vuelta Burgos, I was quite content to have a leader with a quieter approach. I did, however, start to wish that I hadn't so readily accepted the fold-out as it clearly wasn't meant to be there and was positioned on an indoor balcony that stuck out of the front of the building. I slept surrounded by windows on three sides, with no curtains. The wind blew so strongly in the night that I awoke several times and looked at the ceiling light swaying around above my head and thought I must be on a boat. But the biggest problem was that the kit we were training in simply wouldn't dry, and there wasn't enough of it. There was a tumble dryer in the team truck, but it kept breaking down, so each night our washing was handed back to us wet. We would hang the kit all over the room, but it was no use. We were supposed to be wearing the correct kit each day, but we'd only been given one thermal jacket each at this point, and while De Nardi had dutifully provided us with kit and someone to wash it, getting it dry was clearly down to us.

After three years at Mapei it was a shock to find myself in this situation. There were so many things at Mapei that, even though I wasn't a spoilt idiot, I took for granted. In many ways Mapei was what Team Sky are in 2013; that bit more thought and effort goes into the team, which puts it far ahead of its contemporaries. It was a really different environment for me and I found that it wasn't only my 'upbringing' in my previous team that separated me from my new teammates.

While Honchar was off getting a massage on one of the long afternoons during the camp, one of my new teammates, a talented young rider by the name of Matteo Carrara, came swaggering into my room. Carrara was from Bergamo and he'd already been with Colpack for two years. Being new myself I welcomed him in for a chat, as I knew he would be a good yardstick by which to measure the general attitude of the rest of the team riders.

He walked in and sat on Honchar's bed and started talking to me, until suddenly he caught sight of himself in the mirror. To my amazement he broke off the conversation he'd started and jumped up to look at his stomach in the mirror. Impressed by what he saw as he pinched the skin, he said to me, 'See how skinny I am, Charly? You know the secret to how I get skinny?'

I had a feeling he was going to tell me regardless of my response. 'Er, no.'

'When I go home between races in the season, I don't eat food.'

'What?'

'Yeah. I don't eat. No food at all. Nothing. I drink water and that's it. I get so ripped in the season, you should see me: I fly on the climbs.'

As the conversation continued along the same lines, with Matteo telling me things that were most likely exaggerated or simply of no interest to me whatsoever, about himself, the girls he'd slept with, the cars he'd driven and the haircuts he'd had, my heart sank.

Mapei had been a genuinely international team: there were riders from Australia, America and Russia as well as half a dozen different European nations. Interacting in that kind of multicultural environment was in itself interesting, but at Colpack the only non-Italians were a few Eastern Europeans who had come through the Italian amateur system anyway – and me, the outsider, changing my character to fit in once again. As Matteo babbled on about himself, I realised that De Nardi just wasn't the sort of environment where any of my colleagues were ever going to think, 'Fuck me, this guy is English. This could be an interesting cultural experience,' or ask me, 'What's it like in England?' Instead they would be looking at me and thinking, '*Cazzo!* He doesn't put enough gel in his hair.' They weren't bad kids, but they were the most basic bum-bag wearing, mobile-phone wielding Italian bike riders. They were the equivalent of third division footballers in the UK. They didn't really have the kind of money to be flash, but they tried hard at it. One of them had some sort of tiny 1.2 litre hairdresser's car in which he had installed a sound system so loud he could be heard 10 kilometres away. When he arrived at training camp in it the whole team had run out excitedly to look at it – and for the rest of the camp they talked endlessly about that bloody car. One of them ended up in prison a few years later for credit-card fraud. He was an OK guy – they all were – but they were the simplest kind of Italian riders.

In a team like De Nardi there was only one rider who was earning good money, and that was Honchar. The rest of the riders were just like me: expendable bodies, paid the bare minimum and expected to do the best we could with that. I was just different to the rest of them in so many ways; I wasn't overly concerned with my appearance, I regarded a good haircut to be one that required the minimum amount of attention – not a work of art that made you look like a peacock and took hours of preparation each morning. I had a crappy mobile phone that was two years out of date, and I drove a sensible car that I chose because of how economical it was. I couldn't dream of living beyond my means, nor for that matter would I consider getting a giant tattoo of the Colosseum on my calf (as one of my teammates did). The rest of the team probably regarded me as a bloody idiot to start with, but I knew that I *had* to fit in. I worked hard on the bike, but I went further than that. I laughed at all the dumb jokes that flew around, and acted interested in people's exaggerated tales of their prowess. I even went to the hairdresser's and sat there for hours making conversation with housewives with bits of fucking tinfoil in my hair to get highlights put in. It was an attitude that would, throughout the year, gain me a reputation for being a good rider, but it made me feel really shitty about myself. I was really selling myself, and I hated myself for it. People I knew started saying to me, 'So, you're practically Italian now!' and I despised that. I hated it, but it felt it was an inescapable part of being a bike rider. British riders had no credibility at that time, and I wasn't a good enough rider to be allowed to be weird. You have to remember I was just a bumpkin to them, and if I didn't adopt their ways it could all be over. I had to eat shit. I had to prove myself to get to the Giro more than any other Italian rider would and I couldn't put a foot wrong; if the Italian riders were expendable, then so was I – a thousand times more so.

Throughout the year, I suffered. Mapei was an Italian team, but it was also very progressive in its outlook. De Nardi, however, were a basic Italian team who wanted to stick to their very simple traditional methods of getting their riders to go faster. Italians were crazy about being light, and they believed the only way to do it was to not eat. There was little room for real science, no room for accommodating the possibility of people having a metabolism that demanded more fuel than others. The team philosophy was simple: *everyone* eats as little as possible.

The real issue for me was that Italian riders were used to being treated like children to the point that they expected to be told when to stop eating. In another environment I could have got away with quietly eating a bit more, but at De Nardi (and many other teams) when we ate there would always be a masseur standing at the head of the table, watching everything, ready to go and tell the *directeur sportif* if anyone ate the wrong thing or, even worse, ate too much.

I am quite sure I underperformed a lot of my career because I was living to these standards, and I had a physical make-up that needed so much more fuel. It got to a dangerous level, where even on a rest day in a major stage race I would be starving, but I would just be given water or a 17g energy bar and told not to eat too much. Never mind EPO, I could have gone much, much faster if I was just fed properly.

The feeling of being increasingly enveloped in Italy was exacerbated in that first year by our race programme: De Nardi was one of a number of Italian teams that raced almost exclusively in Italy. In Italy there existed a self-sustaining cycling world, mainly because the Italian media don't report on races outside of Italy; or at least they didn't bother to back then. But, that said, the Italian cycling calendar didn't lack anything; there was a logical programme that went through the whole season. We started with all the early season races – Giro di Liguria, Trofeo Laigueglia, Giro di Lucca – and went on to the Settimana Coppi e Bartali before the final Giro warm-up began at Settimana Bergamasca and the Giro del Trentino.

There was so much racing, even just in the build-up to the season's centrepiece, the Giro d'Italia, that despite the names of the races being largely unknown in the rest of Europe, we raced extremely hard consistently through the year. It made me a better rider, but it made my average salary and desperate existence even harder to swallow.

• • •

As I swung the gate open and dragged my bike and kit bag into the courtyard, I saw the window of Zaza's apartment open and the familiar face of Rossana smiling at me. Using the affectionate nickname that the family had given to me, she shouted down: '*Ben tornato, Bagai*. Everything went OK with the race?'

'Hello. Thanks, Rossana. It was OK.'

'Are you hungry? Throw your things in and come up for some dinner. We'll wait for you.'

I was relieved that they were in. Coming back from a race was a challenge for me, especially after a stage race, but this time after yet another build-up race for that year's Giro d'Italia I felt that things were getting tough living on my own, and they were about to get a lot tougher.

When I finally walked through the front door of my apartment after packing my bike away in the garage, my situation hit me like a cartoon anvil. The loose ends that were my life had been frozen there in time. The apartment was exactly how I had left it: nothing had moved, my bed sheets were still open and crumpled where I'd left them in a hurry to head off to the start of the race. Until that moment I had seen the apartment as my salvation, a place where I could hide between races. Now, suddenly, I noticed what a strange place it was: the antique furniture was completely mismatched with the modern interior; the only evidence of my existence was a few unframed photographs stuffed into the doors of the wall cabinet. Nothing about the space was right: it wasn't a family home, it wasn't a bachelor pad, it wasn't even the amateur accommodation I'd lived in in France – it was just nothing. I sat alone at the kitchen table and wept the tears of a lonely, exhausted young man. I had spent all of the last week waiting for the race to be over and to get home, only to find I had no home. I was just a bike rider in transit, waiting for the next race.

I knew that Zaza and his wife Rossana were upstairs with their two sons, Marco and Lucca, patiently waiting for me, as they often were. It would have been generous enough of them to have me up for dinner once or twice a week, but they had me up there eating with them every single day. But what if for once they had been out with friends? I had been worried all the way home that these two adults and their children might not have been home that night, and that I would have been left to fend for myself – even worse, left alone. I had become utterly reliant on their generosity. They had practically adopted me. I became known as *Bagai*, an affectionate term for 'kid' in the local dialect. They were so good to me, but that same warm-hearted generosity that was saving my existence was also, in a profound way, highlighting my loneliness, and made me even sadder. I was a grown man, or so I thought, but I felt like a sad case, adopted by kind strangers. I was 25 years old and I was sat each night having dinner with two grown-ups and their family, and I felt like their third, awkward child.

The thing that really pulled at my heartstrings as I sat there and delayed my inevitable trip upstairs to eat the food that Zaza had paid for was the thought that not all riders lived this way. Most of the Europeans I had been racing with all week were returning to their home towns and the welcoming bosom of what I imagined to be an adoring family. The following day would be even worse. The day after returning from a race is when you are at your most tired; it is the day when you can really benefit from doing absolutely nothing – slowing right down, having a soak in the bath, emptying your mind and filling your legs with good food. For me, these days were spent trying to turn the capsized ship of my life back on to an even keel, something made all the more difficult by my imaginings of the warm and cosy families that others were being welcomed home to. Stefano and Rossana were family to me, but I still felt that they were too kind to risk offending by trying to explain how I felt. I didn't want them to feel that they were in any way inhospitable, but the truth was I hated myself for demanding so much of them, and I had no one to tell.

Many times I felt on the edge of having an irrational outburst. At the supermarket on a Monday morning, for instance. Often there would be no food when I arrived home, so I would have to drive to the shops still in massive calorie deficit from the previous day's super-human race effort, and feeling like my body was trying to eat itself from the inside out. Once I was there I would desperately try to get enough stuff from the shelves to have a decent breakfast, but it was exactly the same each time: my muddled mind, clouded by the lack of blood sugar, couldn't think straight. Instead of getting in and out quickly and efficiently I would find myself wandering up and down the aisles, bumping clumsily into other shoppers, forgetting what I wanted, forgetting what I was even doing there. I often felt like just falling to my knees, right there in the aisle, and screaming for help.

I dealt with it because I had to, but getting back from a race and sitting in my mismatched and desolate flat felt like the moment the bubble burst. The protection of the Mapei years, and the excitement at being a professional cyclist, were stripped away, and my new existence forced me to realise that, after seven years dedicated to nothing but racing, it was time that I found a life outside of cycling, and outside of the family that I had come to rely on. I had my contract and I was racing at the level I had dreamed of, but the horrible thought was lurking: 'Now what?' I was yet to become a man; I was still just a kid. At Mapei it had been all too easy to avoid reality; we were removed from social interaction and there had always been something to be busy with. At De Nardi I had a mere existence and nothing more. I looked around at my teammates and realised that cyclists seemed to have two ways of dealing with the reality that they have sacrificed most of their youth to do something that is, ultimately, just a job: they either started making babies at a furious rate, or spent their time going from training camp to training camp, avoiding reality at altitude in some out-of-season skiing hotel. I had lived enough of my life as an assassin, and finally, as a reaction against it, I dived into the bachelor life.

From then on I knew I had to I busy myself with being in the flat as little as possible.

I still couldn't fully let go, though. I stayed in Italy year round because I still felt that by going 'home' and back to England I was inviting a sort of weakness in. It was a really easy trip to go to the UK and see my family, but I wouldn't consider the idea, because that would have been like admitting defeat. Instead I allowed myself a social life, and Italy became a new world. I discovered that I could go out and have a few beers and still go and do my job at the weekend. I let real life into my life and saw for the first time since I was 17 that I could be a bit more 'normal' than just obsessing about getting an extra 3 per cent out of my performance.

Slowly, I'd started letting the air out of the dreams I had grown up chasing with such fervour. I told myself I didn't care *that* much about anything; it wasn't who I wanted to be. It was easier than saying, 'This is so fucking hard and it makes me want to cry.' The ruthless person I'd been as an amateur, and the eager bike rider that I'd been at Mapei, was, through a few beers at the weekend, modified a little. Inch by inch, I worked towards regaining some of the balance I had completely abandoned for seven years, spurred by the haunting emptiness I had felt for those few months at my desolate flat. It may have been a massive avoidance exercise, but for a time it was a great feeling.

● ● ●

And so it was that De Nardi became the place where I let go of my dreams. It was the Post Office and I developed a Post Office mentality. They paid me minimum wage, and they treated me in endless little ways that I never imagined performance athletes would be treated. They dressed us in tracksuits that made us look like the 1972 Scottish football team, and used something that smelt like lighter fluid to clean our legs after races, but they were never dishonest, which was a relative rarity in Italy. And they paid my pension. So I did what they asked of me, but not more. They didn't give me anything extra and I didn't give them anything extra. That desire to make the superhuman efforts – that which had left me clinging to the barriers short of the finish line when racing for Mapei – was completely absent at De Nardi. I'd started stamping in and stamping out. It was a dangerous attitude to have, and if I didn't do something about it I could spend the rest of my career earning the minimum wage for my efforts.

CHAPTER 6

Giro d'Italia

There were very few races that I was part of that I would call *genuinely special*. But the Giro d'Italia was one of them.

I had always known that Italians were passionate about the sport of cycling, but it took becoming a professional in an Italian team to realise just how much cycling suited the Italian culture, and how much racing in Italy suited me. The Italian style of racing is dictated by so much more than the race routes and the riders themselves. It is a culmination of geography, history, aesthetics, passion, celebrity and that deep-seated Italian desire to see something beautiful. The races in Italy work so well because they pander to what the public want – they want a spectacle, and they want something to talk about. The race routes never follow common sense: why would you if you could deviate to take in a climb with a picturesque backdrop, or go past a historic chapel? The racing keeps the riders on their toes, and in touch with the history of the sport. There are no races that see riders slog it out for hours on end until the last man standing slumps across the line. Italian races are tailored in the same way that Italians like to tailor everything: perfectly designed to get the very best out of the riders and the environment. The race routes take into account what the weather will be doing and where the sunlight will fall. It's no accident that the bookend races of the Italian season – Milan–San Remo and Lombardia – have such beautifully lit finishes; the spring sunlight bathes the finish of the first, and the autumn light fades luxuriantly on the last. And it isn't just aesthetics that the Italians do so well. The Italian races are also designed to suit the cunning mind. In Italy it is never enough just to be strong, like it is in Belgium and northern France, where an ability to bang your head against the freezing wind driving in from the sea can be all you need. In Italy the racing is designed so you have to choose your perfect moment; it requires timing, finesse and an attention to detail to create something brilliant. It is the art of cycling, the balance of perfection.

You only had to glance at me to see my physical frame wasn't suited to taking repeated batterings, but in Italy, where the mind came into play to make every effort count, I was in my element. The Giro is the jewel in the crown of Italian cycling, and from my first days living in Italy I couldn't help but feel its influence and importance. It played a pivotal part in where I was, what I was doing and who I was trying to become. Once I was in Italy the Giro was forever on my mind.

The thing about Italians is they love to talk. They love to talk about anything, but much in line with their Mediterranean cousins in Greece and Spain they love to debate. In Italian the word is *polemica* – it is what keeps bars in business, cafés bustling, and it is what makes cycling, along with football and politics, so important. The drama and aesthetic beauty set against the titanic physical struggle of cycling make it the perfect subject matter for this kind of debate. In Italy, while one-day races might provide reasons for a good debate for a day or two at best, the real winner is the Giro. It provides one whole month of conversation and argument, and the newspapers and television stations delight in fuelling the conversation – they exist purely to stoke the fire of debate.

By the time I started the race for the first time in 2003 I had been living in Italy for three years, and the Giro, being a reflection of all things Italian, helped me understand the people and the country I was living in. It was no real surprise that the Giro got the best out of me over the years, and would ultimately be the race that turned me from a young rider with potential into a polished and highly respected pro, with a reputation that would take me to a new level.

* * *

There were only six short months between my first three-week stage race, the 2002 Vuelta a España, and my first Giro, but the changes within myself as a cyclist, physically and mentally, were very significant. In September of 2002 I had been ill prepared and petrified of the Vuelta, but by the time I was getting ready to take to the start of the Giro the following May I had no fear at all of what was ahead.

My preparation for the Giro began in early April, after I rode strongly in the Coppi Bartali stage race. The race itself was fairly uneventful, and my De Nardi team was less than impressive, but I made my presence felt amongst the riders and staff. It was my first opportunity to really demonstrate to the team that I knew what I was doing in a stage race. Being in late March, the unpredictable weather meant the riders constantly needed to pick up or drop off rain jackets and gloves, and be handed up some warm tea in a *bidon*. I was always first back to the car, staying in contact with Honchar and making sure that the communication lines between the manager and the riders ran smoothly. I had no ambition to win whatsoever, but I had made myself an integral part of the team. Everyone likes the guy who passes them a piece of chocolate and a warm drink on a freezing stage. Those things make all the difference, and being the man who seemed to make it all happen *I* was making a difference.

In a cycling team you can usually tell quite quickly who will make the grade or not: cliques form, and I was good at getting inside them. That year it had become my obsession to find the right configuration of riders and elements, to be in the right place to show my wares. De Nardi were a small team, so I had to be sure that I could make it into the very biggest races to be able to move on to a bigger outfit. Being one of the very few foreigners in an Italian team (and literally the last man to get a contract) prepared me for the shit fight that was about to commence to get myself into the squad for the team's most important race of the season. My performances in the spring were determined and considered and my hard work paid off with my early selection for the Giro. But, unlike with the previous year's Vuelta, coming to the Giro I was allowed the luxury of adequate time to prepare.

My final rides with the team in the build-up races allowed me to feel even more relaxed. In 2003 there were no obligations for the organisers to invite the best twenty teams in the world – that came later with the introduction of the Pro Tour in 2005. Instead, the organisers still invited a lot of the small Italian teams ahead of bigger foreign teams. This meant that going into the 2003 Giro I knew my competition well – 90 per cent of the field were made up of the riders I had been racing with since the Italian season had started in February. I knew the level of competition, I knew who the protagonists were likely to be and how fast the majority of riders in my position could possibly ride. I also, crucially perhaps, knew I could last the distance in a three-week race. Finishing the Vuelta had taught me how my body would react to the effort of twenty-one days of racing, and how I had to deal with the task mentally. I was ready.

The 2003 Giro started in the south of Italy, and that in itself was an education. There are almost no races in the Italian calendar in that part of the country, so when I first arrived there I could smell the change. As you head south in Italy the country seems to downgrade metre by metre; the asphalt gets worse, the landscape changes, and the atmosphere in and around the race is completely different. I was learning about the country, but it wasn't always good things that I saw.

The start that year was down in Lecce. The day before the race, on our short pre-race ride, the team stopped for a natural break, and looking out to sea I saw a boat out off the coast that looked like a trawler. Just for the sake of making conversation I asked an old local guy, sat on a bench with his back to the sea and an air of utter indifference to the world, what they were doing. 'Are they fishing?' I asked. Almost without looking up, he said, 'No, they are pulling out a dead body from the sea.' It wasn't exciting; it was frightening, and quite threatening. That same night after dinner we went for the *passegiata* (a short walk after dinner that is customary in Italy, and

Italian teams) and as we meandered down the pedestrianised street a couple came walking in the other direction. The whole team was there, and we were all chatting amongst ourselves, but as we passed the couple one of our guys turned around to say something to the rider behind him. As he turned, the boyfriend from the couple, who had been looking over his shoulder to make sure no one was looking at his bird, assumed that one of our number was checking her out. Two minutes later the same guy came tearing back down the street with all of his friends on scooters and threatened to shoot us. It might have been an idle threat and a display of childish machismo, but the thing that really disturbed me was the fact we were in the middle of a busy pedestrian street and nobody said a thing.

It was hard to really feel safe at all in the south of Italy, even when I was racing. The people in the south behaved very differently by the side of the road. There would be millions of them, and they loved the Giro, but they had absolutely no respect for the athletes. Kids would push each other in front of the race for a joke, and dogs would run out into the pack. On a climb somewhere down in the south a spectator stole my sunglasses from my face while I was racing, and I wasn't even out the back going slowly – I was right in the action! The funny thing was that they were prescription lenses, and I was half expecting him to come back another year and say, 'Here, have your fucking glasses back, they keep giving me a headache … '

It all went well for me to begin with: in the first week I could feel I that I was able to be involved with the racing and that I was no longer just a spectator like I'd been in the Vuelta. The importance of the Giro had infected me, and at the first mountain stage to Terminillo I committed my first cardinal sin as a *domestique*. It is a unique moment in my career, but on that climb I allowed my heart to rule my head – I completely forgot myself – and I dropped my leader. The stage had started in Avezzano, right in the middle of the country, and the route was practically flat until we hit the final climb to the ski station at Terminillo. This final ascent was a relatively 'small' mountain in comparison with the rest of the race, gaining only 600 m of altitude in 14 km, but when we hit the lower slopes and began the ascent the whole race suddenly went to pieces. Gilberto Simoni's Saeco team drove hard at the front, and very quickly people were in a lot of trouble. Riders started cracking all around me, and letting go of the wheels of the leaders. One of the first to go was Aitor González, the rider who had won the Vuelta only a few months previously. Seeing González backwards was a real kick – knowing how much he had made me suffer in the Vuelta. As the crowds thickened and the group continued to whittle down, I felt like I was finally getting a whiff of the Giro itself. My lungs burned but the Italian voice in my head kept on, '*Tieni duro, tieni duro.*' ('Hold firm, hold firm.') I held tight near the front, incredulous as favourite after favourite seemed to fold and disappear from the group. The thrill of holding on overrode the pain. I found myself in a group with two of the biggest Italian stars of the time, Francseco Casagrande and Marco Pantani. There were ten riders in front of us with 3 km to go. I had finished 109th at my first Vuelta, and now I was amongst the top twenty riders in the Giro. It wasn't where I was used to riding at all, and what felt stranger was that I was doing it so ... *so easily*. After years of suffering in the races there was a momentary flicker of what might have been. Perhaps it was ignited by the passion that the race brings out in people, or perhaps by my desire to make my own history in that great race.

Either way, in an instant the team car shot up alongside us and I saw Stanga's puce head sticking out of the window screaming at me to stop. Overcome by emotion and excitement I had completely forgotten that Honchar had been dropped and now, Stanga told me furiously, he was a minute and a half behind. My excitement switched to despair. I had fucked up. I had broken one of the rules of my job: I had left my leader. I instantly sat up in the group and watched the race ride away from me. I rolled forward, turning one pedal at a time, barely moving quickly enough to keep the bike's momentum. Riders who were still racing passed me in ones and twos before Honchar eventually arrived and I quickly got back to speed and towed him to the finish. I ended up crossing the line in 24th place, 3 minutes 46 seconds behind the winner and 2 minutes behind the group that I had to let go. On paper it was a strong ride, and the climb to Terminillo certainly proved to me that I was capable of performing at that level, but as I rolled across the line I was utterly dejected. I'd had no intention of dropping my team leader, but I had become wrapped up in the racing. In my mind it was unforgivable for a *domestique* to behave this way.

Throughout my career people approached me and questioned me: 'You could have finished in the top twenty in the Giro. Why didn't you?' It's what people don't understand about a *domestique*. I am sure if I could have used all my energies I could often have finished much higher in many races; there were countless occasions when I deliberately slowed to wait for my leader, or simply because I no longer *had* to make an effort. I was paid to do a job, and that job wasn't to finish in the top twenty. I was paid to help a rider who could finish on the podium, even if, on occasion, I was stronger on the day. I felt I had flirted with the passion of the Giro that day, but I vowed never to make that mistake again.

The following two stages across Tuscany were pan-flat and allowed me to go about my business without any issues, while Italian cycling celebrated Mario Cipollini's record 41st and 42nd stage wins in the Giro. Cipollini was adored in Italy: he was a celebrity, and he had flair. For the Italians, these were things that drove the common man wild with delight. Italians love celebrity, and 'Il Re Leone' was one such star who kept the excitement of the race alive. In those days the flat stages were the Cipollini show, from start to finish. A Cipollini win was a win for the race, and a win for Italy. More than just a victory, Cipollini was in charge of the bunch, and, as such, he was an important figure in my working day. When the peloton had a patron like Cipo calling the shots everything was that bit more relaxed. On a flat stage you would know what was going to happen: whether riders would be attacking like mad all day, if anyone would attack in the feed zone, or if a rider wanted to ride through his village in front of the race … you just had to go and ask Cipo, and if he said yes there would be no problem. In Italy Cipollini went beyond cycling, and it wasn't a matter of fear, but of respect amongst the riders, that allowed him to take charge of the group. For me it was ideal: I knew that I could switch off on 'his' stages because the race would be ridden in a certain way. Over three weeks days like these were invaluable – days that I could allow my body a rest, minimising the damage, and let my mind have a few moments to itself.

When the race returned to the mountains in the following days, however, things didn't go so well. The stage from Montecatini to Faenza turned out to be the decisive stage of the race as Gilberto Simoni made his move for the *maglia rosa*. I had covered an early break of sixteen riders to make sure we were represented in the front. After building up a decent lead the group was quite content to be tapping along, but when we reached 40 km to the finish news started coming in from our team manager that Simoni had launched an unexpected move and was attempting to leapfrog across to his teammate Leonardo Bertagnolli, who was with us in the break. All of a sudden the riders in the break started to panic. Before Simoni could get across on the penultimate climb of the day, riders started attacking all over the place to create a gap. The group went over the summit lined out at full bore and started hammering down the steep descent to Faenza.

Not being able to accelerate quick enough at the top of the climb meant that I had to make up ground on the descent. As the leaders sped down the hill ever faster, I started having to take more risks to stay on the wheel. Coming in to a sharp right-hand bend I hit a stretch of rough asphalt and it threw my back wheel into the air: in that moment I grabbed the brake to try to lose some speed to make the corner, but with no contact between my wheel and the road I didn't decelerate at all. I missed the corner completely and smashed into the guardrail. I was thrown into the air and I landed right on the rail, thumping the steel barrier hard with the small of my back. I had taken a beating from an iron girder. I leapt up in agony and hobbled around the side of the road as rider after rider shot past me, yelling to the riders behind them to watch out as they saw me. Their screeching brakes yelped out in surprise. As I stood still feeling the initial effects of the blow I saw our light blue team car pull up and the concerned face of Stanga came rushing towards me.

'*Cazzo, Charly, stai bene?* Are you OK?'

'No fuck. I landed on the fucking barrier. *Porca miseria!*'

'Can you get to the finish?'

I winced and nodded, '*Si.*'

Even in the agony I had known I had to try. Stanga was in a rush to get back to Honchar, and once the mechanic had checked my bike they leapt into the car and sped off down the mountain. There were still 30 km to ride, but I convinced myself I could do it. I slowly set off down the hill. As the adrenaline wore off I felt the swelling on my back increase, and every single second I was on the bike became agonising. Group after group of riders passed me, until eventually I was joined by three of my teammates, Guiseppe Palumbo, Michele Gobbi and Leonardo Zanotti. Zanotti was an ex-mountain biker and was in his first Giro too. He was a really nice kid and he seemed upset to see me in so much difficulty. He organised the three of them to take it in turns to help push me along as much as they could. I couldn't sit on the saddle properly, and I couldn't stand either. I was so twisted I had to unclip my foot every few pedal revolutions to ease my back. I was in tears, but I knew that I had to finish. There was always a chance that I could get better by the next day. I hung on, pedalling with the assistance from my teammates and then stretching out my back every few hundred metres, making increasingly slow progress until we eventually crossed the finish line, 17 minutes behind the winner.

I crossed the line sobbing in agony and my *soigneur* carried me into a team car and drove me (still dressed in my sweaty racing kit) through the chaotic Italian traffic to a local hospital. My back was ballooning, but after several X-rays it was clear that nothing was broken. I so badly wanted to continue the race that I managed to persuade the doctors to syringe out the excess fluid from my back while I lay face down in a hospital bed. It was a process that had to be repeated by our team doctor for the next five nights of the race. From then on the race became a matter of endurance. I wanted to finish, and I wanted to do my job, but I wasn't the same bike rider again. I was so desperate not to be seen as troublesome or as a burden on the team that I suffered in silence. I was still lacking power in my left leg from the skewed position I had adopted on the bike to accommodate the pain in my back. In a way, my disappointment helped me endure the pain.

• • •

That 2003 Giro was also the last that the capricious Italian legend Marco Pantani would ride, and before I made it to Milan I would witness my own little piece of Giro history. Like Cipollini, Pantani was a superstar in Italy. He was quirky and passionate, and he defied the laws of convention. He had been a Giro winner, and the public, who saw in him everything they wanted from the sport, adored him. But by 2003 he had become a sad figure, adored by everyone it seemed bar himself. His problems evidently ran deep, and there was a sense that the end – at least in a cycling sense – was nigh.

On stage 19 I saw with my own eyes the last attack of 'Il Pirata' on the road to Cascata del Toce. Pantani was revered for his attacking style and his last big move was pumped up in the

Italian press to be a huge event, the 'devil may care' stuff his legend was made of. The reality, like a lot of cycling, was quite sad. It was a token attack, really. He was trying to do something, and the bunch let him go out of respect – you could almost see the embarrassed *domestiques*, who could so easily have covered the move, looking the other way so they didn't have to feel responsible for chasing him. He was Pantani, though, and he was allowed a bit of leeway before the real race got underway behind, and the strongest rode straight past him.

In truth, by 2003 Pantani was long past his best. He had never really recovered from the high haematocrit reading that forced him out of the 1999 Giro. It was undeniable that he was a champion cyclist, but he was also a fragile guy, with a huge ego and a coke habit. In the peloton you see riders as people – people with a great deal of talent, but people all the same. Outside of the peloton (and especially in Italy) these legends get blown up in the public's mind so much that they can't handle it in the end. The curse of celebrity, no less. Sadly, nearly a year after that Giro, Pantani would tragically be found dead in a Rimini hotel room. In the Giro of 2003 he must already have been in a pretty dark place, as he was incredibly distant and the slightest of things could set him off on a rant. My lasting impression of Pantani came on stage 18 of that Giro in the Alps. The stage went over the Colle di Sampeyre; it was a long climb, and, as it has a tendency to do in the Giro in May, the weather turned bad. We started the climb in rain, and slowly made our way through sleet, and then into driving snow by the time we reached the summit. The pressure had been on and the race had slowly fallen to pieces behind the leaders. I found myself climbing alone up to Pantani. The Simoni group had dropped him, and as soon as I had caught him I saw that he was fucked. He was creeping along in the darkness, completely surrounded by the television cameras that followed his every move, no matter how undignified it made him look. I wasn't a big fan of the man, but I respected him, and I knew that he was something special. I hated seeing his suffering, and the desperation of the cameras to capture every pedal stroke of his defeat. I barged past the cameras and gave him my wheel; it was not in my interest at all, but I was compelled to help the guy. I rode the final stretch to the top of the climb with him, doing what I could to slowly increase the pace and reduce our gap to the front. He stayed millimetres behind me as we began the descent, but after my crash earlier in the race I just didn't have the nerve to go that fast. My lines into the corners were atrocious and I crept around the first two soaking wet bends way too timidly for Pantani's liking. Suddenly, a torrent of abuse came flooding from behind: he was livid, he was yelling and swearing and suggesting in no uncertain terms that perhaps cycling wasn't the vocation I should have chosen. I couldn't believe it. I had just gone out of my way to help the guy, and he had turned on me.

I felt belittled, humiliated. I was in the presence of a legend, and he was calling me *a piece of fucking shit*. I let him past on the next straight and he shot straight by me and disappeared into the murk. It wasn't long until I saw him again. He was going so fast that when I came round the next corner he was there, still swearing, laid in a ditch at the side of the road. Out of rage and frustration he had gone way too fast and crashed pretty heavily on the corner. He managed to finish the stage, and eventually the race, but that was pretty much the end for him.

. . .

After my first Giro I had plenty to think about. Honchar finished in eighth place overall, which was a respectable ride and reflected well on the team that had helped him. I continued to live and race in Italy throughout the rest of 2003, and the more that I considered the race in context with the people and the country, the more I understood it. The psychology of doing well at the Giro – as far as I could tell – was that you had to *become* a little bit Italian to be able to perform at your best. As a rider, you had to be able to deal with the unexpected, to be relaxed and go with the flow, whatever that might be.

CHAPTER 7

Unfit to Race

I wasn't even supposed to ride the Tour of Lombardy in 2003. I thought my season had finished at the World Road Race Championships in Hamilton the week before 'the race of the falling leaves'. In my mind, the year had ended on a high out there in Canada. By winning the time trial Dave Millar had become Great Britain's first World Champion on the road since 1994, and after a solid year of hard work for De Nardi I had agreed a new contract with Stanga for the following season. If things were far from rosy in my life, at least I felt like I was moving along on an even keel. Little did we know as we celebrated David's win in the team's four-star hotel with champagne and cigars that David's reign as World Time Trial Champion was due to be short lived, and that within one week my own career would be in ruins.

After a big night of drinking, and with still no idea that I would be racing in Lombardy, I flew home from Canada, gave in to jet lag combined with the fatigue from a long season, and collapsed into bed. I slept for what felt like two days straight. On the third day of my convalescence, fate played a hand. De Nardi were one rider short for the Tour of Lombardy, so once again, knowing that I was fairly dependable and that I lived only an hour from the start in Como, Stanga called me up and asked if I could race on Sunday.

Unenthusiastically, I told Stanga that I hadn't ridden at all that week. He assured me that I only had to turn up and start to make sure we had the minimum number of riders. Even though I had already verbally agreed my contract for the following season, I still hadn't signed it, so I saw the race as a decent opportunity to go and put pen to paper, as well as get a massage and give the team my race bike back. It was more like an errand than a race. The following day I dutifully headed out on my bike for the first time since I had crossed the finish line in Hamilton. Forty-five minutes later I was lying on the ground, having been hit by a car. I was unhurt, but I was tired and it was too much. I couldn't even be bothered to ride home, so I called a friend to come and pick me up. I had ridden the grand total of forty-five minutes in a week; it would prove to be a massive error on my part. I had no idea at all, but the perfect storm was brewing in my veins, and I had just unwittingly forsaken my last opportunity to potentially avoid disaster.

The 9.30 a.m. commencement of the Tour of Lombardy meant an even earlier start for us, with breakfast scheduled for 6 a.m. But even before my alarm could go off that morning there was a knock at the door. The fretful knocking meant only one thing: our team had been selected for a random haematocrit test. I didn't wake up well most mornings, and still suffering from jet lag I was especially pissed off to be woken so early to have blood extracted from my body. I was exhausted and paid no real attention to what was going on. I had been through plenty of tests before and, once the blood had been taken, I left the hotel room – where a string of groggy and disgruntled riders were going through the same thing – and completely forgot about it. I went down to breakfast and started my usual race routine. In no time at all we were transferred to the start and were sat in the team camper van idly chatting and filling our pockets with race food. I was in my gear, race number pinned on, ready to go and hoping against hope that the early break would go without much fuss and that I could have a trouble-free ride to the first feed.

There is a lot of noise around a camper van at a race, and having the door closed offers the last bastion of privacy for a rider before they are thrown out to the mercy of the hollering crowds and the juddering of the cars and helicopters. When someone opens that door, the noise completely invades the inside of the camper, so you can't help but notice whenever anyone walks in or out. As we sat there chatting between ourselves on that morning, that very same invasive din pricked up my ears and as I looked up I saw Stanga come bowling in through the door, looking shaky and mumbling. He was looking right at me and talking, but I couldn't tell what he was saying. I wondered why on earth he was so hard to understand all of a sudden, this man who made his living making himself heard by bike riders.

He was mumbling because he knew what I was yet to discover. He could see the livelihood and reputations of those around him crumbling, the careers of his riders and his staff being ruined. His was a team that relied on a good, clean image, and he knew the implications of the news he had just been given. Confused, I asked him to speak up. He said, 'You failed the test. You're not starting.' It was close to a stereotypical movie moment: the clock stopped ticking, everyone in the camper went still, and I could feel my teammates shrinking away from me, as though I had just been diagnosed with a highly contagious disease. I was stunned. I had never taken a banned performance-enhancing drug in my life. My brain scrambled to make sense of the situation, and slowly, like rising floodwaters, the reality began to envelop me. I had exceeded the UCI's 50 per cent haematocrit limit: I fallen headlong into a trap that had been waiting for me.

The UCI had set the limit for a rider's red blood cell count – his haematocrit level – to be at a maximum of 50 per cent in 1998. It was the first real attempt to try to stem the widespread abuse of EPO in the peloton at the time. I could have choked on the irony. Being one of many people in the population with a naturally high haematocrit I couldn't even entertain the idea of taking EPO, and yet I had just failed the test that was supposed to determine who was taking the banned blood booster.

The problem was mostly that, as a test for banned performance-enhancing drugs, the 50 per cent haematocrit was a ridiculous value. A person's haematocrit goes up and down all the time: the haematocrit level is a measure of blood dilution that gives a percentage of oxygen carrying red blood cells compared to white, but that was all. It was easy to manipulate (just by the amount of water in the body, for one) and it didn't show how many of these blood cells were new and at what rate they were appearing in the body. It was so crude and basic and the figure of 50 per cent might as well have been plucked right out of thin air. A lot of scientific literature puts

53 per cent or 54 per cent amongst the normal limits. Fifty per cent must have seemed like a nice round figure for the UCI to plump for, because it was the safest limit someone whose natural level was 37 per cent or so could go to without killing themselves. It was a 'best-fit' type strategy, but at the same time that limit, and those tests, completely reshaped the landscape of professional cycling for almost a decade.

The 50 per cent limit never stopped anyone from doping; all it did was give people a limit of how *much* doping they could do. It completely redressed the balance in favour of people with less natural talent. In any other generation the riders with the naturally higher haematocrit would have had a *natural* advantage over those with a lower limit. With the 50 per cent rule in place, however, a rider who naturally had a low haematocrit, of 35 per cent, say, could improve himself chemically by up to 14 per cent without any kind of worry that he would even become suspect in the eyes of the UCI, whereas a rider whose haematocrit was naturally 47 per cent had only a 2 per cent margin to improve. It gave those who had smaller internal engines a massive advantage over those riders who were genetically better suited to being an endurance athlete. Having a 35 per cent haematocrit level should have meant you were a weaker athlete. Instead it was like a licence to print money.

The fright I'd had at the Mapei offices in 1999 had made me realise that I needed to know something about the complex world of blood, and once my career had begun I went about educating myself as quickly as possible on the subject. During my years at Mapei the sheer professionalism and organisation of the team put my fears of one day failing a test completely aside. I couldn't forget about it, because there was so much to be taken into consideration, but I felt the team doctors were all aware of my situation and supported me. They frequently spoke to me about it, and tested me to make sure I was under the limit.

There were occasions that I had gone over 50 per cent on a centrifuge (a simple hand-held device that separated the white and red blood cells to give an approximate haematocrit reading) the day before the race, and subsequently I would have to go through the process of bringing my haematocrit back down, as the testers could potentially be coming around the next day. It became routine for me, but remained disturbing for anyone who didn't know my situation. At the start of the Peace Race in my first season, the doctor from the 'older riders' team had come with us, and wasn't used to dealing with me. We had been in Sierra Nevada for altitude training. As a result my levels were higher than normal. The doctor tested me with a centrifuge and, after looking at it, rushed out of the room, returning moments later, red faced and dragging an entire cool box full of water that had been left out in the corridor for the riders. He dumped eight litres of bottled water at the foot of my bed and said, 'Drink that, now!' The poor guy was completely shitting himself.

Drinking a lot of water is one of the things you can do to naturally bring your haematocrit back down; it is a very basic way of diluting the blood in the body. It was crude but effective for short periods, and it became something I had to be prepared to do. There were dozens of races, even in those first five years, where I was far from my best because, instead of concentrating on the race, I was thinking more about keeping my haematocrit in check. I had to sit in hotel rooms drinking and drinking and drinking, and then getting a bad night's sleep because I had to get up every hour to piss. There were times, the night before a race, where I had two sugar-solution drips attached to my arms because I was too high (the drips had the same effect of diluting the blood). It was ridiculous: every time we went to an altitude camp I would come back and throw away any potential gains I had made by wasting all my energy worrying about my haematocrit and drinking litre after litre of water.

During my three years at Mapei I had felt OK about the situation, because I felt protected: after that first test at the team centre they had demonstrated that they trusted me. I also knew that Aldo Sassi was writing letters to the UCI on my behalf. Aldo had wanted to know what the UCI were going to do about me, because sooner or later it would be a problem. I was pretty unimpressed with their response. They practically told him that until I failed a test they wouldn't do anything about it. I felt like they were playing Russian roulette with my career, and they didn't give a shit. Where Mapei had kept me protected, De Nardi were much more lackadaisical. I had lived with the knowledge that things could fall apart like this, and somehow over my first year outside the organised world of Mapei I had let things slip. Now I realised, as I sat there vacantly staring at Stanga's terrified face, that the shit storm that had hung over me for the last four years had finally been unleashed.

• • •

Stanga ushered me through the door and away from the sanctity of the camper van. The first person I saw as I stepped out was a friend of mine from Varese, Mauro. Mauro was a neighbour and a typical

Italian *tifoso*, a guy who just loved the sport, and got no greater thrill than being able to come to the start of a race and know someone in it. He saw me all the time at home, but it was very important for him to be able to say hello to me in that environment. I knew he was stood outside the camper van expressly to see me, but when his eyes met mine it freaked me out even more. I walked straight past him. I knew in no time at all he would know, and I felt like such a fraud. I wanted to put a coat over my head and hide.

Stanga may have been worried, but once he was through the initial shock he managed to regain calm and became, thankfully, quite business-like. He took me back over to the team cars and handed me to the other director, Oscar Pellicioli, whom he instructed to get me to the race hotel for re-testing immediately. This was a routine procedure, the haematocrit test equivalent of getting a B-sample analysis. It was a short walk to the doctor's hotel but the streets were packed with fans. I walked through the throngs of people like a zombie; I had no idea of what was happening. Pellicioli led me down a side street to dodge the crowds. As soon as we were away from people I started crying, pleading, 'I didn't do it, I didn't do it. I haven't taken anything.' I was confused and upset, and Pellicioli had no idea what to say to me. No answer at all; he just kept walking. He had every right to be freaking out as well: I had put his job, and the existence of the team, on the line. The negative publicity was bound to upset the sponsor; the knock-on effect for the team would surely be huge. My mind rushed to the horrible conclusion that thirty people were about to lose their jobs, and it felt like it was all my fault. It was a living nightmare. Throughout my life I have always hated the feeling that I have done something wrong. I hated guilt – more than that I hated blame: there had been times at school when I was called to the headmaster's office for something absolutely routine, and I would be bawling before I got there because I assumed that I was going to be chucked out. As a 25-year-old man I was right back there, petrified of the shame, the disappointment and the blame that I felt was heading my way.

When we arrived at the hotel I felt every set of eyes looking at me. The race organisation were there and they all knew who I was; the news of my test hadn't been announced, but the race was minutes away from starting and it was clear to them that something was wrong with the scenario. I hated it. I hated every face I saw. We passed the lobby of the hotel and went upstairs to a small room where the doctors were waiting for me. I recognised a Swiss doctor whom I'd seen at a lot of races. I knew that she also worked in a mortuary. I remember I had tried chatting her up once by jovially saying, 'I bet we're all a bit like corpses, aren't we?' referring to our skeletal look – to which she had coolly replied, 'Yes, but corpses don't have so many needle marks.' She was frightening, and I knew that she didn't care about cycling or the rules of the sport – she was just earning some extra cash doing some weekend work, and it showed. No one there seemed to give the slightest shit that this was my whole life in their hands. The doctor's disinterest was infuriating. I became hysterical. I *knew* I was innocent. I could have told them that I had a naturally high haematocrit until I was blue in the face, but it would have made no difference; there was a limit and, natural or not, I was over it, and that was all there was to it to them. I stood there in tears berating each and every one of the doctors. A different female doctor eventually reacted, snapping at me, 'Look!

My kids waiting for me. It's the weekend and I've got better things to do than listen to you.' I was so angry I yelled right back at her, 'I don't give a fuck about your kids. My whole life is on the line and you're sitting here complaining about going to the supermarket with your kids. GET ANOTHER FUCKING JOB THEN!' My anger was misguided, and I was lashing out at everyone around me. Nothing made any sense to me.

While I stood there kicking and screaming, the doctors got on with their work. They took more of my blood and ran the tests again six more times. The machine went over and over and it was always exactly the same: 51.4 per cent. I couldn't understand it at all: blood never came back *exactly* the same. The final test was done on a different machine to make sure everything was accurate, but I didn't need to see the result. I knew that by now it was too late, the race had started without me and in no time at all I would be passing through this purgatory and straight into hell.

I went back out of the hotel still trembling. Pellicioli had to catch up with the race in the second team car, so he bundled me back into the camper van and told the driver to take me to meet another mechanic outside of Como who would drive me back to the service course in Bergamo. As the camper pulled out of Como and away from the race, the race radio in the van crackled into life. That was when I heard it:

'Welcome to the 97th Giro di Lombardia, over 249 km … The race start was given at 9.35 … We have 190 riders taking the start this morning … One non-starter: Charles Wegelius, De Nardi …'

It was like hearing news of my own death being read out over the radio. I sank into my seat. I wanted to believe they were talking about somebody else entirely. I wanted to shut my eyes and listen to nothing but the sound of the camper van's engine whining as it hauled us up the hill out of Como. When I tried to force my ears to listen to the van's mechanical hum, I heard my name crackling over the radio and on the lips of the public, and the sound of my name being scratched in pencil into the notebooks of journalists. It felt like every person in the world was saying my name in the same surprised yet disappointed tone: Wegelius? I squeezed my eyes closed tighter still as tears welled up in them, but all I saw were sets of eyebrows being raised and heads shaking in disgust. I felt like I had been swallowed into the unknown. I was sick to the pit of my stomach.

And then, as I tried to prise myself out of my shell-shock, I realised with even more horror that the world was already starting to catch up with me. As journalists became aware of the results, they came to find me. Stephen Farrand, *Cycling Weekly*'s Italian correspondent, had been after me all morning. Pellicioli's knowledge of Como's side streets had helped me to evade him at the start, but he had seen me leave, and now he was tailing the camper van and calling my phone from the car behind. I had known Steve for a while, and I always spoke to him when he called, but I couldn't bring myself to answer. I just looked at the screen of my phone and let it ring.

I didn't want to talk to a journalist about my situation because I just didn't know what to say, nor did I want to get dragged into any kind of moral debate on doping. I had no interest in damning dopers during my career. Former riders and members of the press talked of the *omertà* that existed in cycling like it was a *Godfather*-type 'horse head in your bed' mafia story. It was nothing like that: doping was routine and quite dull, described by people who worked in the sport as being like 'putting your socks on in the morning'. The idea of the *omertà* being something that people swore allegiance to, like the magician's code, was total bollocks. I never worried that if I spoke out I would be pushed off a mountain. It wasn't threatening or sinister, it was just easier to develop the attitude that I did. A rider like me didn't talk about things that weren't 'cool' to bring up. You wouldn't talk about doping in the same way that you wouldn't start lecturing your mates in a nightclub about infidelity. You might well remain faithful to your wife, but there are plenty of your friends who don't. In professional cycling you don't want to piss people off, full stop, by attacking at kilometre 0, or attacking when people are pissing. If someone falls off you don't laugh, because at the next corner you might fall off. I felt strongly that if somebody did dope it was their own business and they were doing it for their own reasons.

With Steve hounding me I felt like a fugitive. I could see him in the wing mirror, as my phone continued to ring. When we drove into the service course and shut the gate I knew I was safe, but I also knew that I was cornered. I waited as long as I could before I eventually pressed the button to open the electric gate and drove out, hoping against hope he might have given up. As I pulled out Steve's tall figure stepped straight into the road in front of my car, forcing me to stop. I had no idea what to say to him. I was still stunned, fearful and emotional. The team had told me not to say anything on record, but, after all, I wasn't a criminal or a politician. I was panicked by the situation and by the chase. I wound down my window and said the first stupid thing that came into my head: 'I don't want to say anything because anything I say will just make things worse.'

I could see it in print on the pages of *Cycling Weekly* as soon as I said it, and I knew it was a statement that could so easily be construed to make me look guilty. But by 2003 there wasn't a lot left to say. In the past five years there had been so many positive results, and so many riders had already abused so many excuses that even protesting my innocence could appear to make me seem guilty. My statement was ridiculous. I knew I would get crucified for it, but I just wanted some solace. I drove towards home in a total daze, aiming for the only place that I knew I would be looked after.

Stefano Zanini was already waiting for me when I arrived at his apartment and he took me straight in. His house was a sanctuary; I was amongst friends and I felt safe again. I walked in without a word and Rossana came straight over and hugged me. Mauro was there too – as soon as he had seen me leave the camper van he must have understood – and he wanted me to know that he still supported me. I walked in like a mute and didn't say a word. I sat on the floor with Stefano's four-year-old son, and started playing games while everything slowly closed down around me. It was like someone went to the very edge of my world and started to slowly paint it black from the outside, working their way in. The rest of reality ceased to exist. The fire in the centre of the room became my only focus, until I fell sound asleep there on the rug.

People say that a guilty person will fall asleep in their prison cell when they are arrested because there is a subconscious sense of relief in being caught. Passed out there on the rug, I had the mentality of a guilty man, not because I had actually taken anything or broken any rules, but because I had spent my entire career until then being made to feel like I was guilty of *something*. The drama at the start of the race and the ridiculous car chase across Lombardy that morning had been the tip of the iceberg. My mentality was an accumulation of all the things I'd done throughout my career to take into account my haematocrit: studying blood, and basing my race routine on avoiding all the things that might raise it, like dehydration, altitude or even a day's rest. The constant fight to keep my natural levels below what they should have been had made me feel that I had something to hide. It made me feel that I really was guilty.

For me, the problem with the haematocrit level was enormous: I wasted so much energy at races desperately trying to get my levels down, with no benefit to my performance, and, what was more, I couldn't dope if I wanted to, *but I could still be punished for it.*

 * * *

The papers all ran the story the next day. De Nardi made a feeble attempt at explaining the result away, citing the removal of my spleen after my quad bike accident as the thing that could have caused my haematocrit to vary. To me, if felt like an insult – the kind of vague excuse someone who was guilty would love to make. Of course it was partly possible that the removal of my spleen made a difference, but the truth of the matter was that I'd always had a high haematocrit, even when I had a spleen. My high haematocrit should have been something that was seen by people as a blessing, a part of my raw talent, my natural disposition to be a bike rider. Saying that I had a high haematocrit because I had no spleen was explaining away my talent because I was missing body parts. The whole landscape was warped. There I was, taking a beating from guys who I knew were less talented than me, week in and week out, and even then when I failed the test no one said, 'He just happens to be talented.' They said, 'Well, he's got no spleen ...' I was a bitter, furious mess.

After putting out the press release, the team promptly decided to fire me. It was classic Stanga: obey the rules, do everything to protect the company. He called me that day while I was still trying to piece together what was going on and told me straight, 'Look, Charly, I believe you, but I can't have you in my team any longer. We can't have this kind of negative publicity. It's too bad, but I'm letting you go.' There wasn't a single shred of emotion. He just walked away. I was devastated. I was at absolute rock bottom. I understood his reasons but I still felt so bitter that the world seemed to be treating me this way.

My feelings were horrible and uncontrollable. Claudio Sprenger, the team doctor from De Nardi, went out of his way to contact me to try to help, but in my muddled state I resented him for letting me get in this mess to begin with. I felt that because he had known that I wasn't taking EPO he'd stopped worrying about me. It felt like I was ending my career in the most undignified way possible. People tried hard to look after me, but I lashed out at everyone. I wallowed in my self-pity and drank myself stupid every night. I had no idea what to do and no direction to turn. It had to end. I needed to think of a way out. Thankfully, after a week or so of self-destruction I found the motivation – or rather it found me.

I came stumbling through the gate of my apartment block. I was drunk enough to have forgotten how I got home. As I crashed into the wall by my own front door, I realised that I was going to have to find my keys and get through yet another fucking door. Why did an apartment block need so many fucking doors? I dropped my keys once, twice, and fell. As I stood up and tried again, I felt the presence of someone behind me. I turned and saw Zaza looking on.

'Ah, Zaza! Good evening!'

'Charly, what are you doing, eh? It's 3 a.m.!'

I knew Zaza wanted to look after me and keep me quiet, but my gutful of alcohol convinced me that I didn't need muzzling. 'I have been drinking … I know Rossana said don't give him any more wine, but … I don't fucking care.' By this point I had raised my voice to a yell.

From the moment he'd heard the news Zaza had patiently allowed me to get my anger out of my system. But right then things changed. I turned back to face him, ready to moan about the injustice of the world. Instead, I felt rough hands grab me and my body felt like it wasn't mine. I couldn't move it. Zaza had me pinned against the wall, and his face was an inch away from mine. Zaza was a gentleman, and I had never even seen him get angry. I saw through my drunken haze right into his eyes. Quietly but incredibly clearly he said two words: 'That's enough.'

I'd be lying if I said I had an epiphany right there and then – I was far too drunk for that – but while nursing my hangover the next day I realised that I had to take charge. If I wanted to clear my name and be a bike rider again, I had to *do* something more than wallow in the injustice of it all. I reminded myself that my cycling career had always been down to me, and getting through this mess would be down to me too. Giving in was no longer an option. I had to prove my innocence, and prove it beyond doubt.

The first thing I did was think through the technicalities of the situation. Even though being declared 'unfit to race' only prevented me from racing for three weeks, there was no actual ban on me as such. If De Nardi had wanted to, they could have trusted me and said, 'Oh well, come back next year.' But Stanga wasn't like that. He wanted to stay safe. That meant the only option available to me was to go and prove to a standard that suited Stanga and De Nardi that I had a naturally high haematocrit and I wasn't a risk for their team. I made a call to Stanga to see where I stood, but he was too cautious to guarantee that, even with proof of a high haematocrit, I could come back to the team. I was chasing shadows and I was clinging on to nothing at all, but it was all I had.

I contacted the UCI, who were genuinely surprised to hear from me. As far as they were concerned I had taken a slap on the wrist and that should have been it; it was like they had sent me on some sort of three-week vacation and I should have been pleased with the break. I was suspended for twenty-one days, but that wasn't my issue – it was the implication that I had doped that came along with the suspension that I thought could ruin me. Begrudgingly they explained there was a process I could go through to prove that I had a naturally high haematocrit. Going through it would be expensive and came with very few guarantees, least of all whether or not Stanga would be compelled to give me my job back, even if I did manage to prove that it was completely natural.

To make sure the process was done in a controlled environment, I had to go to the UCI headquarters in Lausanne to be put under laboratory conditions, to be tested over a number of days and exposed to differing conditions to see how my body reacted. If the UCI thought they saw good enough grounds they would grant me a special licence that accounted for my high haematocrit. It would cost me thousands: I had to fly to Geneva and take the train to Lausanne, I had to pay for a hotel and a week's worth of meals, plus I had to pay for the procedure and the blood tests. The bill for the blood tests alone was €2,500, money that I didn't really have to throw away on my €1,400 a month salary. By the time I finished this procedure I would be virtually bankrupt.

I was nervous before I left, but I was sick to my stomach when I arrived in Lausanne. The testing procedure was fairly rudimentary: I would be tested in different conditions, early in the morning, late at night, dehydrated and rehydrated. I had spent three years fighting to keep my haematocrit down and now I was being told I had to do the opposite. I knew the value they wanted to measure was subject to fluctuations, and, being so used to fighting to make it go the other way, I started to panic: if I couldn't get the bloody thing to go up now, I really *was* finished. It didn't seem to be a world where the athlete had a lot of rights. I could start the process but there was absolutely no guarantee that it would work.

The foulest pill I had to swallow came when I met the doctor in charge of my case. He told me straight away that he knew the haematocrit test wasn't ideal, but that it was simply the best that they could do at the time, even if that meant that a few people a year were wrongly stopped from racing. Once again, I was (rightly) infuriated. He gave me his big spiel about how bad things were in cycling and that I should be prepared to be sacrificed for the 'greater good' of keeping all those riders loading up on EPO from killing themselves. He was talking to me as though I was supposed to give a fuck about what anyone else was up to, like I could be reasoned into adopting a philanthropic attitude. I was 25, and had fought tooth and nail for everything that I had. He, along with everyone else, seemed to take my career so lightly. I refused to believe I could lose it all simply because I was caught in some bureaucratic medical crossfire. At that moment my last shred of faith in anyone bar myself was ripped away.

After four days of needles and testing, I went home to my apartment and sat there, dejected. I had to wait for two weeks to get the results, and I had no team, no money and no idea what I was supposed to be doing. I had gone through so much by now that I knew the only option was to try summoning the energy to get back into a routine. It was December, so I began doing what I knew: I started training again. Two agonising weeks of abortive and uncommitted training rides later I received a phone call from the UCI. It was as if the garage were calling me to tell me they had finished the service on my car. Some anonymous secretary spoke down the line: 'Mr Wegelius, we're just calling to let you know everything is OK.' They were so casual, and yet I immediately broke down into tears and wept. The UCI sent the certificate straight to Stanga, and he called me to confirm that he would rehire me. Once again with Stanga it was as if nothing had happened at all. It was just business: I was useful to him as a rider, and I was employable once again, so he rehired me (on slightly less money than he had initially offered me before this whole débâcle, of course).

* * *

From that time on I raced with a certificate that said I had a naturally high haematocrit. I was allowed to go up to 52 per cent, a meagre two points above the limit that everyone else was allowed to reach. Hardly earth-shattering stuff, but I'd had to fight for it. It made a tiny difference to me as a rider, in that I could stress just *slightly* less: I didn't have to worry quite as much about drinking litres of water the day before a race. I, and others, continued to suffer for a long time at the hands of people who were still using widespread doping techniques to make massive gains in their performance.

Ironically, things didn't get any easier for me as far as testing was concerned. Having been granted my certificate, it meant they tested me more often. I was immediately put into the UCI's 'high risk' pool (along with the top 100 or so riders in the World rankings, and riders who had previously failed tests) which meant that not only was I constantly pulled over for random meetings at races but I also had to repeatedly fill in a form by hand and fax it to the UCI, giving them an hour of the day in which I could guarantee to be in a certain place, where they could find me and give me a random out-of-competition test. If I wasn't there at the appointed hour it would count as a failed test. Again, it felt as if I was being treated as a criminal. There was absolutely no understanding from them as an organisation, and, surely, I couldn't have been the only one dealing with this issue? I still dragged suspicion around with me. I went through testing systems and whereabouts procedures that were entirely unbefitting a rider of my level. I had an asterisk next to my name, all because I was a naturally talented athlete with a high haematocrit.

What really stung me, more than any other of the injustices that I'd had to deal with, was that I saw what a thin and fragile thread my career hung by. I had given so much to cycling and yet in my position, as a *domestique* in particular, it could all be over in no time at all. My life as a cyclist was so precarious that it was frightening to even try to think about the future. I had no family and no responsibilities, and in a way I was glad of that. Had I been the breadwinner for a family and the same thing had happened, I cannot begin to think of how much more catastrophic things would have felt. The ground beneath my feet felt like it wasn't firm. How could I ever try to plan a life, if at any moment the whole thing could be taken away from me? I now saw that it wasn't just the obvious things, like a lack of decent performances, that were a threat to my existence; it was the things that I couldn't see or predict – a rule change, forgetting to drink enough water, a crash, a sponsor's change of heart. It wasn't just the issue of my haematocrit. I felt so vulnerable, and so unsafe right down to my core, that the feeling that it could all end at any second never really left me.

CHAPTER 8
'Tieni Duro'

'Great Britain's Charles Wegelius (De Nardi) has had a relatively uneventful career thus far, despite being groomed in the best possible manner in his early years at Mapei-Quick Step. In his five years as a professional, his best result is a third place on Stage Four of the 2002 Tour de Suisse, where he was involved in a breakaway with his then teammate Daniele Nardello and stage winner Leon van Bon. In the Giro, Wegelius will most likely be assigned the task of helping this year's Veenendaal–Veenendaal winner Simone Cadamuro in the sprints, as well as being given the freedom to go for stage wins. The 25-year-old may have youth on his side, but this could well be a make or break year for him.'

CYCLINGNEWS.COM'S PREVIEW OF THE 2004 GIRO D'ITALIA

When I stumbled upon the preview to the 2004 Giro on the cyclingnews website, as I whiled away a few hours in a hotel room the day before the race, I couldn't help but feel a little disappointed about what I read. It was my fourth year in Italy, and I was about to start my second Giro, but I felt that I had disappeared behind enemy lines in the eyes of the British press and public. Eclipsed by its megalomaniac brother – the Tour de France – the Giro suffered in the press outside of Italy, and similarly I found I had started to as well.

It was a curious thing but British riders had a way of 'disappearing' when they raced in Italy. Harry Lodge, for example, was a really good professional bike rider, who finished the Giro at a time when there were virtually no other British riders even close to achieving something like that, and yet the whole thing went almost unnoticed because it was in Italy. A lot of journalists didn't really take the initiative to look for things outside of their comfort zone. There was plenty of information in the English-speaking press about the Tour de France, but there was very little about the Giro. Perhaps, as I had myself thought when I was young, it was just too foreign. I don't think the race, or my achievements at the time, got the attention either of us deserved. A preview on cyclingnews describing me as the type of rider who was going to look after a sprinter or go for stage wins was so off the mark it was untrue. Never in my life had I looked after a sprinter, nor would I be doing so this time. I wasn't going for stage wins; I was there to do a job for a rider in contention for a podium finish. But the journalist had done maybe a ten-second scan and seen the only rider from the team with results was a sprinter, so assumed my job was to help him. I was working as hard as I could to perform at a high level as a professional cyclist, and, despite living in Italy, I still considered myself British. Reading this kind of nonsense hurt, and it made me start to question why

I wasn't being recognised amongst the English-speaking cycling audience. It felt like 'either/or': the more recognition I got in Italy, the less I got in the UK.

The results did come for me, though, whether they were recognised in the media or not. In that second Giro in 2004 things changed for me. As a *domestique*, your on worth is gauged in a large part, not by your own performances, but by the performances of your team leader. I had been able to contribute to the team in 2003, but my leader Honchar had struggled in the mountains. In 2004 it was a different story. Honchar was riding the Giro of his life and I suddenly became vitally important. Honchar possessed an incredible natural strength. He had the ability to push an enormous gear for an impressive length of time, which made him a great time triallist, but also meant he wasn't a natural climber. So the gains he could make against the clock we had to defend with everything we had in the mountains. With my climbing ability I became the ideal teammate for him. I was always there when he was in danger, and capable of making the difference when he couldn't.

My biggest feat, and the ride that I would be remembered for (in Italy at least) throughout the rest of my career, came on the final mountain stage of the race in 2004. The Italian sense of drama meant that stage 19, the penultimate stage of the race, was perhaps the most brutal of the whole three weeks. The 121 km stage went over two massive mountains – Passo di Mortirolo and Passo del Vivione – before finishing at the summit of the Passo della Presolana. With only the processional final stage into Milan the following day, and things tight amongst the riders vying for podium spots, the stage became a showdown for the overall victory.

At De Nardi we knew that this would be the final hurdle for Honchar. He had limited his losses brilliantly throughout the race and was hanging on to an incredible second place at the time. For a small team like De Nardi the lure of the final podium of the Giro in Milan was almost too good to dare to imagine. We knew that it would be a day of reckoning for our team, and I knew it could be the making or breaking of me as a *domestique*. Sure enough, sparks began to fly as soon as the race hit the first mountain of the day: Gilberto Simoni and Stefano Garzelli, my former teammate, attacked the *maglia rosa* Damiano Cunego on the Mortirolo. It was a dangerous move by Simoni, the previous winner, who was in third overall at the time. As a natural climber Simoni had a major advantage on the stage, and he knew he had to push Honchar as hard as he could from as far out as possible if he was to overtake him on the podium. If Honchar chased too hard too soon, or found himself isolated, he could not only have lost second, but everything that we had collectively been working for during the past three weeks.

Simoni and Garzelli started taking time quite quickly on the steep slopes of the Mortirolo, and I was still with the *maglia rosa* group when the order came crackling through my earpiece to ride. It was the moment I had been waiting for. As soon as I took up the riding on the front of the group I knew that day I could make the difference. I lifted the pace and the chase began, and with it came the onslaught of pain. Racing up a mountain is like putting your hand into a flame – it hurts and you want to do anything you can to make it stop, only in racing, if you stop you lose, and then the pain only lasts longer. You have to find whatever it is that switches off that reflex, and when you do, you can hold it. You learn to stay still in the pain. '*Tieni duro, tieni duro.*' Those words in my mind again.

Now was the time to put my hand in the fire. I was on a mountain, in the Giro, with the race happening right before me. It was everything I needed. All the other shit that made cycling complicated or difficult was wiped away. I could take the hurt and give everything I had to give. I didn't have to worry about who was sitting on the wheel, or who was going to beat me in a sprint. I just rode. That was the cyclist I had become, and that was the role I fulfilled. I could hurt myself as much as anyone, but trying to win races as a professional had opened the door to the things that I didn't want to face: responsibility and pressure. On the Mortirolo, every metre I rode reduced that pressure. I pushed harder and harder and harder and with every pedal stroke I felt unburdened. The only pressure I had now was to do what I could; there was no failure because now it came from inside. It was welcome and it somehow drove me. Everything that I dealt with in all those other races disappeared and I was finally left with the chance to make a difference.

I buried myself on the front of the pink jersey group for almost the entire Mortirolo until, when there were just five riders left, I was distanced over the top as the group accelerated to the summit. I was exhausted but I knew I wasn't finished. I descended back to the group in the next valley. Simoni and Garzelli were working hard together in the break but I marked a new finish line down in my head. There were 50 kilometres to go and I told myself, 'There are twenty kilometres left in this race: after that nothing matters.' I went to the front of the group and rode as if my life depended on it. I pulled the group along through the entire valley without looking behind for a turn, and still I kept on pushing. I towed the group half-way up the Passo del Vivione before finally I could give no more, and the last burst of electricity that had been firing through every circuit board in my brain to keep my muscles pumping seemed to flicker and die. I was finished. When I had taken up the chase behind Simoni and Garzelli, the duo had a lead of over two minutes; when I eventually cracked, their lead was down to 60 seconds.

As soon as I was dropped I was done. Rider after rider rode past me. The hard work wasn't totally over; it never is for a *domestique*. Riding up a mountain on a bicycle is a hard thing, no matter how much time you have to do it in. There were no wheels for me to sit on, and there was no team car to help. That day I knew I had given everything; I lost 22 minutes as I rode exhausted to the finish. Amazingly, Honchar hung on to his second place overall by a slender three seconds. For De Nardi it was a huge result; for me, it was life changing.

The top of the Mortirolo that day was lined four-deep with fans, and it felt like the few Italians who weren't there watching on the road were certainly watching on TV. The stage was broadcast live, and people had seen with their own eyes what went in to being a *domestique*. I had sacrificed everything, and had ridden myself into the ground for my leader, who had succeeded by the slimmest of margins. It was dramatic stuff. I hadn't thought about it before, but riding at the front during a race like the Giro put me in the limelight all over the country. I was on television for long stretches of time and people really got to know my face. It might have hurt me that I was shunned in the English-speaking media, but the reception I got in Italy following that exploit was really special. It is a cliché to say it, but that ride is something that people I meet in Italy still remember to this day.

The following afternoon the race reached Milan, and Honchar climbed on to the podium. We toasted our success that evening with a team dinner, in which Honchar made a big effort to thank everyone. I felt the warm satisfaction of a job well done, but the real feeling of success didn't come until after we had finished our private celebrations and I saw for the first time just how success at the Giro could change things. The Giro is to Italy what Wimbledon is to England: everyone is a fan, and for the month after the race the Giro is all everybody wants to talk about. From the first day back home people started to recognise me in the street. A lot of things in my daily life started to change: I didn't have to wait in queues in the supermarket, I didn't have to pay for a haircut or a coffee. Pretty much anything that anyone could do to show their appreciation – anything they thought would help me – they did. It was crazy and, like any young man, I enjoyed the privileges while I could. These little things made a difference. I was already leading a privileged lifestyle, just by being a professional cyclist in Italy; now all of a sudden everything was upgraded, and for a while it felt great.

There was one area in particular where I would have been a fool not to profit from my fifteen minutes of fame.

'Hey, Charly, get over here!'

My mate Massimo, a local bike rider who rode with our group on occasion, who had some time previously abandoned me to go and get some *aperitivo* for us both, shouted at me across the busy bar. As I looked up I saw him stood at the far end of the bar grinning ear to ear with a glass of *spumante* in each hand, and two rather attractive young girls stood either side of him, as if he was in the middle of a podium ceremony. As I walked over, I heard Massimo's mischievous introduction.

'Girls, here he is: Charly Wegelius, Giro d'Italia finisher!'

Massimo had been around bike riders a long time and clearly knew the game. June was hunting season for anyone who could claim to have had anything to do with the Giro – especially a rider.

Taking my cue, I joined in. 'Yep, that's me.'

'Really? Oh, wow: a real-life Giro rider. Have we seen you on TV?'

'Uh, yeah.'

The girl stood closest to the bar looked up at me through beautiful dark eyes, and giggled before she cooed at me, 'That's so amazing. You must be so tired …'

Her look was so intent and I was so unused to that level of attention from a stranger in a bar that I brushed the side of my face expecting there to be a lump of food stuck to my cheek. I looked over at Massimo and he raised his eyebrows in delight, before intently engaging the other girl in a conversation. The two of us had been coming to this same bar on and off all year, and while Massimo was always keen to have a crack at any ladies he had his eye on we never usually got any further than a polite brush-off. Now suddenly, almost unbelievably, I realised that it was me who held all the power in the situation; girls who I wouldn't have dreamed of chancing my hand at talking to were suddenly hitting on *me*. I (like everybody, I believe) knew my natural level with girls. I knew who I could expect to be able to chat up in a bar, but this was ridiculous.

It was like shooting fish in a bucket. I looked back at the girl by the bar, now ready to hang from every word that I said, and thought to myself, with a chuckle, 'Charles, you are batting way above your average.' I wasn't foolish enough to think that I was about to fall in love, or believe I was about to get myself into a relationship with the girl. The whole thing was ludicrously superficial, but it was a thrill, and a self-confidence appeared over that period that made the experience so much sweeter. But that confidence wasn't really from all the attention that I was getting. What gave me the real thrill was knowing that in the race I had done my job, and I had done it well.

. . .

My love of the Giro was enhanced because I felt it allowed me to tap into my talent. The Giro became 'my race', and over the years more and more success came from it. What I learnt there was that I could create the niche for myself as a cyclist that would keep me in a job, and also perhaps help me find the satisfaction in other areas of my life that I craved. I could never win the Giro, nor even ride towards a general classification there, but I could have an influence on the race, and make myself a part of it.

CHAPTER 9
Liquigas

'Wegelius! That is not a body! Where are you going to go with that body?'

Mario Cipollini's eyes had fixed themselves on me, and I could tell by the size of his delighted grin that we were all about to be treated to one of his trademark performances. The man was prone to these larger-than-life parades, and, sure enough, his captivated audience looked on as he announced, 'This is a body!' before stripping down to his underpants and flexing in the conference room of the hotel to howls of admiring laughter from his new teammates.

It was late November 2004, and the Liquigas team were assembled together for the first time in the Grand Hotel Porro in Salsomaggiore for a short training camp to measure up for our new bikes and clothing, and to start to get to know each other. Mario Cipollini certainly knew how to break the ice.

In any other team, or at another stage of my career, I would have been quietly annoyed at being the butt of a joke like that. I knew, too, that I would have taken it well because I had to. But at Liquigas things felt different. Finally, after five years in the Italian peloton, I was feeling really at home. The room was full of laughing bike riders, but while I was the prop in one of the master showman's jokes, I felt no mocking. I felt no sense that I was humiliating myself to fit in. I was just able to laugh along with everyone else.

At Mapei I justified my subservient behaviour because it was my first professional team, and I was desperate to ingratiate myself with my peers and my bosses. At De Nardi it went even further – I'd spent two years laughing along, and acting interested at the most idiotic behaviour. But now I could really laugh, because finally it all made sense – in signing for Liquigas I felt that I was finally 'at home' and in a team that valued me. Liquigas had started from scratch and it meant a great deal to me that I was one of the first riders on their shopping list.

Even before the end of the 2004 Giro I had been contacted by my former Mapei *directeur sportif*, Roberto Damiani, telling me that a new team would be starting in Italy in 2005, and on the basis of the performances he'd seen from me since Mapei had closed its doors he wanted me in it.

If the collapse of a big team changes the balance of the peloton in a negative way, the creation of a new team does the opposite. A new team is a major boost to the economy of the peloton, creating a whole new set of jobs that, in turn, boost riders' values and job security in the group as a whole.

Damiani was astute and he recognised that my stock was about to mature as a rider. After my years of schooling at Mapei, and two further years of physical development at De Nardi, I was the finished product. I knew what the job entailed, I knew the races, I had the legs to make the difference and, after bouncing back from my haematocrit crisis, I had found reason to renew my determination again. I was singled out as someone who could fulfil the role of the kind of *domestique* they needed, perfectly.

I knew from the conversations we had at the Giro that, while being a big team by Italian standards, Liquigas wasn't going to be anything like the size of Mapei. But during the summer I did my homework and I was encouraged by what I saw. The fundamental difference between Liquigas and De Nardi was so microscopic no one outside of the team would even notice, but to me it was huge. My contract would be with Liquigas Sport SpA, which sounded like a minor technical detail but actually changed everything. It meant everybody in the company – even the boss – would be an employee. Meaning the man in charge of the whole set up, Roberto Amadio, was the chief executive officer of a company owned by the sponsor, and so, unlike in almost all other teams in Italy, at no stage did Amadio stand to personally gain by saving money and cutting corners on riders, equipment or support. It gave me comfort to know that my second set of race wheels weren't likely to be sold off half-way through the year because my manager wanted to buy a new dining table or something. I signed the contract with Liquigas as quickly as I could. It was reassuring to find myself back at a big team and I relished the job security; I was to be a bike rider for another season at least. I was still a long way from the financial heights of the top riders, but, after earning little more than enough to survive for the past two seasons, my return to a professional's salary felt like a small victory. Returning to this kind of money also meant that I could finally start to work on the things that had been so painfully absent in my life at De Nardi: getting a mortgage

At Liquigas I finally felt at home. There I found myself riding alongside riders like Dario Cioni who respected me, and knew how to get the best out of me.

I enjoyed the best years of my career at Liquigas, but despite being close to victory on several occasions myself I never once held any personal ambition beyond doing the best job I could for the team.

Working for Danilo Di Luca at the 2005 Giro. A real *domestique* becomes invaluable when he is the only rider left in the front who is riding for someone else and not to win himself.

The Grand Départ of the 2007 Tour de France in London. My Italian teammates were less than impressed by the hotel food, asking me, 'Does the Queen have to eat *beans* in *tomato sauce* for breakfast?'

© OFFSIDE/L'EQUIPE

Starting a wet Tour time trial on stage 13 of the 2007 race. That TT was tough, but I was about to experience another hazard of cycling the Tour – staying in the worst hotels known to man.

Liquigas made the very most of my talents, they knew exactly when and how to use me as a rider. Leaving them at the end of 2008 would prove to be a costly mistake.

At the 2009 Tour de France. On the outside I had become the rider that I had always wanted to be, but my professional cyclist's exterior hid an inner turmoil that was making me ask questions of myself, and my profession.

Descending in the 2009 Tour. Once Cadel lost hope of a high overall finish the team that had been built around him became a sinking ship.

Cadel Evans's intensity ran me ragged in the first week of the 2009 Tour, and left me with nothing for the mountain stages where he needed me.

The race I couldn't finish – the Omega Pharma-Lotto team celebrate without me on the Champs Elysee at the end of the 2010 Tour de France. It was an image and a world I knew that I no longer wanted to be a part of.

Happy at home. With my wife Camilla, our son Emil and my mother Jane in Janakkala, Finland, 2012.

and buying a house. It was an important box to tick in my life, and proof to me that I was 'succeeding' in some way, that my personal life as well as my professional one was starting to slowly feel like it was getting fuller and more meaningful.

* * *

By the time we were all gathered together in Salsomaggiore the team had filled the roster, and the biggest name in the line-up was undoubtedly Mario Cipollini. Cipollini was a Giro stage-win record holder, former World Champion and, at 37, in his final season. He had signed to Liquigas, in part, to have a stab at winning his beloved Milano–San Remo for the second time; he was also a major publicity coup for the new team. His personality was so big it was magnetic, and I was pleased to be in his presence. Knowing cycling as I did, I always knew that there would never be competition between us, because he was a giant of a man, and I, as he had pointed out, was his physical opposite.

Cipollini's high jinx continued over the next two days of the camp and I saw just how important a role he could play in creating a good team atmosphere. The camp was a fairly relaxed affair, and on the last evening we all had a few drinks. Most teams like to encourage this – nothing helps men bond like a few drinks – but being an Italian cycling team (and not, say, a Belgian one) a few drinks really did mean *very* few drinks. On the whole the Italians are remarkably well behaved when it comes to alcohol, and there are rarely any of binge-drinking piss-ups you might find elsewhere.

But, drunk or not, Cipo had the entertainment all planned out: an inauguration for the young riders. Once we'd finished dinner he stood everyone up and frog-marched the group of nervous neo-pros outside into the freezing November night. The first race of the new season was about to begin. As the rest of us followed the group out, guffawing with laughter, Cipo appeared with 6 ft 4 in Swede Magnus Bäckstedt's bike in tow. 'Now, gentlemen, it is time for the *cronometro*.' Cipo had come up with the idea of running a two-lap time trial around the tiny ring road that ran around the outside of our hotel. The rules were quite simple: each of the four neo-pros would do the TT stripped down to his waist, and could only leave the start gate after downing a carafe of wine. The course was two laps of the circuit (to allow us the opportunity to chuck freezing water on the riders after the first lap), and just to make sure the riders were properly motivated Cipo would be following behind each rider in his own car.

The sight of the first rider coming around the bend on the first lap on Bäckstedt's enormous bike, with Mario Cipollini's Bentley behind him, horn blaring and lights flashing, while Dario Andriotto leant out of the window yelling, '*Vai, vai, vai, Porco Dio!*' like the most rabid *directeur sportif* you've ever seen, was side-splittingly funny. I had no idea what the other guests at the hotel must have thought, but all of us – including the neo-pros – were in stitches. It was pandemonium.

It was a typical Cipollini masterstroke, instantly taking it upon himself to create a good ambience amongst his new teammates. It was something that, despite the cynic in me, I really admired. He knew that a good working atmosphere got the most out of everyone, and he went about creating that within the team as quickly as he could.

• • •

In December 2004 I received a call from Damiani asking me whether or not I wanted to go to Mexico in February. Damiani was a man who always had a project on the go, and his current one was to try to re-launch the career of one of Liquigas' other big signings: Danilo Di Luca. Di Luca was already a high-profile rider: he'd had the kind of glittering amateur career that screamed 'future superstar', and duly shot straight to prominence with an incredible second place in the 1999 Tour of Lombardy in only his second year as a professional. In the following years he had taken his share of big wins, but in 2004, while at another Italian team, Saeco, he had gone through some problems with a doping investigation that stopped him from participating in the Tour de France. While missing the Tour wasn't too much of an issue in itself for Danilo, the experience had damaged both his reputation and his confidence. He had signed for Liquigas on a fairly small salary for a rider of his results, but he knew that the step back was needed for him to regain the ground he had lost in the previous season.

Damiani's concept was quite simple. He wanted to take a small team of four riders (Di Luca, Dario Cioni, Devis Miorin and myself) and three members of staff to somewhere isolated and at altitude to get right back to basics. Mexico was chosen as the place; the weather was good, it was at the right altitude, and Damiani knew that he had to toughen Danilo up a little bit. Danilo had been treated as a star from the moment he began winning bike races as a kid, and putting him well out of his element could be just the ticket to get him back on his feet. I didn't know Danilo at all on a personal level then, but when Damiani called and offered me the chance to go I knew that I couldn't say no – it was a golden opportunity to get myself straight into the heart of the team.

The seven of us flew to Toluca in Mexico, and when we arrived I immediately saw why Damiani had chosen the place. In the informed climate, post Tyler Hamilton's (and others') revelations about riders' doping practices in that era, and the methods by which riders would avoid detection from out-of-competition doping tests, it is easy to raise an eyebrow about disappearing off to isolated places to train. I knew this at the time too, but the UCI knew of our whereabouts, and the team made no secret of where we were going, continually publicising the fact that we were in Mexico. More to the point, I shared a room with Danilo (who would later be found guilty of such practices himself) for the entire time, and I never once saw him do anything illegal or that constituted doping *in any way*. Whatever was going on had either been done before we had gone there, or it was being done incredibly secretively, because I can hand on heart say that I didn't see a thing – and I wasn't a fucking idiot either.

What worked well for me was the fact that we couldn't do anything else for twenty-six days except ride our bikes and sleep. There was nothing there at all; we were in a wilderness that felt just about unsafe enough to prevent us venturing out of the hotel in the evening. For twenty-six days I was blissfully disconnected from the world, and it felt like a textbook exercise in how an athlete should live. The camp went well. It was hard work on the road, and thanks to Damiani's little project it was hard off the bike too. Damiani was trying very hard to calm down some of Damilo's prima-donna tendencies. We had to wash our training clothes by hand there, which was standard for a rider like me, but to Danilo this was a shock, as he would always have his masseur wash his stuff. Our masseur, Michele, had brought 15 kg of De Cecco pasta with him because he knew that was the pasta that Danilo liked. But Damiani was having none of it, so he forced poor Michele to keep it hidden from Danilo for an entire month because he wanted him to eat the Mexican hotel food and have to deal with it. All of this, for Damiani, was a big deal. He publicised it all, making sure the press were up to date with pictures of Danilo washing his shorts by hand and so forth. In fairness, Danilo reacted very well to what must have been an alien world for him. He had been a superstar his whole life, and this was surely a shock to his system.

The differences in Danilo's and my worldview were made very apparent to me on that camp. I had the plans for my newly purchased but as-yet-unbuilt house with me, and on a quiet afternoon I was looking through them when he came into the room. He immediately grabbed the blueprints and started going through them, asking, 'Charly, what are these? What are you doing?' and with that he pulled out a marker pen from his kit bag and decided that he would add his recommendations to the plans. Sure enough, they were returned to me with a good few hundred thousand Euros worth of additions, including another floor, a swimming pool and a sauna.

Danilo had that air of the cheeky chap, the scoundrel who you couldn't help but like. But instead of driving around the village in a modified Golf GTI – as I'm sure he would have been if he wasn't a superstar cyclist – he was tearing around in a Porsche. He was kind of like Toad of Toad Hall (if that incredibly English reference can extend to someone as Italian as Danilo). He was enthusiastic about everything and yet somehow comically reckless with it. At a later date there was a story doing the rounds that his mother had to intervene so that he wouldn't lose his driving licence. In Italy, at the time, it was commonplace to say someone else was driving your car if you got caught speeding. His mother was a typical elderly Italian housewife who wouldn't say boo to a goose but – according to legend – she had to toddle into the police station in her woollen stockings and confess to driving at 240 km/h. down the motorway in a Porsche Boxster, or something similar.

But it was when we started racing together that I really saw the best side of Danilo. I saw how genuine and generous a character, and a rider, he was. Before every single race we went to he'd stand in front of the mirror, shaking his legs. 'My God, look at the condition I've got!' he'd proudly say to anyone who would listen. He told everyone there in the team he was going to win. When he didn't win, everyone just shrugged their shoulders and said, 'Ah well, that's Danilo.' But when he *did* win, everyone said, 'He told me he was going to win this morning!' He would prove to be one of the best leaders I had because he never tried to be something that he wasn't.

The training we did in Mexico was hard, but being in a group of four meant that we could do good-quality work without the usual competitiveness that creeps in. Altitude can be a curious thing for athletes, and my reaction was always the same. I would really suffer when I was there – in Mexico we were staying at a camp at 2,500 metres – but when I returned back down to ground level I could really feel the benefits. By the time we left, in mid-February, I was ready to return to racing in the best condition I could have hoped for.

• • •

When we did return to Europe my début for Liquigas came very quickly. I was called up to ride two one-day races in Switzerland only forty-eight hours after stepping off the plane from Mexico. I struggled bitterly with the sudden return to cold temperatures, and instead focused my ambitions on my next race, the appropriately nicknamed 'race to the sun'. Paris–Nice is a one-week stage race that traverses France from north to south, and seems to bring about the arrival of spring. On the early stages across snow-covered northern Europe I suffered just as I had done in Chiasso. I was last overall, the cold completely biting into my form, and my team and friends were genuinely concerned that something was wrong with me. For three days I was grovelling along as the *lanterne rouge*, the last place in the overall standings. But as we raced south, the sun began to break through the gloom and with it I managed to conjure spring in my form, too. By the time we reached the final ascent of the race, at the Col d'Eze, I was flying. As I raced to the foot of the final climb as part of the day-long break, sweating in the first rays of the Mediterranean spring, I could hear Laurent Jalabert's commentary from the French TV motorbike, saying, *'Wegelius marche super bien en tête,'* and it felt like everything was coming together. I did a perfect job setting up my new teammate Franco Pellizotti, who took an encouraging second place on the stage. Flying all the way out to a remote town in Mexico instead of staying in Europe for the winter may have been a bit of a gamble, but it was about to pay off with the richest vein of form that I would ever have.

After Paris–Nice I had a short pause at home, and, as always, stepping off the hamster wheel was hard. A hollowness would frequently set in at moments like this, where the distraction of racing would dissolve away and my life as a man would be laid bare in all its emptiness. I had signed the deeds on a new apartment a few kilometres down the road from Varese in Gorla Maggiore the previous December, and I had at first been thrilled to think of myself as a homeowner. Getting out of that shitty rented apartment where I could barely stand to be alone had been a big goal for me. But now, while I waited for my new apartment to be finished, and went about the very adult errands of looking for furniture and choosing what was going to go fill it, that all-too-familiar hollowness returned.

It had been one thing to sit in a mismatched rented apartment and feel sorry for myself, pining about how removed I felt from normality. Now that my life was starting to finally look nice, and my home was no longer going to be little more than a waiting room, I started to feel terribly alone. Why invest in a home, when no one is there to share it, save for a few bike racers and, occasionally, my mum? I walked around designer furniture stores with a cloud over me: who is going to sit in these dining chairs, on this sofa, or on these kitchen stools? It hadn't been a question that I had ever had to ask myself when I was young. When my mother drove off and left me in France with a group of total strangers, I barely even looked over my shoulder as she left. Now that I had arrived at my desired goal, to be a respected professional cyclist with a nice house, a decent car and a big team, I could see how much had fallen by the wayside on the journey there. Now, more than ever, I needed to find a balance.

As the year continued I could feel that my form was exceptional and it felt like I had made huge progress physically. I was ambitious and I was hungry, and I channelled it all into doing a good job for other people, rather than striving for wins of my own: when I scored the best individual result of my professional career that April at the Vuelta Aragón, it came as a very pleasant surprise, but I didn't let myself entertain the idea of it leading to anything other than good form to help Danilo at the Giro. The Vuelta Aragón was on the programme for the Giro riders who weren't doing the Ardennes Classics, so we hadn't gone there with any expectations. It was strictly a preparation race for me, and, whether he recognised that I was going well or not, Damiani knew my psychology well enough not to ask me for anything in terms of results.

For the first flat stages I went about my business without any stress and, without really paying much attention, I managed not to lose any time. The fourth stage was an 11 km uphill time trial – a race that, given my time-trialling ability and climber's frame, suited me well. Before the start Damiani gently suggested that we take a drive to the top of the climb to look at the course. As we drove up the dull skies darkened and the rain began to fall. I made a mental note of the steep sections and where the climb levelled off. At the summit, satisfied that I had a good understanding of what was ahead of me, Damiani swung the car around and we drove back down towards the start. As we reached the junction where the narrow climb joined the main road, a serious-looking Spanish policeman halted us. It dawned on us that the road closure must have happened already. It was a disaster: from where we were it was a mere 3 km to the start, descending via the race route – but a 35 km loop to go in the direction that the officer was gesticulating that we should take.

Damiani was incredulous. We were in a team car with an athlete in it and a bike on the roof, and it couldn't have been more obvious that we were going to the start ourselves. In Italy this would never have happened. Italian police regarded the rules with that kind of generous elasticity that can often be useful. Damiani wound down the window and started to explain, but this particular Spanish policeman seemed to be under the impression that Franco was still in power and had personally requested the road closure. There was absolutely no budging him. Negotiations quickly escalated into a heated row. I sank into my seat and started to panic. After flinging his hands in the air for the final time Damiani gave in. He was livid; we knew that there wasn't time to drive to the start the long way round. He switched the car engine off, and sent me off to go and ride my way back to the start. By now the earliest starters would be getting ready to go … I grabbed my bike and rode back down the hill in my tracksuit in the pissing rain. By the time I made it to the team camper I was cutting it fine. I threw on my skinsuit and managed a panicked warm-up before rushing off to the start gate.

Amazingly, just as the haphazard nature of the cycling world quite often screwed me over, this time it worked in my favour. My pulse was racing as I quickly signed on, and with thirty seconds to my start time I shot up to the gate. I was rushing everything, and as soon as the countdown ended I started hammering it up the road like I was still running late. I was completely alone for the first few kilometres until I picked up the following car at the junction where Damiani had stayed waiting for me. In the rush I hadn't taken a radio or an earpiece, so I had absolutely no idea how fast I was going, or how I was doing; I just rode as hard as I could. Half-way up the climb the rain turned through sleet into snow and I felt it melting on my burning skin. I pushed on, surrounded only by my effort and a blissful uncertainty. I heard the mechanic screaming at me from the team car behind that I was 'going like a bloody motorbike!' I felt a twinge of pride, and without any other voices, orders or doubts I pushed on against the gradient and the weather. When I crossed the line at the top I had completely smashed the previous best time. I had no idea where it had come from, but I had done it. My time of 24 minutes and 23 seconds was fast, but as I wrapped up to protect myself from the freezing cold I was too cautious to even begin to believe that I might have done enough to win. Even when the German Tour de France winner, Jan Ullrich, finished almost a minute and a half behind my time, I steadfastly refused to think that I was going to win. I was protecting myself mentally, and I knew it, but there was no other option. Sure enough, after sitting at the finish shivering for half an hour, I listened as the PA announcer excitedly called out: 'New best time ... Ruben Plaza team Comunidad Valenciana ... 24 minutes 16 seconds.'

My response was symbolic of how deeply I had buried any sense of personal aspiration: I treated my achievement with utter indifference. I was happy, but not really for myself. Instead, I saw second place in a pure event like the uphill TT as a sign that I was going in the right direction for the Giro. Once again, I plotted this event on my career trajectory – this result had just taken me a couple of steps further along. I gauged my happiness from the reaction of those around me, too. Damiani was pleased for me as the ride put me up into third place overall, my first ever podium position in a professional stage race, but that was all. At Liquigas I was the perfect cog in the machine. That is what I had wanted to be. Early the next morning I flew to the Giro del Trentino, which started two days later, to play my role again.

● ● ●

While I had been busy surprising myself in the build-up for the Giro, elsewhere Danilo Di Luca had returned in a big way, winning both the Flèche Wallonne and the Amstel Gold Race in the space of ten days. This was a brilliant Ardennes double that had also seen him take the lead in the UCI Pro Tour classification. The team was already on a roll in its first season and we went into our first Giro together with high hopes. True to form, success came quickly for us at the Giro. We detonated the race with 30 km to go on stage three and Danilo took the win, inching himself to within seconds of taking the *maglia rosa*. As soon as he had won the stage, in typical Danilo fashion he was already announcing just how important it was for him to win *another* stage *and* take the pink jersey on home turf in L'Aquila two days later. On that stage we hit the race with a definitive plan, and I relished playing my part in it: I infiltrated the break of twenty or so riders that took off at the start and sat on the back of it all day refusing to work (and remaining thick skinned, as rider after rider came back and tried coaxing me into riding). The team wanted me to cover the move and be ready for action in the finale. Coming into the final 20 kilometres the break still hadn't been caught and my radio earpiece crackled into life. 'Charly, we need you to sit up and come back to the bunch right away.' It goes against every instinct of a bike rider to stop pedalling and let a race disappear down the road, but without question I stopped imme- diately and waited by the side of the road for two minutes before the peloton eventually came into sight. It was then that my real job started. I immediately set to work driving the bunch as hard as I could back across to the break that I had let go of. Along with Dario Andriotto and Marco Milesi, I pulled the bunch all the way back to the break before Andrea Noè gave Danilo the perfect lead-out for his dream win and Liquigas' first *maglia rosa*.

Danilo was delighted with the team, and he was delighted with me too. I was still selling myself like I had been at De Nardi, but this was different. Here, I was happy, and I was selling my skill as a *domestique* to a team who knew what that skill meant. Danilo was a big champion as a cyclist, albeit a slightly eccentric human being; but what struck me above all was that I was valued as a person, financially remunerated for my efforts, taken into the fold as an essential part of the team, and thanked. I was physically capable being there with Danilo in the mountains when things were getting hard and he needed me, and I had the right character that I could share a room with him for three weeks and make him feel comfortable and happy with himself.

It is a fallacy that gets perpetuated in the media, as a way of crudely explaining the role of a *domestique*, that they are good guys who go around doing good deeds. *Domestiques* aren't simply kind-hearted folk who just want to help others; real *domestiques* are hired killers like everyone else. They do what they do out of professionalism. It is a job with many facets and innumerable intricacies and, put simply, you have to be fucking good to be able to do it well.

For the public, the complexity of bike racing often has to be condensed, so that it can be easily digestible as short news bites or sensationalist coverage. Spectators turn on the TV and see one team's *domestiques* plodding away on the front, riding behind a break, and think it is an easy job. But what often goes unrecognised by the general public is the effort these *domestiques* have made to create the situation where they can confidently ride steadily on the front in the first place. There may have been countless break-away attempts before the one that sticks, but for one reason or another these other combinations would have been too dangerous to let go. It could mean these *domestiques* have been chasing moves down at full tilt for an hour before the one move that is weak enough not to be a problem is allowed some freedom and they can ride a steady tempo.

Bad bike riders were just as guilty as the media of devaluing the term '*domestique*'. It is all too easy for weak riders, when they find themselves without a contract, to explain away poor performances by saying that 'they fell into the role of a *domestique*' – a bad work-man blames his tools, and all that. But a team will *never* end the contract of a real *domestique* without a really good reason. Anyone can bring feed bottles to someone when the group is taking a piss in the first 100 km of a race. But you prove your real value as a *domestique* when there are twenty guys left in the race and every single one of them thinks they can win, and you're the only one working for someone else, that's when a real *domestique* is priceless. By 2005 that was how I saw myself. I wasn't a *domestique* by default, or because I couldn't think of what else to do. I was a skilled professional, and I was fucking good at my job.

CHAPTER 10

Madrid

'Greg LeMond still waits … the punch he requires seemingly not there as he relies on Robert Millar, his teammate all year round, to set the pace at the front. Loyalties are always to one's racing team, even though a World Championships is fought out between nations. For this reason too Sean Kelly of Ireland cannot chase the leaders ahead because the two Belgians are both on his team.'

PHIL LIGGETT, FROM THE COVERAGE OF THE FINAL LAP
OF THE 1990 WORLD ROAD RACE CHAMPIONSHIPS

'Do you have any plans for Sunday?'

'Nothing special … The circuit is pan-flat …'

'Who is your team leader?'

'Hammond.'

'A sprinter … OK, then … well, if you want to make a little extra cash there is an opportunity that should suit us both. Let me know if you're interested.'

I should have seen that the 2005 World Road Race Championship was going to be more trouble to me than it was worth. When I arrived in the team hotel near Madrid airport two days before the race, as ever, I was picking my way through a raft of decisions to try to keep my career on track. The choice that I made following this brief phone conversation two nights before the race with a member of the Italian team was one that I admittedly got horribly wrong, and one that would haunt me for the rest of my cycling career.

One week before the World Championships I had also been in Madrid, riding the final stage of my second Vuelta España. The race had been the usual stinking hot bucking bronco ride around Spain. I made it through to the finish in Madrid, but as I was sitting at the airport waiting to fly home I had some rather unsettling news. I took a call from a very concerned Aldo Sassi, who had just seen that I was announced as a member of the Great Britain team for the World Championships. Knowing my body like he did, he'd done some worrying calculations.

Following a big effort like the Vuelta it is natural for a rider's haematocrit to dip, but the amount of red blood cells in your body doesn't actually change that much. Instead it is a matter of haemoconcentration. My exhausted body was likely to bloat with water over the coming two days as it tried to redress the balance, making my red blood cell count appear to go down. Aldo sagely informed me that after a few days of rest, 'You will start pissing like a racehorse,' and as a result my haematocrit would rocket. I didn't normally race for a long time after a three-week Tour, but now, thanks to my high blood values, Aldo predicted that on the day of the World Championships the following Sunday my haematocrit would be 'sky high'.

My heart sank as I realised what this meant. With no biological passport system in place, despite the fact that I had a certificate for a high haematocrit, I knew there was a very real possibility of failing another UCI health check. I couldn't face going through more heartache while I proved to the world (yet again) that I wasn't taking EPO. I was tired from a long season in which I'd ridden both the Giro and the Vuelta. The thought of going through all that stress to ride a one-day event on a virtually flat circuit seemed counterproductive. I quickly decided that it probably wasn't worth my time or the risk. I wasn't going to ride.

I called John Herety, the national team manager, while I was still sat in the departure lounge in Madrid airport, and through the continual interruptions from flight announcements I made him aware of the situation and suggested that I shouldn't ride. John understood, but advised me to speak to the British Cycling doctor, Roger Palfreeman. The noise at the airport was too much to consider making a serious call such as that straight away so I waited until I had returned to Italy to call Dr Palfreeman to explain the situation.

The GB team, it seemed, were very keen that I rode. As one of only six British riders racing professionally in Europe my influence was needed, not simply in the race, but as a way of giving the team credibility. My attitude, however, was quite different towards them. At the time I was completely indifferent to riding the World Championships for the national team: I wasn't a traitor, I didn't want to blow up the Houses of Parliament or burn the Union Jack, but, in all honesty, my attitude towards the British Cycling team was an ambivalent one, formed from a series of negative experiences I had from riding with them over the years.

My first time riding for GB was the 1995 Junior Worlds in San Marino. I was already the driven youth who wanted to do everything he could to become a professional cyclist, but even with my then-limited experience I found the team to be a misguided shambles. The Great Britain team was the whipping boy of European cycling; we felt disorganised, amateurish and so penniless that when one rider tried to keep his jersey as a souvenir it was noted as missing by the team management, and all of the riders on the trip were forced to empty out their suitcases.

Over the years certain things had changed in the organisation. Some bright spark suggested that 'Federation' be dropped from the name and the 'BCF' became just 'BC'. BC was different in many respects. They were rich and they completely dominated track cycling, and yet, equally, some things really hadn't changed at all: notably their attitude to road racing. A little over a year before I had been selected for Madrid in 2005 I had been a part of the GB team that went to the Athens Olympics. The event should have been a big deal for me: my father had represented Finland at the Moscow Olympics, so it felt like quite an achievement. And yet the total indifference of the national team towards the road race, due to the unlikelihood of us winning a medal, made the whole thing feel like a tourist trip. I arrived in Athens at the last minute and met up with a woeful squad made up of myself and one other European-based professional, Roger Hammond, and two British-based riders, one of whom hadn't even won a decent road race in his life! So uninterested were the team that they didn't even fill the fifth spot that was allocated and we started with four men instead of five. It was a joke.

It was typical of the GB team. In the previous Olympic road race at the 2000 games in Sydney, mountain biker Nick Craig had to be *coaxed* into doing the event after competing in his mountain bike race. He rode an important and serious road-racing event in a peaked helmet and mountain bike shoes.

After lengthy discussions with both Dr Palfreeman and John I eventually changed my mind. I was persuaded that, given my clear history of a high haematocrit, there would be no repeat of 2003, and that having notified British Cycling early on they weren't worried about the possible implications of me racing with high blood values. I relaxed just a little. I had at least notified the right people, and if there were to be a shit storm they would fight my corner. I was sure that the team was better off with me than without me, and I didn't want to see a mountain biker drafted in. Making the decision to go through with it would turn out to be my first mistake.

● ● ●

I arrived in Madrid with a lot on my mind and I felt everything suggested that the GB team was behaving as it always had in the past. Unlike many of the riders who went through the WCPP system after I did, I hadn't maintained any kind of relationship with the GB team. Even as soon as my first professional World Championships, only one year after signing my contract in Verona, I'd felt estranged from the national team. The situation worsened at that race when a dispute between Mapei and the GB team started. GB refused to let Mapei put their logos on the jersey – which GB had the right to do, but still seemed highly irregular at the time. Mapei were forced to back down and the issue eventually diffused, but the incident felt highly embarrassing for me. Instantly I felt there was a conflict between the professional world I lived in and the amateur world that I felt the GB team still represented. In 2005 I had been so busy in the past twelve months at Liquigas that I was still completely out of touch with the GB team. When I arrived I soon realised that I didn't know anyone in the GB set-up apart from John Herety and, once again, I felt marginalised by a staff I didn't know and an organisation I didn't really understand.

My haematocrit problem was still gnawing away at me. There was no one there I really felt that I knew well enough, or whom I felt would be able to offer any kind of valuable help on the matter, even though they had assured me otherwise. I had already spoken to John about it, but, in truth, I couldn't really trust anyone else. I felt completely alienated.

From my perspective, I felt there was a very strange and insular attitude that some of the GB team had towards all of the 'foreigners' they assumed were doping – which I think was, in part, just an excuse to explain away decades of dreadful GB performances. So I felt that I too must be under suspicion because I wasn't a part of their system. Even there in the presence of the team, I felt the distance between us widening.

By the time dinner came and I sat around a large circular table and looked about my teammates as they tucked into their plates of hotel pasta and bread rolls, I felt uncomfortable enough to start asking myself what on earth I was doing there.

I headed back to my room. And then the phone rang.

The caller was known to me but he will remain unnamed here. I am not seeking to explain or condemn the actions of others, but mine alone. The following account of what followed is my recollection of events – even if others remember things differently.

The conversation, to begin with, wasn't anything special or untoward. We chatted for a while, as I lounged in an armchair at the end of the corridor, not wanting to disturb my roommate, Steve Cummings, by jabbering away in Italian. We talked about how the Vuelta had been, how my form was and what the GB hotel was like. Just before the conversation drew to a close, though, the exchange took place that left me feeling like I had just been told I was going to become a made man – and, in a way, I had.

The question of me being able to assist someone other than my own team leader's chances in the race wasn't unexpected or even out of place. For years these types of incidents had been happening at the World Road Race Championships. The entire format of the race was completely flawed in this respect. The World Championships is the one race of the year where riders compete for national teams instead of their professional teams, so how is it then possible that a rider who wins a race made up of national teams can wear the rainbow jersey for his trade team? The World Championships *only* made sense in the national team format for a brief period when the sport was much smaller and professional teams didn't employ many foreign riders. It meant that the Belgian team was an amalgamation of the best Belgian squads, the Dutch team was made up of riders from the top Dutch squads, and so on. Once professional teams were employing riders from twelve different nations the idea of a

World Championships run off in national teams should have become obsolete as allegiances amongst professionals were always going to be skewed. But it didn't, and so instead the race became what it was: a race that masqueraded as one that was based on national pride, but was in fact as mercenary as any other professional bike race. There were riders who could win, and then there were others – who rode for small nations – who every so often were looked at for a little bit of help. The Italians had come to the race with Alessandro Petacchi as their leader, and were desperate for the race to end in a bunch sprint. It hadn't been discussed in the phone conversation but I knew that they would want help to keep the race well controlled.

I went back to my room feeling a mixture of elation and anxiety. It struck me that I hadn't even thought to ask about the money. I knew it wasn't a factor in my decision-making. A bit of money would be a nice bonus, but being asked was the real success. This was a big thing, but I knew it would separate me further from my GB team-mates, at least in the run up and on the day itself. But even knowing that, I was still sure that it couldn't possibly be an issue. The entire GB set-up seemed to be geared towards its riders making inroads into the world of professional racing, and for me this was a massive step right into the heart of the sport. That phone call, and the offer that had just been put my way, was recognition I was regarded as reliable and a professional. If I did the job well it had the potential to elevate my status to being one of the most useful and important *domestiques* in the eyes of the very best riders in the world.

As I went to bed my mind was racing. I was edging towards a decision, but I was still unsure of myself. Why shouldn't I take up the offer that I had on the table? I didn't have to think for long to see that amongst the team of six I was the only rider there who stood to gain absolutely nothing from being at the race riding in GB colours. Roger Hammond, our team leader, had just finished the Tour of Britain riding for the national team and was quite involved with BC; Steve Cummings and Bradley Wiggins were both part of the track team and were looked after very closely by BC. The other two riders there, Tom Southam and Robin Sharman, were at a stage in their careers where simply being a part of any kind of success would benefit them. All of those other riders would have something good coming their way if we did well: either a direct pay rise, more job security or some kind of comeback. But not me.

As I lay there thinking it through, something else came creeping up in my mind. I had known for a while that, post-Athens, British Cycling were actively trying to encourage European teams to accept their riders by paying for them to be in teams. British Cycling were 'sponsoring' small professional teams who were then paying that money back to the riders in exactly the same way the rich uncles and father-in-laws were doing to get their boys into crooked Italian teams. While it was all well and good for the British riders who got these opportunities, it was still incredibly damaging to the few others who were trying to make their way *outside* of this system.

Professional teams were always on the look-out to save money. The fact was that a rider in my position was always at the back of the queue when it came to allocating the budget for wages. The big stars took up the budget and the rest of it was divided between the guys who weren't going to win the big races. This meant that if a team could have a rider, even of a slightly lower quality, whose salary would be taken care of, they would no doubt consider it. If I (or any other British rider who wasn't part of the GB/BC system) had been looking for a contract but a team had an approach from BC offering one of a number of other British riders to the team for free, nine teams out of ten would do what saved them money. By introducing riders at no cost to teams, I felt BC were devaluing good British riders to zero Euros – a situation almost impossible to compete with.

After everything I had done to try to integrate myself into European professional cycling, I felt British Cycling were ruining one of the very few natural advantages that I held as an athlete – the fact that I was British. As ridiculous as it sounds, being British was of value to me. You never knew when a sponsor would have some sort of affiliation to the UK that would make taking on a British rider an attractive proposition.

. . .

The next morning the team gathered after breakfast for our first ride together as a group. As we headed out of the hotel into the scrublands around the back of the airport, I knew this was my opportunity to test the waters. It was a bright, windy day, and as we trundled about loosening our legs and chatting I rode up alongside our nominal team leader, Roger Hammond. I had known Roger since 1997 when, for a brief spell, he had come to race for Vendée U. Roger was a little older than me and, as he'd spent most of his career racing in Belgium, our paths had very rarely crossed. I knew Roger, though, and I knew that he had been a pro for a long time. There was no doubt in my mind that he knew how racing worked, and what was expected of him as team leader.

As we pedalled along I asked Roger about his form and made small talk, and then I asked straight out if he had any bonuses for the race. His response was that he had a decent win bonus available from his team (a fairly standard type of bonus from a team of that size for riders of his level). I reckoned Roger knew the score, and he and I both knew that there would be no incentives offered from the GB team itself.

Back in Athens (where Roger was also our protected rider), having been advised on the matter by various people, I had broached the subject of performance-based bonuses while riding for the national team. The way I and almost all other professional cyclists saw it was that, because the Olympic Games (just like the Worlds) was an event for national teams, it meant that I was effectively doing my job for no pay that day. It was standard amongst European national teams that, while there was no 'match fee' for taking part (as there is in football, rugby and cricket at international level), there was a bonus scheme in place to reward the riders in the team for doing a successful job.

If you are an amateur then it is enough that someone pays your flight and hotel and you get the chance to race. But I was no longer an amateur. I was a *professional* and this was about me being expected to sacrifice my ride for another. In Athens it was all well and good for me to help Roger Hammond to become an Olympic medallist for the honour of the country, instead of just riding my own race and trying to win a medal myself, but after the race was done Roger would be the person who benefited financially and personally from the currency of his Olympic medal. When I asked what I thought was a fairly reasonable question for a professional athlete in our team meeting the night before the road race in Athens, the assembled staff and riders laughed in my face. Who did I think I was, asking for money to ride for Great Britain? It was made abundantly clear to me that everything I did in a GB jersey – including potentially enhancing the career of another rider who rode for another professional team – I was expected to do for free.

· · ·

In Madrid, I assumed Roger would know that if he was serious about winning the race he should put some of his bonus on the line for his teammates. As far as I was concerned that was the very reason bonuses were even offered in the first place; they were an incentive, not only for the rider to do well, but to make sure that he had something to inspire his professional colleagues with, to dedicate themselves to him and his win.

The way I perceived it, Roger's reaction, rightly or wrongly, meant either one of two things to me: he expected us to dedicate ourselves to him for free and watch him take the plaudits *as well as* the money, or he simply didn't back himself enough to believe that he could really win the race.

As we continued to ride on, I pushed the conversation further. I don't know how, or even if, Roger remembers it, but I recall I told him, 'I've got an offer on the table to perhaps do a little bit of work for someone else … if the opportunity arises.' I spoke to Roger openly about it because I felt it was the professional thing to do.

By the time we finished the ride my mind was closer to being made up. There were still things to do, however, before I could return the call to my Italian 'friend' and confirm that I would act.

I wanted to tell Roger, and I also wanted to tell the GB team. Whatever people think of me, I wasn't a total fucking idiot, nor was I a mercenary cowboy. I was going about the process of making a professional decision and I was being as informed as I could about it. That afternoon I went to John Herety's room to seek his opinion.

It wasn't at all unusual for me (or any rider for that matter) to go and knock on John's door. John had been involved in the national team for a long time, and he was always available to his riders. I knocked; John yelled over the din of Ryan Adams's alt-country blaring out of his tinny computer speakers. I walked in but the room was empty. I found John shaving in the bathroom and, being comfortable with him, I went and perched on the side of the bath. John continued shaving. He had been the manager who looked after me in my final year as an Under-23, and he had been my only real link to the British Cycling team throughout my time as a professional on the Continent. Whenever I was selected for the national team it was John who called, and whenever I wanted to get hold of anyone or anything in British Cycling it was John whom I spoke to. It made sense for me to talk honestly to him, because as a former European professional cyclist himself he understood that having influential people on your side kept you in a job.

'John. What do you reckon for Sunday?'

I didn't know if he knew where I was going yet, but I didn't give him time to reply.

'The thing is, I've got an offer to do a bit of work for someone else.'

I saw his eyes flick across to look at me in the mirror. His face tightened ever so slightly. He didn't say anything at all.

Looking away, I rushed back in to keep the conversation going.

'It won't be anything serious. I don't have the legs to be there at the end and I am pretty sure we all know how the race is going to go on this circuit.'

John carried on looking at me, but still didn't speak. I was surprised. I didn't expect a big pat on the back but I had thought John, of all people, would be happy for me. He had been with me at countless World Championships where we were humiliated by the Italians – it was just how it was in cycling – and he knew how important those riders were in my life.

I started thinking that maybe he was going to say no; that he was going to say it was a woefully bad idea. But he didn't. What I didn't realise at the time was that he simply couldn't. In hindsight, I can understand that in John's mind our relationship had changed: I had been a pro for much longer, and had been much more successful, than he was as a cyclist. For this reason, and knowing how the Worlds worked, he didn't feel he could say 'no' to me. But, simultaneously, I think he knew that the British team had changed, whereas I hadn't quite clocked that it wasn't the amateur flophouse it had been for so long. He knew that potentially there could be an issue. I let the conversation peter out. John played the cards he thought he had to, to protect me, and to protect BC: he didn't say anything at all.

I left John's room and entered the corridors of the hotel once again. You get used to hotel corridors when you are a bike rider – the shimmy of tracksuits and the idle chatter drifting out of the open doors as riders get their afternoon massages. After feeling like John's reaction wasn't enough to suggest that it was a bad idea, my thoughts became clear: there was one other thing to do before I made the call. I wanted to make sure that the whole thing was definitely worthwhile, and so I thought that the best thing I could do was to at least use a little bit of my influence to help another British cyclist along at the same time.

Tom Southam was a young British professional whom I'd met years earlier through Mike Taylor. With Mike it was like family: if, as a young rider, you showed you were worth the effort, he would always introduce you to other riders who had made it in Europe. In a time when no one in British Cycling really had any connections to the continental European cycling scene, those kinds of contacts were invaluable. When Tom had popped up in Italy riding for an Italian team I saw it as only natural that I helped him out a little.

Tom had turned pro with a small Italian team, and he was a strong rider who had a decent amount of natural talent. The thing that struck me about his situation was that he was equally as good as, if not better than, so many Italian riders who were destined to have an easier time than him. But being English in an Italian system meant he was due to eat a lot of shit in his career – and I knew just what that tasted like. I wanted to help, and the previous season I had set about it in the only way I knew how: he stayed with me in Varese and I introduced him to all the right people. I took him training with my group and explained how things worked. We got along well, and as two of only three British pro riders in Italy we spent a bit of time together at races.

Getting Tom involved in the action in Madrid would be a massive leg up into the right circles for a rider like him. I made a diversion past his room, and knocked on the door. His roommate was out having a massage so I ran the idea past him there. He was a rider who wanted to be a reliable professional and he instantly understood the importance of the offer. To him this was a godsend, a way to get his name known by the riders to whom he one day hoped to prove his worth. He agreed without much hesitation and I left it at that.

I made the call.

This time it was an even shorter conversation. I asked if more help was needed, and the reply was yes. I put Tom's name forward and, in turn, I was told what we were expected to do, and what the price would be.

'When the early break has gone, we need a little help to take up the chase just to get it started so the bunch keeps within ten minutes of the break for the first 100 km. There is 2,500 Euro a head on offer.' I agreed, and it was done. My country was sold out for €2,500. Or was it?

Two and half thousand Euros is not a great deal of money in cycling – the amount didn't surprise me at all. The role that we were due to play in the race was so trivial and insignificant that the money was an illustration of what it represented in cycling: nothing. It was a symbolic payment, that was all. I knew I wasn't going to be building a swimming pool or buying a Maserati after the race. Of course it depends on how you look at it: €2,500 is a very cheap price to sell out my allegiance to my country, but I couldn't even begin to see it that way. To me, I was making a decision that would gain me the reputation and respect amongst the people I saw as my peers, that was to provide me with invaluable gains in my career as a professional cyclist in Italy, and in the international peloton.

The fact that I would be wearing a Great Britain jersey on the day was a double-edged sword. I felt I was representing my country, but also a self-appointed professional organisation. I had been involved with the GB team for years, but when Lottery money came in to the national team it became more like a business that traded under the banner of a national flag.

My Great Britain, the country I believed in, and the national team that I would have been proud to represent, didn't look anything like this one. By now everyone I knew who worked in British Cycling had been either fired or marginalised by the creation of the regimen now in place. If people wanted pride out of me, and loyalty and all the things that went into patriotism, then they had to do a bit more than just point at the flag on their T-shirt. There is a lot of pressure on athletes to portray their exploits as being patriotic, as part of some public service. I am sure there are a lot of patriotic athletes out there but I struggle to believe that the Union Jack is really foremost in their minds when the shit hits the fan. But this, of course, is not something that can be said out loud without risk of crucifixion from the media and the fans. As much as it had been important for me to represent my country as an amateur, at a professional level things had changed. When I made that decision I was honest with myself: I didn't race my bike for Great Britain, I raced for myself and my future. If my racing brought something to GB and to British Cycling then I would be delighted about that (my medal at the European Championships had certainly done no harm to the WCPP in its first year of existence) but I wasn't about to lie to myself. In my future I needed the people who had offered me the opportunity – the Italians – and, if I was honest, I needed a bit of spare cash so I could get a new kitchen while I was at it. That was my motivation: my job security and my home life.

I'd made the call and the die was cast, but the reality was really quite unexciting. Just like the riders who make the choice to take drugs, the decision wasn't harrowing or difficult, this was the simple reality of life for a cyclist like me.

● ● ●

After I had returned the call the time passed quickly as we prepared for the event. On the morning of the race itself, though, things felt a little strange. I woke up to the relief of not having to go through a blood test, and that should have calmed me, but deep inside I felt uncomfortable knowing something the other riders didn't. When we arrived in the pit lane an hour before the start I hopped on my bike and rolled the 500 m or so down to the start to sign on. As I got there I saw the rider from the Italian team who would be orchestrating things on the road. As we walked back to our bikes after scrawling our names on the start sheet, he looked at me. 'When I say, you start riding. OK?' he said quietly. I looked back at his casually smiling face. This was no dramatic movie scene. I didn't feel like a boxer getting told to take a dive. I saw someone I knew pushing some of the business of cycling my way. I said, 'OK.'

Once the race rolled off it took the predictable shape of a one-day professional race run on the flat. Three unknown riders duly set off in the suicide move as the bunch yawned its way around the circuit in the early morning sunlight. By the end of the fourth lap the break had established itself with a ten-minute lead and, as we went through the twists and turns in the tall buildings on the back of the circuit, the word came. The light blue of the Italian team jersey popped up alongside me. 'Can you ride? Just *regolare*? No need to do any damage.' It wasn't a demand; it was a question.

I gave the nod back and I couldn't believe my luck. Until now a little part of me had been worried that the race might take another shape and I would be asked to do something that contravened our team orders. As I started my push towards the front to begin the pace-setting I knew that by riding behind the break I wasn't doing any damage whatsoever to Roger's chances. Our plan was to ride for a sprint for Roger, but I wasn't a lead-out man, nor did I have the punch in my legs to be anywhere near the end of a 270 km flat one-day race like this one. By taking the initiative now, I saw that I could actually have a constructive influence on the race. I picked up Tom, who was hovering a little closer to the front, and as I passed him I gestured with a nod of the head that it was time to go to work. We slid up to the front of the peloton and I started it. For the first time that day I had open road in front of me, and I ever so gently lifted my speed up from 32 to 37 km/h. and settled down to it. 'In a few hours,' I thought, 'I can hop off, grab a shower and watch the finish.' If Roger had the legs he'd be there, and if the Italians could keep Petacchi in the game then they'd be over the moon with me too. Job done.

When the steady pace slowly started to halt the break's progress and we began to ride the bunch (including Roger, who had three teammates with him) back into the race, I noticed things weren't right. Before we took the U-turn back up past the finish, I saw the GB staff had run out of the pits and were staring intently at the race. Instead of wearing the knowing looks that I had expected, I saw panic amongst the staff.

As I continued my work, my mind started to rush. The radio stayed silent, but even if the order came to stop it was too late now.

Each time I passed the pits I could feel myself sinking. There was activity there, but none of it was positive. I caught my old friend Rod Ellingworth's eye. He looked like a man who knew my girlfriend was shagging someone else and saw I was about to walk in on her. His expression said, 'Don't go in there,' but I already had. I had already waded right in. I buried my thoughts in my work on the front of the bunch.

What I also noted about the commotion in our pit area was the number of press and TV suddenly hanging around. When I had overheard a few days previously that the race was being broadcast in its entirety for the first time, I took little notice. But, really, I should have. What I thought was a completely uninteresting footnote would actually make all the difference in the end. The early broadcast of the race meant that the part that I was involved in was shown on TV. Usually, the early, rather uninteresting laps wouldn't even be shown to the public, but now there were a lot of people watching and a lot of people – commentators, journalists and fans – were struggling to find things to talk about. Inevitably, at the first spark of action, people had found something interesting to latch on to: why the hell was GB, of all teams, suddenly picking up the chase?

It was a good question only because the team was so bad. Nobody could ascribe a legitimate reason to why GB would ride the front of a World Championship with two riders. Until then the GB team hadn't ever dared show themselves on the front of a World Championships Road Race. The team's chances were clearly regarded as slim at best, even by the British press. After a couple of hours I duly abandoned and slunk behind the pits and into our tour bus to change. As the race continued around the circuit and I sat on the bus, the staff came on one by one to take a look at the naughty schoolboy. It became apparent that I was now accountable for something that I had thought would be of no consequence whatsoever. I knew that once the press broke the story, they would scratch at the wound and things could start to get worse. Roger Hammond failed to make the final selection of twenty-seven riders who contested the race, and eventually took 14th in the bunch sprint, ending up in 41st place. As soon as he got off his bike he had a microphone shoved under his nose. He had just finished the race and probably knew less than anyone about the shit storm that had been brewing. He agreed with a journalist that it hadn't seemed to be in our best interests to ride, and once he gave that answer we were news, and there was suddenly something for the British press to write about in the wake of what was a fairly uneventful Championships for the team.

After the finish we packed into the team cars and headed back to the hotel. By now the roads were overrun with spectators, and I looked through the window at them as we made our way slowly through the mob. The Spanish fans cheered out for Alejandro Valverde, the French waved their flags, and the delirious Belgian fans were celebrating Tom Boonen's victory. I thought about the fact that almost an entire bike race had taken place after I had retired from the action. The race had gone the way it was expected to; it was only amongst the GB team staff that it felt like the world had ended. I shrugged the whole thing off. I decided that the judgement from the British team was just another example of how little they understood about the world that I lived in, and I vowed to forget about it.

But things slowly and painfully worsened. I didn't fly home until the next day so I still had another night to spend in the GB hotel, another day to walk around in a Great Britain cycling team T-shirt surrounded by the staff and riders.

That night I sat talking to Tom on one of the couches on the first floor landing, waiting to head out to dinner with the other riders from the team. Most of the GB staff were in the dining hall eating, and as we waited there one of the GB coaches who I'd never really had anything to do with, and who'd barely even ever spoken to me – caught sight of us as he walked past. His eyes lit up with delight.

'Evening, gentlemen.'

It was like he was so happy that he'd seen the 'naughty boys' together he could barely wipe the smile off his face; he was practically giggling with excitement. It was as if I'd finally proved what some of them had known all along; that I was *dirty*, that all my time in Italy had made me one of the riders who cheated their way to be good at cycling. Again, it seemed to me that a lot of people from BC were consoling themselves with the idea that everyone else *had* to be cheating to be better than them, and for me to succeed I had to be up to something.

• • •

I returned home to Italy and ate dinner with my Italian friends. They were from a culture that understood cycling, and were completely unfazed by the story of my Championships when I did eventually explain it to them. In the following days I mentioned it a couple of times in training with the group and amongst friends in the evening, and people just laughed at me. The reaction was always the same. 'It's the Worlds! What else would someone go there for?' I consoled myself with the thought that Roger had never been in with the slightest chance for the win, and that what I had done had no influence whatsoever on his final result.

But still, I felt the rumble of discontent growing. My phone started buzzing with calls from increasingly irate cycling journalists. I decided the only safe response was to not talk to anyone. I was stubborn about it because I didn't feel that it was something that could be explained away in a news item on half a page of a weekly magazine. How could I possibly explain the situation? It was my entire life that was on trial, and my very existence as a cyclist would have been in jeopardy if I started pointing the finger at the people who had offered me the chance in the first place.

Things turned increasingly sour. One quick search of my name on the internet a few days later revealed a whole world of anger and conjecture from the public about what I had been up to. At first I was bemused – there was no way on earth that anyone could have known anything by that stage. But then it started to dawn on me that something was going to have to be done to appease the rabid press and public. While people talked and the discontent rumbled on, I began to think there *must* be someone somewhere within the organisation who would understand why I did it and the dynamics behind it. At the time the British team were happily working to support David Millar, who was in training for his comeback from a suspension for taking EPO to *win* the World Championships Time Trial *in a Great Britain jersey*. What I had done was so harmless, and so insignificant, that I really thought people would have understood what was going on. But the goalposts had moved and I hadn't seen it coming. I knew deep down that the choice I had made had been the wrong one, but what I found so confusing was that out of all the people who claimed to understand the world of professional cycling I didn't hear one single voice speak out in my defence, or seek to understand why I did what I did. Instead, it seemed that British Cycling had another agenda and decided to use the opportunity to reshuffle their staff once more.

After nearly a week of ignoring my phone, a number I recognised called and I picked it up.

'John, how are you?'

'Pretty bad, mate …' John Herety's voice sounded tired and stressed. 'This is turning out to be pretty serious. It is looking very bad. I'm sorry but I'm going to have to tell them the truth about what happened.'

Throughout the race John had refused to tell us to stop riding. He knew as well as we did that once we had said yes it would be career suicide to stop. He knew the reasons that we were riding, and I felt that he saw his job was to help British riders succeed in European professional cycling as best he could.

I asked the question that I dreaded the answer to: 'Shit, John, are you going to be OK?'

'It is not looking good.'

When John answered it felt like I had been punched in the stomach. The wind went out of me and I groped for something to say and some oxygen to think. In that moment I recalled an uneasy feeling I had in Madrid, but had ignored. BC had become big business and there was an air of people scrapping and plotting to move up in the organisation. From one major championship to the next BC would shift direction and cull a bunch of jobs at the same time. Even with my limited experience in the team I had seen it plenty of times before and, in Madrid in particular, even in my distant state of mind I had picked up on the less than harmonious state of the BC organisation. To me it felt cliquey and political; the kind of place where if people got wind that someone was out of favour then they would do all they could to cut ties to save their own behinds. In Madrid I couldn't help but notice that it was John who now seemed to be out in the cold. What hadn't been clear to me in Madrid, but was becoming rapidly so in the events that followed, was that John perhaps didn't quite fit into the plans of British Cycling. He was very good at his job; there would be no way that he could be sacked under normal circumstances. I had unwittingly provided the perfect excuse for his dismissal. I saw every person who'd complained about John that week – who was seeking to gain from his dismissal – rubbing his hands with glee, and I felt disgusted that I had given them their opportunity.

I hung up the phone dejected and stressed. I didn't know what punishment awaited me, but I sensed that it was swiftly on its way. A few days later as I was driving my VW Golf across town to go and visit Dario Andriotto, John called again. I pulled the car into a dirty car park, full of puddles and surrounded by posters for a circus that had long since left town. I turned down the shrill voice of an Italian transvestite comedian on the radio and took the call. With no intervention from myself – no chance to speak or explain myself – it had been decided. I hadn't spoken a word to the press, nor had I spoken a word to anyone in the organisation, and yet the punishment had already been measured out. John explained it: Tom and

I would be billed for all of our expenses from the race and banned for life from the national team.

The stress of not knowing what was going to happen had been mounting in me that week. It was an unpleasant few days and when John finally told me what I would be facing there was a small sense of relief. My conscience had already been churning, and my nerves were thrown into overdrive when a friend had told me that BC were looking into having my racing licence taken away. I knew by now that BC wanted to throw everything they could at me, but I still couldn't understand the ban. The fine I could comprehend, but even convicted dopers didn't get lifetime bans from the national team! Stupidly, I was earning too little and I was naturally too guilty-feeling a person to go and seek legal advice on the matter.

John continued to relay the bad news. He gave me Dave Brailsford's number and told me I had to call him and apologise, and that, for me at least, would be the end of it. For John it wasn't the end. He'd had to resign. I was devastated for him and apologised profusely, but he put a brave face on it and we ended the call.

Dario Andritto was one of my closest mates in Italy; his infectious good humour meant I could normally rely on him to pick me up when I was low. He was the guy who would manage to drag me out to go training when I just couldn't face it, or keep me motivated through a grim race. This time, though, I was so dejected I turned the car right around and drove home through the rain without bothering to visit him. I was sick of everything.

Given that my punishment had already been doled out I thought twice about calling Brailsford. What reason was there for me to apologise? I had been given my punishment. I would never ride for

GB again and I had four nights in a Spanish hotel and an Alitalia flight from Milan to Madrid to pay for. I felt that they were rubbing my face in it, yet at the same time I knew that I had made a mistake. Regardless of what I had believed, I *was* in the wrong. Someone I respected and called a friend had lost his job and I had done little to stem the tide of ill-feeling and speculation, especially in the press. Dave had been pretty chummy in the past, and I'd got on well with him. But when I made the call I knew things had changed.

In a brief, cold exchange, I apologised to Brailsford for disobeying team orders during the race. He wanted to know how much I had been paid. I resisted at first because I considered it pointless. In fact, I was incredulous: wasn't it enough that I was apologising and refunding my costs? My mind was tired. I was fed up. I was damned if I did and damned if I didn't, and the constant fucking battle that was my life fighting to survive in professional cycling was wearing me down. I had told myself I didn't care so often, and I knew that my fate had long since been sealed anyway. So I told him: 'Two and a half thousand Euros.' We finished the call, and that was the end of it.

* * *

From that moment, I sensed things changed for me. The British press, who I felt took umbrage at the fact that I didn't want to make a confession in their magazines, never forgave me. The way I saw it, to spill the beans would only involve me pointing the finger at the very people I had gone through all of this to impress. It was hard; I felt that there was nothing I could do but keep my mouth shut and get on with my job. I had apologised to Dave Brailsford and I paid the expenses of the trip, and yet I was never, ever forgiven. I never again rode for GB, even at times when I was an obvious candidate for selection (the Olympic Games Road Race in Bejing, for example, where the British team was as hopeless on that kind of course as the 2004 team had been in Athens) and I never once publicly bemoaned that.

In the days following that very first phone call in Madrid, I had made a decision based on what I thought were the acceptable parameters of the world I inhabited. In many ways, I was wrong. I misunderstood many things about my actions that day in Madrid, including the strength of feeling that the British fans had towards the national team and the sense of pride that others took in my actions.

I made a mistake in Madrid and I was left alone with my choices. The few ties that were left between the British Cycling scene and me felt like they had now been severed permanently. I was banished from the Kingdom, and forced further into the dark corners of the European peloton.

• • •

In 2008 I read this quote from the national coach, Rod Elling-worth, discussing British Cycling's plans for Mark Cavendish's planned assault on the 2010 World Championships:

'We've got to be realistic about it – these are professional bike riders we're talking about. They ride for their professional teams all year and then we expect them to turn up and do it for free? It's not realistic. Yes, there's pride and honour in riding for your country, but if one guy is going to win a world title, the others in the team should be rewarded too.'

CHAPTER 11

Falling into Place

Despite the sour taste of the trouble with the national team in the last race of 2005, I felt that in my first year with Liquigas my professional life had finally all fallen into place. And, with wonderful synchronicity, at the end of my first year with Liquigas my personal life started to come together too.

It is freezing cold in Finland in November. On a bad day when the rain falls and the sky closes in and the ground becomes as dark as a peat bog, it feels like the only light that you see is electric, and that natural light will never again return.

On one such winter day in November 2005, as the rain pissed down, I found myself walking out of the gloom into a showjumping hall that I knew very well. The hall was at my father's former home, a place called Gustafsbäck, where I had spent most of my summers after my parents' divorce. He had sold the buildings a few years previously, and they were now a commercial stable. Like many of the slightly older halls, it was cold and damp in the winter months, not something that bothered the horse riders, but it was a real killer for anyone stood about doing nothing, as I often was.

I'd come down with my father, a showjumping trainer, who I was visiting during my off-season break. I loved being in the building because I was so attached to it, but I didn't usually hang around while my father trained his poor students, as I found his tough (and very vocal) methods excruciating to watch. As per usual I planned to take my father's black Labrador, Lida, for a walk and to leave him to it. But as we walked into the hall and I glanced over the usual mix of riders forming their patterns of what looked like organised chaos – people coming and going in different directions, some jumping fences, others doing flat work – I was halted in my tracks, and my Wellington boots became rooted to the freezing muddy floor. It might sound like a terrible cliché, but a beautiful girl on horseback stunned me from across the hall. I was taken completely off guard and a tremor of excitement passed through me. That tremor turned into a full-blown heart-thumping moment when the girl trotted her horse over to go and talk to my father, who'd walked off ahead of me. My father was only training one rider of the six who were there, and she was the one. I couldn't believe my luck.

On such a dank, dull day she seemed like a ray of pure light. She was beautiful, but she also had a determination about her that you could see a mile off. Much to Lida's disappointment, I gave up on the idea of a walk and stayed instead to watch the whole session. I was lost in her already; there is something so special about seeing someone concentrating on doing the thing they love. I stood there in the freezing cold, under the harsh electric light, oblivious to Lida's whining. I was transfixed.

By the time it ended I panicked. I didn't have the guts to say anything to her, and made myself scarce before she was finished. In the car on the way home I asked my old man about her while trying to sound casual and disinterested. He snapped back that she was the only student he had ever taught who had the guts to answer back to him during one of his sessions. I could see that although he didn't like her insubordination he also kind of admired it. Knowing my father, I was very impressed. But the reality of my life was all too close. I was only visiting Finland, and in two days' time I was due to return to Italy, and back to my busy life, so I resigned myself to doing nothing more about it. And deep down I knew that a beautiful, confident girl like that would never be interested in me. But that evening, while I was sat around still torturing myself with what might have been, my mobile phone buzzed with a text message. An unknown number: 'Don't tell your dad, but do you want to go out for a drink tomorrow? Camilla.'

It was her! I couldn't believe it. I had no idea who had given her my number but I was thrilled by the chance to see her again.

The following evening was yet another dark, rainy winter night. We went out in Helsinki. We hit it off straight away; we talked about her love of showjumping, her horses, and her life in Helsinki. I tried my best to explain my life travelling the world with my bike and I was amazed at how she took it all in. Her outlook on life was so beautifully uncomplicated that her very presence seemed to relax me. I walked her back to her apartment in the rain and kissed her in the doorway. Moments like these seem a cliché when they happen to other people, but when it is your own love story it makes perfect sense. As I walked away I realised that this was the very street that my brother had been born in, and where my own parents had lived in the sixties. Suddenly I felt that I had come full circle. My head was spinning, and I drove back to my father's house at 30 km/h. because I was struggling so hard to process just what was going on. I was flying away tomorrow, and yet I had just fallen in love, and it was impossible to take in.

I climbed into bed and lay awake all night wondering what the hell I was going to do. My mind flirted with the idea of making the huge romantic gesture of missing my flight and turning up on her doorstep in Helsinki ready to start a life together. I knew even then that she was the one for me. It felt like I'd met another part of me, but better. But in the end old habits die hard, and after a sleepless night I was still too cheap to waste my money by throwing away a plane ticket. I went home to Italy and called her as soon as I landed asking if she would like to come and visit as soon as she could.

Camilla flew out to visit me in Varese in December 2005, and this time it was confirmation for me that it was true love. It was an exciting love that made my throat dry and my heart race. I could see that she was going to bring so much more into my life. As we got to know each other I saw that Camilla was a lot of things that I wasn't: she was organised and strong; she seemed to possess in her character all the things that I felt I was lacking. It felt like I hadn't been functioning correctly without her and she immediately made me stronger.

As soon as Camilla arrived to stay with me in Italy, I knew that I didn't want to be without her. The problem was, the logistics of our lives felt so complicated that I was petrified that we couldn't make it work, or that the thought of trying to be with a man who was away half the year racing would put her off. I worried about it to myself, but I didn't dare talk directly about it, for fear of not liking the answer. As her stay came to an end and I drove Camilla to the airport to go home, nervous with apprehension over what was going to happen once we were separated again, Camilla turned to me and said, 'So, what do we have to do to make this work?'

The logistics of my career and our lives meant that over the next year we would be snatching time and taking flights to see each other when we could. But, despite this, Camilla never let it feel complicated for a second. We did what we had to do to make it work, and there was never a moment of doubt that our love wasn't strong enough to see us through. Within a year Camilla packed up and moved with me to Italy full time and we started to build a home together. It was the most profound, positive influence on my cycling career that I ever had. Up until now I had been trying to race my way to happiness, but that year I realised that was unachievable without a family whom I could love and care for, and who in turn would give my racing some meaning. I completely changed as a person.

• • •

By 2007, my third year with Liquigas, my career had reached another level. Liquigas suited me down to the ground as a team. My salary had increased dramatically every year and I knew that I was valued in my job. Camilla had brought everything that was missing to my life and, for a brief moment, before the challenges of my chosen career would take on a new form, I had my moment of glory at the 2007 Giro d'Italia.

After building his season around a Grand Tour for the first time, Danilo failed to hit top form and flopped in the 2006 Giro, so he returned in 2007 determined to win. The race opened with a team time trial in Sardinia: gaining an advantage here was really important. The team time trial was a discipline that suited me like no other. It seemed to push all the buttons, to bring out the best in me. Increasingly, I had grown to understand the skill required for a team time trial: every single person there has different strengths and weaknesses, but the event rewards a united effort. The key skill – more so than raw power or strength – is an ability to work with other people, to be able to react and adapt yourself to the strengths and weaknesses of those around you, to keep the team together as a cohesive unit. A good team time triallist is like a current-regulating diode – constantly adapting to keep the flow of electricity stable. In Liquigas the rider who could do all that was me.

I was confident that I could perform well, but when we rode the course the day before the event I was struck by how technical it was. It was a big worry for me. In a team time trial, where the key to cohesion and getting the whole squad to go quickly is to keep as tight together as possible, corners and sharp turns are a real challenge. Even a small gap in the line on a circuit like this could mean a team in pieces. Ever since my accident on the back of the quad in Ireland I had struggled psychologically with descents. I was terrified of falling again. My instincts simply didn't trust that the person in front of me had full control. I couldn't blindly follow the rider in front like many could. In races I could normally manage my way around this by leaving a little bit of a gap between myself and the wheel in front for security, but that wasn't an option here. After two laps of the circuit in training on the Friday, I went through forty-eight stressful hours as I tried to calm myself and switch off my natural instincts.

On the day of the race I felt enormous pressure not to let my teammates down. We set off and I used all of the agility I had in my pedalling to stay as tight as I could to my teammates. I was petrified of the technical descents, but for twenty minutes I managed to shut down those instinctual fears. I let go of everything as we shot through turn after turn without touching the brakes and I clung in desperation to the wheel in front. The first turns were terrifying, but I worked so hard at quelling my fears that in a way I overcompensated and I didn't miss a single turn on the front during the stage. I was one of the strongest riders there.

We crossed the line with the best time and with only a few teams left to finish behind us. Every one of us knew straight away from the sheer sensation of the ride that we were going to be almost unbeatable. We rolled back to the bus and embraced each other for a job well done. It felt like no time at all before Stefano Zanatta jumped on to the bus and yelled, 'We won! We won!' The bus erupted. We'd done it. I had never won an individual race, but if I did I couldn't imagine that the feeling would be greater than on that bus. Every single rider there felt himself a part of that win. It was a shared joy. The release of pressure for all of us was enormous. The Giro was the biggest race of the year for the team, and the previous year's poor performance was still weighing heavily on us. I could have cried with joy and relief. As we all bounded off the bus to walk the short distance to the podium I had an emotional moment when I saw the proud faces of Mike and Pat Taylor. Mike and Pat often travelled out to watch the big European races, and having them there to share in the achievement felt so special. I was literally bouncing around with joy and ran over to give them a hug before I finally stood on the Giro podium, a winner.

It felt appropriate to me that I stood there on the podium linked arm in arm with my teammates. Winning a team time trial is regarded by some people as a 'half' victory, but I could never see the logic in that. Every one of us had worked for it and we all deserved it. As we stood there grinning ear to ear while the crowd applauded us, Di Luca turned to me and said with a satisfied smile (despite having lost his cool at the finish when Enrico Gasparotto crossed the line first), 'Winning a team TT is not like a normal win, because *everyone* gets to share this.' It meant a lot to me, because I understood, and *he* understood. We worked our backsides off for Danilo and he knew what we did for him, but because of the way the sport works those wins were always a little bit more his than ours, no matter how he thanked us in the press. This was different, though; this win really was ours, and I allowed myself a rare moment of true pride. This win was in no small part mine.

The 2007 Giro continued brilliantly for us, and for me personally it was a dream race. The team knew what to ask of me and I knew how to do it. I loved my job there. On eighteen of the twenty-one stages I took up riding on the front of the bunch. It was fucking hard work physically, but it was enjoyable, not simply because I was doing my job but also because I didn't have to think about anything when I was riding on the front; when you are not up to it it is awful, but doing it when you are going well can be incredibly satisfying. There is a sadist in every cyclist that is fuelled by the suffering of others; no matter how much you are hurting, hearing or seeing that others are in more pain somehow allows you to push harder. There are all kinds of rewards and incentives that you can find while driving a peloton along, and I picked up a few tricks in my time at the Giro. For example, the fact that there were so many race motorbikes at the head of those races meant I could quite easily (and almost embarrassingly) sit in their slipstream and effortlessly tear the legs off the riders at the back of the bunch. Whenever I was on the front it felt incredibly good to look over my shoulder and see a long lined-out peloton, with people crumpled over their bikes fighting to keep up, or to hear on the race radio that riders were being dropped from the group, or that the time gap to the break was coming down.

When you are on the front of a race you are in control. You control how quickly the bunch comes out of a corner, and if you feel like it, by accelerating at just the right time you can make life harder for the poor sods at the back. I might not have been winning the race, but I was letting everyone know I was undoubtedly there at the Giro, and it felt great. I loved it when riders would come up to me in the hotel bar in the evening and say, 'Fucking hell, you made that hard for us out there today!' It was an ego trip, of course, but these little things became the recognition that I decided I wanted. I didn't measure my success through media exposure or what non-cyclists wrote about me in newspapers or magazines, but through the little things like that: acknowledgement from the people who *knew*.

After nearly three full weeks of the best work I had done in my career, Danilo Di Luca rode into Milan the winner of the Giro d'Italia. As he crossed the line victorious, he was surrounded by all of his teammates bar one: me. Instead, I was sat at home on the couch with Camilla, refusing to switch on the TV for fear of catching a glimpse of the victory parade that I was cruelly absent from. I had been forced to pull out of the race with one stage to go when I had contracted a fever. I had emptied the tank throughout the whole race, and I was so exhausted at the end of the final mountain stage (which finished atop the Zoncolan) that I stood in the shower fully dressed in my cycling kit and began to shake uncontrollably. Without a spleen, my body couldn't cope with the fever and I reacted badly. There was nothing to do but pull out. I felt it was fucking typical of my luck that I was forced to abandon after all the hard work was done, and that I couldn't be there on that final day to be one of the riders who rolled into Milan at the head of the peloton with pink bar tape on my bike and a champagne glass in my hand.

However, despite this bad luck, my move to Liquigas proved to be the best thing I ever did in my career. Liquigas put me in races that suited me and I was given a role that was perfect for me. Finally, I felt incredibly rewarded as a cyclist, and as a man.

CHAPTER 12
The Tour

On the day of the prologue of my first ever Tour de France, things felt different. For starters the race that I had spent my youth dreaming of, and trying to trace on Michelin maps of France, started not on the mythical roads of Europe, but instead in England, on the streets of London, of all places. The London start of the 2007 Tour was only the third time in history that the race had visited the UK and the first time since 1994. The prologue course was set to be a 7.9 km tourist trail of the city's most iconic sights: Buckingham Palace, the Houses of Parliament, Hyde Park and the Mall. I may have been born in Finland, but I grew up in Britain. British was the nationality of my passport and it was in Britain that I had grown up dreaming of one day racing in the Tour de France.

Driving down Whitehall in the Liquigas team bus, I was taken aback by the size of the crowds. Deep down I expected something profound from the Tour. I had grown up with it on television each summer, and I had answered the question, 'Do you think you'll be in the Tour de France one day?' more times than I could possibly remember. Now, after nearly seven years as a professional, I was.

When we arrived in the allotted parking spaces, I climbed down the steps of the bus and walked out into the expectant crowds. Big crowds never really did anything for me; the faces I knew were the ones that really counted, and as I looked past the row of lime green bikes that the mechanics had hastily arranged on our arrival I was greeted by the marvellous sight of practically my entire family patiently waiting to see me. My face broke into a grin as I saw the group – my mother, my brother, Camilla, and Mike and Pat Taylor, all huddled together waiting to enjoy the moment that I had worked towards for so long. It was a special moment, made all the more incredible by the next face I saw: stood waiting in the wings was my father's ex-partner, a Finnish woman called Gun Järnefelt.

After my parents' divorce, during the summers spent in Finland with my father, I had talked incessantly about the Tour de France, insisting to anyone who would listen that I would ride in it myself one day. Gun promised me that if I ever rode the Tour she would bake me my favourite blueberry pie. Sure enough, there she was, arms extended, holding out a blueberry pie she had baked and transported as hand luggage all the way from Finland.

It was more than a blast from the past. Gun and my father had parted ways many years previously, but she had remembered all this time, and the gesture bowled me over. I stood there for a moment, surrounded by the people I loved most in the world, about to partake in the event I had worked my entire adult life to get to.

I knew by now I was never going to be really recognised for what I did by the British public – I was as good as Italian to them, and, equally, I would always be British to the Italians (as for the Finns, they really had no interest in me or cycling at all), but to my family, and to Camilla, I was important, and that made me feel very special that bright morning in London.

I felt like I shouldn't really have had a lot to prove to the outside world when I arrived at that Tour. I had worked hard throughout my career to that point. I had already been part of the winning team at the Giro that year. I knew I was at the top of my game. There was no doubting that I was considered to be a consummate professional by my peers, but until now I had managed to go about my career without ever really having to be the focus of attention or worry about playing any games with the media. The Tour de France, however, is different. Compared to other professional races the Tour can have relatively little action in the race over the three weeks, but it is a feeding frenzy for the world media.

Despite a few requests for interviews from the home press, the build-up to the Tour felt remarkably similar to every other race I had ridden. Even selection for the 2007 Tour had been relatively low key. In a lot of teams, the Tour is such a focal point of the year that making the Tour selection is a really big deal. Typically, though, for a rider like me in a team like mine, selection came in an off-hand way. My *directeur sportif*, Stefano Zanatta, casually informed me over the phone in May – before the start of the Giro – that I was going to the Tour. There was no room for discussion, and certainly no allusion to the fact that I was any kind of outstanding athlete who'd been selected to go to one of the greatest sporting events on the planet. I just simply fitted the mould of the generic type of rider that was needed at the time.

This disappointingly mundane feeling was exacerbated by the blasé attitude of my Liquigas team. In the aftermath of Di Luca's Giro win there was no buzz of excitement about doing the Tour; after the emotional high we had all felt there it was as if no one could really muster any more energy. We were just *there*. To make matters worse we had Dario Mariuzzo as our manager, who, in my opinion, was the worst manager I ever had as a rider. He lacked the necessary language skills, and sometimes seemed only to be able to communicate by swearing in a Venetian dialect. This made the entire build-up to the race feel incredibly trying, but it wasn't only him.

I had learnt by now that, for many Italians, being outside of their comfort zone was a big challenge. Unfortunately in this case, because I was English, everything was my fault, and every Italian rider in the peloton thought it worthwhile to let me know this. If the coffee was no good, then someone had to tell me. If they didn't like the hotel breakfast, then it was worth asking me, 'Does the Queen have to eat *beans* in *tomato sauce* for breakfast?' If the cars were suddenly coming at them on the left-hand side of the road then it was worth yelling at me about out the stupidity of driving on 'the other side of the road, *cazzo*!'

At the Tour de France the team was looking to do something to merit their inclusion and please their American bike sponsor, Cannondale – and it didn't really matter what that was. The strategy they decided on for the race was quite simple: they would send a group of riders from the Classics squad who could try for a stage early on, and pad the team out with guys who were consistent enough to keep Liquigas in the running for the team classification by finishing close to the front on the big mountain stages. The team classification is something that no one in their right mind pays attention to; it is of zero interest to the public, because all eyes are fixed on the overall winners. To a company looking to show off its ethic of 'cohesive teamwork', however, it is an acceptable consolation prize.

Liquigas' whole outlook on the race was more like something you'd expect on the B-programme: we even had a rented team bus (hired from Manolo Sainz, the disgraced former manager of the ONCE team). The night before the race I watched completely impassively as the mechanics decided it was a good time to stick our sponsor's transfers on the side of the bus, so people could actually recognise the team. I laughed aloud at the thought that the next day cycling fans would be gazing in awe as the bus pulled into the car park covered in exotic-looking logos and sponsors, which had just been slapped on by two uninterested mechanics the night before. It was typical of a professional cycling team, and even more so of the Tour: gleaming and shiny on the outside, but chaotic and unnerving on the inside.

*   *   *

By the time the start of the race came around, the emotional high of seeing my family felt like such a warm and happy contrast that I didn't want to leave them. But in no time at all I received a tap on the shoulder from a team *soigneur* who wanted to know what drink I would like on my bike, which was being set up on the Turbo trainer waiting for me to begin my warm-up. I suddenly remembered it was nearly time to go to work and, after I thanked everyone for coming, I went back to shutting the world out of my mind to allow myself to prepare for the TT effort.

A prologue is always such an immense effort. As per my race programme I hadn't turned a pedal in anger since the Giro, and I knew that this would be a shock to the system. The course was slightly less than 8 km, which would translate to just under ten minutes of searing pain. In that kind of event, if you felt comfortable you were undoubtedly going too slowly.

There are lots of things that I'd love to say about my first kilometres becoming a Tour de France rider on the roads of my nation's capital. I'd love to say that the crowds were so loud that the deafening noise spurred me on – but my aero helmet had cowlings that covered my ears, and the only noise I could make out was the gasping of my breath and the furious yelling of the *directeur sportif* down the radio. I would love to say that the majestic sights of the city encouraged me, but I could only concentrate on the few metres in front of my face – that same view of the tarmac stretching out in front of me that I had seen the world over. I would love to say that I couldn't feel my legs, or the burning in my lungs, but I could – the sudden jolt back into racing felt like someone had put their hand down my throat and was trying to wrench my internal organs out from my body. I would also love to say that the occasion encouraged me to perform way above expectation ... but I finished in 91st place, lost somewhere in the middle of the 190 starters.

If that felt like an underwhelming start, things were even less exciting the following day. As the race hit British roads for the first stage, and the action got underway, David Millar was soon off the front. Dave had always exuded that star quality, and this was his big comeback from a suspension. He instantly inspired the hearts and minds of the British public with a spirited display of bravura, trying to ensure that there would be a British rider on the podium that night. But while Dave was floating along out front, surrounded by the television cameras and the approval of the cycling world, my ride, in contrast, felt more like being dragged along the bottom of the riverbed.

The new frame that Cannondale had given me for the race had been fine during the previous few days of easy training, but as soon as the action had started I found I had a problem with my cranks, which were now loose, and I was going to have to change bikes. As the fresh-legged Tour peloton had charged off down the road, I swapped my race bike. The thing about spare bikes: they get used so little that, as the season goes on, they simply become used for parts when things break and a mechanic needs a quick fix. They slowly degrade, and the less they are used, the less they resemble your own race machine. I hopped up on to a bike with no computer, the most basic training wheels that the team must have found lying around and, worst of all, a brand new saddle. My old saddle was nicely worn in and the sagging was equivalent to roughly 4 mm of saddle height. I was so used to my position with the worn saddle that even the tiniest change made the bike feel wildly different. As I rode back into the cars and began to chase the bunch the first time check was given to David's break. His gap was well over a minute now, and his day in the spotlight was assured. And there I was, on what felt like someone else's bike, crawling through the team cars just trying desperately and uncomfortably to get back into the race. There is a great deal of glory to be had in cycling, but none of it can be found back there.

As early as that first road stage, I realised why the Tour is so different. In most of the races I took part in, particularly in Italy, there was a certain place in the bunch that I liked to call 'the office', behind the riders at the front who were fighting to get into position. I knew I could find a group of riders whose job it was just to stay out of trouble at that moment, or during that stage, and so they would be a bit more relaxed and give each other a bit of space. There was no pushing or shoving, and every now and again there would be a bit of chat and a few jokes to try to lighten the mood. No one in the office was ever really suffering – the guys who were suffering were the guys hanging on at the back. The office was where I liked to spend my time on the days that I wasn't going to be in a position to do a job for anyone, or just to wait, in case my leader needed me later on. On a four-hour flat stage of a stage race, the office was my salvation. While I still had to physically hold the speed dictated by the front of the race I could switch off enough in my head to save some of the precious mental energy that I would need to do my job later. In the Tour, though, there was no 'office' – instead it was all-out war.

The perceived importance of the Tour de France means that everyone there sees the race as his chance to strike gold. Every single second-rate sprinter is fighting for the wheel that they think will deliver them to the big time; every opportunist is looking for the break that might just catapult them into the limelight. No team leader can take the risk of crashing and losing time, so they, and their entire teams, want to be at the front from the beginning of the race until the end. Bike riders will fight tooth and nail in most races for any kind of success, but at the Tour that is all amplified. It is bike racing with the volume turned up.

The absence of an office to go to in the first week of the race meant there wasn't a moment to relax. It felt like I had a brake lever shoved up my arse the entire time, and if I so much as left a two-inch gap to the wheel in front then someone would whip round me and push me off the wheel. Riders whom I knew well, and whom I could normally spend a bit of time chatting to in the bunch, didn't even say hello. It wasn't because they wanted to ignore me, but simply because they didn't see me – they were so stressed by the race they could only focus on what they were doing.

This increasing tension and the continually rising speeds can add up to only one grim conclusion: crashes. By 2007 it was already customary for the first week to be plagued by crashes in the tightly packed peloton. Crashes are a part of racing, but in the Tour's first week they are really horrible. They aren't a result of the natural hazards of the race which typically cause them – slippery descents or dangerous corners – they are senseless, caused by too much tension, and too many riders trying to be in the same place at the same time.

Crashes weren't only a risk for me because of injury. For a *domestique* they can make a tough day even harder, and the frequency of them in the Tour is exhausting. Once a crash went down, presuming I had managed to avoid falling off myself, it was my job to make sure that none of our riders needed help after the crash. If they did, it meant waiting for them to get their bike fixed (for what inevitably felt like an eternity) as the bunch continued to speed down the road. Then I had to help whomever it was get back to the race as smoothly and as quickly as possible. In most races it was enough to cover the distance to the back of the team cars before I could relax and start to feel safe. At the Tour, though, the convoy is so long that even when I spied the tail lights of the last car up ahead there was often still a full kilometre between me and the back of the race. Making up ground at the speed of the Tour peloton is fucking hard, and I knew that saving my leaders from disaster in the treacherous first week would mean serious difficulties for me later in the race.

While I was suffering a personal hell in the first week, things went extremely well for the team. My roommate for the race, Pippo Pozzato, got in early and won the fifth stage. The team was delighted; we had won the Giro and now we'd taken out a Tour stage. In only five stages our job was practically done. In any other race that release would have meant the whole thing became relaxing and fun, but that was the Tour, it just couldn't be that simple. That same evening Maurizzo, the *directeur sportif*, walked into the room on his rounds, and after finishing congratulating Pippo in one breath, in the next he reinforced the importance of the team classification to me. What he seemed to fail to realise was that instead of bringing three climbers (as the team had planned) he had only brought two, Manuel 'Trixi' Beltrán and myself. Beltrán was a nice guy. He had been one of Ábraham Olano's *domestiques* at Banesto and one of Armstrong's mountain men at US Postal, but he was a bit lost at Liquigas – he served no real purpose, and sending a guy to the Tour to ride the team classification who is used to riding for the overall win was completely unbefitting to his talents. He seemed to think the same thing too, and he sat up every day as soon as he felt like he'd had enough, and eased off.

When we hit the mountains things got nasty on the descent of the Cormet du Roselend during the stage from Le Grand-Bornand to Tignes. As we charged down the descent, and my triceps burned with the strain of my weight being unusually distributed all over the bike, as per usual the world disappeared from my consciousness as I focused intently on the back wheel in front of me. Part way down the descent I shot out of a fast bend, pulled hard on the bars and stamped on the pedals, sprinting full bore after the wheel in front. Suddenly the bike bucked like a rodeo bull. I was flung from my machine and over the handlebars at 70 km/h. and came thumping down on the back of my head before I even knew what was happening.

Crashing is always unexpected, but often when you hear or see a rider fall ahead of you, or you slide out on a bend, you have a microsecond for your brain to register. The feeling of knowing that you are going to fall is perhaps the worst feeling that any professional cyclist can imagine. It is nothing to do with the anticipation of the pain, the potential for broken limbs, the stinging intensity of cleaning the wound out in the shower, or the nights stuck sleeping on one side to avoid touching the parts of your body that have had the top layers of skin grated off ... It is much more serious than that. With every slip, overshot bend or unavoidable pile of riders in front of you, as a professional rider about to go down you know in that moment your very career is in jeopardy. For a professional cyclist, just being hurt by a crash is the best possible scenario. A crash, no matter how seemingly innocuous, can be all it takes to start off a chain of events that can end a career. I had known, all too well after my haematocrit issue, that if you are left behind for even a moment, cycling will move on and there can often be no way back in. A crash could have just the same effect. A broken bone would mean time off the bike; time off the bike would mean missing racing and the loss of condition, both of which could potentially put you in a bad position with team management, consciously or not. There is nothing worse for a manager than having one of their twenty-five riders unable to compete. The pressure is passed on to other riders and the management themselves while they try to fill the gap left by an injured rider. When it comes to contract-renewal time the things that count aren't excuses, they are numbers of wins, numbers of race days and performances. There is simply no room in the twelve or twenty-four months on a rider's contract for time out for crashes. People often marvel that cyclists continue to race with horrific injuries, and think that cyclists are tough. It isn't that cyclists are particularly robust guys; it's just that they don't have a choice. A rider climbs back on to his bike bloodied and hurt and tries to keep going because he *has* to. If a rider can get to the finish then at least he has a chance to race the next day. If he can do that then he won't abandon his team in the race, he won't lose race days, and he won't be seen as a problem to anyone.

All of those things are usually what flashes through a rider's mind as the balance goes beneath him, the split second before the whole deck of cards hits the floor. This time, though, I had no time to see my career flash before my eyes, or wonder about the months of hard work that I might be throwing away if I landed slightly wrong. I hit the floor before I knew I had even fallen. I was completely disorientated.

The recently delivered new frames that we had received from Cannondale for the Tour were pre-production models and weren't anywhere near rigid enough. The lateral force was too much for the sloppy frame and the chain shipped off the outside of the big chain-ring as the bike flexed through the bottom bracket. I hadn't stood a chance.

I felt around my head and the back of my helmet was completely caved in. I was shaken, but as the helmet had taken the impact I quickly realised nothing was broken. With my adrenaline still pumping from the descent, I was in a rush to remount, and I picked up my bike and started riding off, only to suddenly realise, by the terrified and confused looks of the riders coming towards me, that I was going the wrong way. By the time I had turned around the effects of the shock hit me and I felt I had suddenly folded in on myself like a burning scrap of paper. All my strength and my nerves had been smashed out of me when I hit the floor. I rode crumpled and slow towards the finish. I eventually crossed the line in 172nd place, dead last.

In the mountains the pressure of the Tour mounted on me even more. Liquigas was hell-bent on going for the team classification, and while Beltrán didn't seem to care I was too diligent to try to not care. On the road, though, this made my life really hard. In the Tour (as with most races) once the front group has gone off to fight for the victory most riders want to stop racing hard. This is especially true in the groups just behind the leaders, where a lot of the riders have been dropped from the front, having done their job, and want to conserve as much energy as possible by riding at a steady tempo to the finish. I was normally one of those riders. I would do my job, and then find a group that I could ride in to the finish with as conservatively as possible. I knew as well as anyone how irritating it was to have one person amongst the group who wanted to continue racing. The trouble was, with Liquigas dead set on the team classification I knew that I was going to make myself very unpopular.

I was the best Liquigas rider on the road on these stages, and while the riders I was with just wanted to get to the finish with as little effort as possible, I had the number one team car behind the group, with Mariuzzo's balding head stuck out of the window barking swear words at me and hammering the car horn to get me to keep racing. I found his attitude humiliating rather than motivating, and just about the worst approach I could have imagined as I tried to get through the mountain stages. I felt so irritated about it that I started jumping away from the groups I was with before the final climb of the day and riding alone to the finish, not because I was desperate to get myself a better placing on the stage, but because I was just so embarrassed by the situation.

● ● ●

On stage ten, during the second week, things took on a new dimension. Seventy kilometres into the stage, as we hurtled down another tiny *départmental* road at Mach 3, I turned to my Brazilian Liquigas teammate Murilo Fischer and said, 'Jesus suffering fuck! Has that break not gotten away yet?'

'Nah, sounds like Schumacher is going to get caught too. Could be a while yet till they let it go.'

'If some fucker doesn't get clear soon, I am going to be finished. It's fucking forty degrees …'

The prospect of having to keep racing at this speed while the endless flurries of attacks and counter-attacks nullified each other and forced the speed of the peloton ever higher was almost too much.

The intensity of the fast flat sprint stages that dominated the first week had been replaced by the wild ride of the transitional stages. In any Tour there are far more specialist stages than there are stages that can be won by an 'average' rider. Most Tour de France routes have at least ten stages for pure sprinters, four mountain stages for the climbers, and two time trials for the general classification favourites. Every other rider in the race is forced to focus his energies on a short period in the second week when the stages are open for a breakaway to succeed. In a normal race these stages would be the moment where the race relaxes a little and allows the riders who really want it to try for the win: in the Tour, though, *everybody* really wants it.

Instead of the usual flurry of attacks that quickly sort out who will go in the breakaway on days like this, in the Tour the peloton becomes a raging mass of riders all desperate to get what they think could be the winning ticket to a better life. As the days go by and these opportunities decrease, then the intensity amongst the riders trying to get in the break increases.

The second week was hard going; at the end of stage 13 of the race I was an exhausted man. But if I was at least prepared for the racing to be hard, nothing could have prepared me for my accommodation for the next two nights. Hotels at bike races are far worse than most people would imagine, and the hotels at the Tour de France were notoriously bad even by the standards of a bike race. I had seen some things in my time as a cyclist, but nothing quite like Hotel Belle Vue in Albi. I mean, by 2007 I had raced all over the world, in tiny unknown places in all sorts of 'developing nations' – South America and all over Eastern Europe – but the Hotel Belle Vue, where our team lodged for what was supposed to be the greatest race on earth, was what any civilised person could only describe as a hovel.

We arrived there after a soaking wet time trial (another anonymous hundred-and-something position for me). By this stage of the Tour I was so accustomed to hurting myself that all of the stinging shock I had felt making my effort in the prologue had turned into a kind of dull ache, something I could just about feel if I pushed through the layers of fatigue. What mattered now wasn't the ability to hurt myself; it was every little thing I could do to make myself comfortable when I wasn't on the road squeezing the life out of myself. Each night I hoped that we would stay somewhere comfortable, and I could at least relax. As soon as I pushed the door open to our room at the Belle Vue I heard the bump as the back of the door banged into the suitcase that had been squeezed into the only available space in the room by the *soigneur*. I felt my heart sink.

The room was so cramped that Pippo and I had to remove the desk and a chair to make enough space to open our suitcases, and even then the situation was chaotic. The rain on the stage meant that we had to find a way to dry our shoes and damp clothes. My attempt to enter the bathroom to find some extra space was abruptly halted when I opened the door to a waft of cleaning detergent that was so strong it took me right back to the RSPCA kennels in York where we used to go and get stray dogs when I was a kid. I slammed the door back shut but it was too late: the whole room now stank like a crime scene. Still, at least there was a bed. But when I opened the bed sheets, to my utter disbelief a fucking cockroach was already making itself comfortable!

In the evening events began to resemble an episode of *Fawlty Towers*. While we were waiting for dinner a row erupted between the owner and his wife. The débâcle escalated to such a level that eventually the owner's wife called the gendarmes in a desperate attempt to get the owner under control. The upshot of this drama was that our team went without dinner, and the riders had no option but to eat the food we had with us. This was the era before teams travelled with chefs, so it was ham and cheese baguettes and boxes of cereal and protein bars all round. As I slumped into bed that night the old mattress sagged so much my back touched the floor. I listened to the thumping music that was coming out of the nightclub next door, and couldn't help but think of the many tourists I would ride past the next day who were probably at that moment just finishing a nice meal, washed down with some French wine, before heading back to their four-star hotels for a comfortable night's rest. The very next day those same people would be standing at the side of the road, marvelling at us shiny bike riders. It felt like a cruel joke. I felt so far from the pinnacle of anything that I didn't know whether to laugh or cry, and I didn't honestly have the energy to do either.

* * *

If it was possible to descend any lower than the Hotel Belle Vue, in the third week of the race things seemed to do just that, only with a much more sinister twist. Cycling was in the midst of its toughest period in terms of doping positives. For the decade leading up to the 2007 race it felt like not one Tour de France had passed without some sort of incident involving doping. The reality of doping had forever been held back from the world by a seemingly unbreakable dam wall, but now the dam had sprung leaks all over the place. Cracks were appearing and more and more uncomfortable truths were flowing out. The Tour was the centrepiece of European cycling, and it duly supplied the most explosive and scandalous stories each year.

In that Tour of 2007, one depressing débâcle followed another. T-Mobile's Patrik Sinkewitz was the first to test positive, followed by double stage winner Alexander Vinokourov (who left the race with his entire team on stage 15). It was like a forest fire was ripping through the group. Doping at the Tour was such big news, it felt as if TV stations kept people on standby ready to pounce on us if there was news of a positive. As soon as anything happened with a doping story, the media presence at the race would swell to another level again.

The first real shock that I experienced personally was the positive test result of Cristian Moreni on stage 16. We were staying in the same hotel as the Cofidis team, and one evening, after a tough six and a half hour stage that finished on top of the Col d'Aubisque, we returned to the sight of police swarming all over the hotel. The French police were so heavy-handed it was ridiculous. They had set up a makeshift command centre in a conference room, with banks of computers and phone lines. They even had police dogs being led about the place. Even though I knew beyond any doubt that there were no pharmaceuticals in my body or in my suitcase, under that kind of scrutiny it was impossible not to feel guilty.

When I eventually made it to the sanctity of my room, I shut the door behind me and peered out from behind the curtain at the scene outside the hotel. It looked like a hostage situation was underway, and if I hadn't been made to feel so guilty then I'm sure it would have been quite exciting – rather like watching an action movie – but this was really disturbing. Having been on our bikes for the best part of the day, none of the riders had any idea what was going on, nor who was being arrested. We had less information than anyone and we were under siege in our own hotel. There was such an atmosphere of paranoia that I didn't even want to leave my room to go for a massage, just in case Axel Foley from *Beverly Hills Cop* pounced on me and started reading me my rights. Still, the intimidating glares of the gendarmes were preferable to the scene outside the hotel, where hordes of press were waiting, desperately looking for a comment from anyone.

The situation was horrible, but I had no energy at all to be wondering about what was going on, or what my reaction should be. I didn't spend the evening looking at the news on the internet. I did what I could to stay focused and recover from the race and prepare for the next day. In the morning I was still so tired it was a major effort to just get a decent breakfast and re-pack my suitcase. Yet, when I stepped off the bus an hour or so later at the start, such was the media scrum in the road it looked like we'd arrived at a protest march. They had all been following every development in the last twelve hours like their jobs depended on it, and now they wanted an opinion from anyone and everyone.

I'd had no media training, and despite being smart enough to normally avoid the kinds of traps that could be laid in a question I was exhausted mentally from the effort of riding the race. But things had started to change. It wasn't enough to just ride dope-free; you were expected to take a stand, to *say something*.

My problem, aside from the obvious one – i.e., not wanting to have to wonder what drugs everyone else had been using to make my job of chasing them around France for the past two weeks so fucking hard – was that I was full of empathy for the people around me. I knew enough to understand that a majority of the riders at the time were 'second-class' dopers, who would just as happily have raced *without* drugs as they would with drugs. I didn't have the luxury of being able to call all my colleagues dickheads. I understood the immense pressures on them, on all of us. I saw no point in standing there giving an ill-informed soundbite stating the bloody obvious, which would only serve to drag my teammates into the mire and throw mud at most of my colleagues, whom I'd then have to work with. My only wish was to keep my head down and get to the finish of the race, so that my job was done.

But things kept getting worse. Information had been slowly seeping out about the race leader, Michael Rasmussen, who was in trouble with his own Danish federation for missing several out-of-competition tests. The race was thrown into disarray, and the pressure continued to intensify on everyone. Tensions were high even as we raced through the mountains. It would begin from the moment we all woke up; riders tried to stay hidden in their team buses, and rushed to and from the sign-on trying to avoid having to give a quote. Then the tension between the group would grow throughout the day, until we crossed the line at the finish of the stage, where it felt like whatever news had come out was about to be unleashed on us while we struggled for breath amidst the pandemonium. The first rider I can remember to crack was the Dutchman Michael Boogerd of Rabobank, who ended up punching someone.

At the time the only surprise registered in the group was that things like that didn't occur more often. There was almost no way to keep it together in that environment. Riders no longer wanted to be associated with old acquaintances, and the peloton became a very unpleasant place to be.

• • •

It wasn't until we rolled into Paris on a very relaxed final stage that I finally let go of my stress and slipped to the back of the bunch. In London, at the start, like at the beginning of most Grand Tours, I had been blinkered by the process of what I was about to do. Throughout the race I had felt like a bull in the final act of a bull-fight, whose head had been forced lower and lower by the taunts of the matador, but finally, on the very last stage, I felt that I could afford to lift up my head and take look at where I was.

Even more than the impressive sight of the Arc de Triomphe was the feeling of release – of almost being *free* from the Tour. The pressure cooker had been so demanding that in the final days I reduced my mental focus to the basic mechanical process of simply turning the pedals and nothing more. I had no idea of anything superfluous, like town names; often, my mind zoned out from the fact I was in the Tour de France at all. I knew how long the next day's stage was, and how much downhill there would be (so I could tell myself the stage was that little bit shorter). My blinkers were on: 'Drink a bit, eat a bit and stay in front.' Maybe, if I had thought more, I could have fired myself up somehow, but in the end I found that the only way to survive the scale of the Tour and the drama was to try to sterilise things as much as I could to make them manageable.

What perked me up somewhat as we swept through the streets of another European capital was that I knew Camilla would be there waiting for me at the finish. That was a major boost. Camilla, along with several of the other wives and girlfriends of the Liquigas riders, had made the trip to Paris. I felt a sense of pride, as I always did when she was at a race, and I enjoyed my ride on the cobbled incline up and down the Champs-Elysées to the end of first Tour de France.

If the last stage was rewarding, my final experience with the Tour was just comical. I had endured doping scandals, police raids, crashes, and the charms of the Hotel Belle Vue, and yet as it turned out I still had to sample the delights of the after-Tour party – an event so talked up by so many riders during the last week that I was quite looking forward to it. But as soon as I crossed the line and realised I was actually freed from the race, after three weeks of racing each other, sleeping within two feet of my roommate and never being more than an arm's length from someone involved in the Tour, all I wanted to do was to spend some time with Camilla. The last thing on my mind was looking at the same ugly bunch of faces I had become overly familiar with during the previous three weeks. But the Tour party – like the Tour itself – was hailed as something you *had* to do. So after some dinner and a bit of time to rest, Camilla and I found ourselves walking around the middle of Paris on a Sunday night looking for the location of the 'official' night out. By now Paris was totally deserted, apart from a few bars filled with alcoholics and tourists – a stark contrast to the day, when the packed streets of fans had made the city feel as if it was bursting at the seams.

After a while we eventually stumbled across the nightclub where it was all supposed to be taking place. There were serious-looking doormen outside and they told me in gruff French that a private party was going on. After the great performance of finding my name on the list, they showed us through the entrance, and we walked into a dingy and half-empty nightclub. My suitably low expectations meant that I wasn't in the least bit taken aback to see that the big Tour de France party had all the atmosphere of an out-of-season holiday camp disco in Blackpool.

Camilla and I exchanged awkward glances, but felt too many expectant sets of eyes on us to disappear instantly. As we worked out what we were going to do, I excused myself to nip to the bathroom to pee. By the time I returned I was unsurprised to find the tall Belgian Gert Steegmans already chatting Camilla up. I walked over to them and, catching my eye, he asked, 'Do you want a drink, mate?' I replied, 'Yeah. Do you want to buy one for my girlfriend too?' He just said, 'Oh, this is your bird, is it?' and wandered off without a care in the world.

That was enough. My first Tour was done, and we left the party after one quick drink. It wouldn't be my last Tour de France, but my impression of the race never changed: it was big, it was brash, it was tiring, and nowhere near as glamorous as it looked. What was more, it definitely wasn't for me.

CHAPTER 13
Big Time

I arrived in Monaco at midnight. The team had already checked me in to the hotel, so I crept quickly through the reception and into the elevators up to my room. It was late, so I was quiet: I slipped the key-card in and out, excusing myself in hushed tones as I heard my Belgian roommate Johan Vansummeren stirring in his bed. I quickly put down my bags and fumbled around with the light switches, taking a wild guess as to which one would switch the bathroom light on, rather than illuminate the room my teammate was trying to sleep in. Waking him now would be inconsiderate; we were forty-eight hours away from the 2009 Tour de France, and nine hours away from having to present ourselves at the pre-Tour medical tests. I guessed correctly, and as the light flickered on I crept into the bathroom. Under the unforgiving bathroom light I looked at my face in the mirror. My head was held firm on my shoulders, but internally it was spinning like a centrifuge. Only hours earlier, that very afternoon, I had been in Milan dressed in jeans and a T-shirt rattling around on the Metro with Camilla on our way back from the British consulate. It was then that I felt my phone vibrating in my pocket.

I was alarmed as soon as I fished my mobile from my jeans and saw the caller ID on the screen. Marc Sergeant was the general manager at Silence-Lotto, and he never called me. In the few months since I had made the huge career decision to leave Liquigas at the end of the 2008 season and join Silence-Lotto to help Cadel Evans's ambition to win the Tour, I had spoken to Marc only a dozen times. My heart filled with dread. My first thought was that I had tested positive, for some reason. I knew I wasn't taking any banned substances, but after what I had gone through in 2004 I had never stopped being paranoid that something similar would happen again. I answered the phone, 'Hi … how are you, Marc?'

His response momentarily added to my fears. 'Not very good, Charly.' I paused to let him continue. I didn't dare ask what the problem was.

'We had some very bad news today. Thomas Dekker has tested positive. I need you to come to Monaco for the Tour, and I need you to come now.'

A mixture of emotions ran through my mind: Thomas's positive test was really bad news, but a part of me was relieved that *I* wasn't the reason that Marc sounded so glum. I should perhaps have been excited about being called up for the Tour, but it was only ten days previously that, following a disagreement with the team management, I had been unceremoniously dumped from the Tour selection and told at the last minute that I wouldn't be riding.

It was not how things had been planned. Unlike in 2007, when Liquigas sent me to the Tour as an afterthought, at Silence-Lotto things were different: in Cadel Evans my new team thought they had a realistic contender to win the Tour, and so I was sent to the Giro merely as a warm-up for the main event, or at least that is what I was told. But, once the Giro started and the team (myself included) weren't getting any results, what had sounded fine in theory started to seem less of a good idea to the team management. The pressure mounted on everyone day by day, and for some reason I bore the brunt of it. At Silence-Lotto I had been reunited with Roberto Damiani, and he had, naturally, been my point of contact for the team. Perhaps at that Giro he had secretly thought I could ride a good GC and, knowing my psychology, he had tried to take the pressure off in the hope that I would do well. But in my mind I was only there to train, and I rode accordingly.

Each day that I lost time Damiani became increasingly sour towards me, and it slowly dawned on me that he was actually expecting a lot more than he originally asked for. This angered me. Our relations became strained and, with two days to go, things came to a head. Damiani announced that, instead of going home after the race, I had to fly to Zolder in Belgium to do team time trial training with the Tour squad. I snapped. Springing a surprise like that on me at the end of a three-week Grand Tour was totally unfair, and Damiani knew that. I stood my ground and we flew into a blazing row. I felt that Damiani had misled me, and, with hindsight, he may have felt disappointed that I'd not risen to the challenge in the way he thought I would. In truth we were both frustrated, and we both held valid opinions, but the problem was that we no longer saw eye to eye.

Knowing that I had angered the management, it came as no surprise to receive the call, ten days before the Tour, saying that

I was no longer in the team. It was a kick in the teeth, and I knew that the team would find a way to 'punish' me, but, as annoyed as I was, it wasn't devastating. Firstly, I had a two-year contract with Silence-Lotto, and I knew that if I didn't ride the Tour I could ride a good Vuelta, and that that would be enough to redeem me in the fickle eyes of cycling management. Secondly, after only a few months of riding as a teammate for Cadel Evans, I was quite glad not to be going to the pressure cooker of the Tour in support of the man.

My only issue about missing the race was something quite trivial indeed: I'd already booked and paid for a hotel at altitude in Livigno to do my final preparations for the Tour. Deciding that I would look for the silver lining in this particular cloud, with nothing to train for I took Camilla with me instead, so we could have a bit of time away from home together. Instead of training in the run up to the Tour, I spent a few days walking around, shopping and relaxing. I was a world away from the three-week race. We'd had a fantastic time in the Alps, and on the way home we made use of passing through Milan to go to the British consulate to collect the papers we needed to get married. Then the phone rang.

As I hung up the call I was in shock. With a stunned look I told Camilla that I had to go to the Tour as soon as I got home. It was far from ideal, as we had a wedding to plan in August. I was effectively telling her that she was on her own throughout July. What made me feel more uncomfortable still, apart from having to leave my fiancée high and dry at short notice, was that from the moment I had been told I wasn't riding I had been on holiday. After three days with no riding, eating out in restaurants and an exhausting day spent walking around Milan, I felt about as bloated and healthy as a drowned corpse. It wasn't what you'd call Tour de France form, but it was too late to do anything about it now.

We went home and I hurriedly packed my suitcases. Camilla, being as no-nonsense as she is, looked past any feelings of disappointment at being left alone and volunteered to drive me down the motorway towards Monaco. We were used to my lifestyle being unpredictable at best, but in the six months that I had been at Silence-Lotto both of us had noticed an erratic, chaotic manner about the team. My move into the big time wasn't turning out to be quite what we had expected.

Going to Silence-Lotto was the move that I had always dreamed of making. Liquigas were a big team, but they were still very Italian in their mindset. They followed a traditional approach to cycling that, while effective, I had begun to question. During the early summer of 2008 I had engaged in tentative talks with the management at Lotto. After nearly three decades of focusing on the Northern Classics, and since signing and reviving the career of Australian stage racer Cadel Evans, the Belgian team started to entertain stage-race ambitions. They adopted relatively progressive ways of working (for an established European team) in order to help them climb out of the rut that had seen them underperform throughout the nineties. I was interested in them, and in their new ethos, and now that Roberto Damiani was working there I knew I had a good connection. After nine years on Italian teams there was a little voice in my head that was curious to know what life might be like elsewhere. I had as much recognition as I could ever want in Italy, amongst the riders, managers, race organisers and the *tifosi*, but still, the part of my ego that wanted recognition on an international stage pinched at me, pushing me towards the notion that a change of team would be beneficial.

Just as quickly as Lotto had shown interest, though, suddenly it seemed to be withdrawn. The trail went cold. My contract was up at the end of the year with Liquigas, and I decided I would tell my agent Alex Carera, the brother of Jonny (who many years previously had forced Stanga to honour his letter of intent), to put the word out that I was available. The response, for the first time in my career, was genuinely exciting. In a short space of time I had a few offers from various Spanish and Italian teams; it seemed my value had soared in the last two years. I realised then, while I sat down to talk with Alex over a coffee in a hotel bar, that without really noticing it I had made it. There is nothing more satisfying for a professional cyclist than to know that more than one team wants to pay you to ride your bike.

In that moment I recalled a long-buried memory of riding on a club run with VC York when I was 13. I had been talking to an older rider about professional cyclists and he had sagely informed me, 'That Sean Yates, he is a *real* professional cyclist. They say that every team in the world would sign him.' It was an off-hand comment, and probably quite misinformed, but it had stuck in my mind. He hadn't said that Yates was good because he had won a Tour time trial, or that he'd won a Vuelta stage. Yates was the archetypal *domestique*, and whether or not the old club member really knew what he was talking about I had come to understand more and more over the years that if you were a *domestique* there was no greater accolade than having teams queuing up to sign you. 'That Charly Wegelius, he is a *real* professional.'

My only difficulty at that point was to make the right decision for my future. I thought long and hard about the offers I had, but I couldn't convince myself that a move to Spain was the right thing to do. In the end, satisfied at least by getting an impression of my value, I fell back on what I knew and agreed to renew my contract with Liquigas. There was nothing wrong at Liquigas, after all, I told myself, and they matched the best offer I'd had, which was considerably more money than I was already on.

But after the 2008 Tour de France everything changed. Cadel managed second place to Alberto Contador, but with a weaker team than the Spaniard he'd found himself isolated in the mountains. Suddenly Silence-Lotto were scrambling to find strong climbers who could help make the difference and I was back at the top of their shopping list. I was the ideal candidate for the job. Not only was I an exemplary mountain *domestique*, I knew Cadel from our brief spell at Mapei together, and I conveniently lived only 20 km away from him on the other side of Varese. As it turned out, Lotto were willing to invest heavily in Cadel's chances of winning the Tour. In late summer of 2008 they contacted my agent and immediately offered a sum that dwarfed what I would have been getting at Liquigas. I had agreed a new contract in principle with Liquigas, but nothing was signed. I knew full well that Liquigas wouldn't be able to match the offer, and I couldn't possibly turn down that kind of money. A cycling career is startlingly short. My mind was made up.

Leaving Liquigas was difficult. Things had gone so well there it was impossible for me to dislike them, and I knew that they really wanted to keep me. It felt like breaking up with a girlfriend whom you really liked, but who wanted to stay at home while you went off to travel the world. I made sure that when I gave them the news I called the general manager at Liquigas, Roberto Amadio, myself, instead of making my agent do it. I wanted to be honest and straightforward, not to have him feel like I was trying to black-mail him into paying me more. I called and simply said, 'Roberto, Lotto have made me an offer I can't refuse.' I didn't even need to tell him how much it was. Amadio was a good manager and he understood a rider's need to explore different paths in their short career. He was disappointed for the team, but accepted my decision and respected me for making the call myself. I left Liquigas, but I left them with my head held high. It was the right end to a very productive chapter in my career.

Once I put pen to paper with Silence-Lotto, I felt like I was getting the reward for everything I'd done at Liquigas and De Nardi before that. At De Nardi I was paid poorly for a professional athlete; at Liquigas things were better but I was still stuck earning an average wage. But now at Lotto I would be earning what felt like the wage of a proper sports star. Professional cyclists don't go through it all for nothing. A love of the sport gets you out of the junior catego-ries and around a bunch of local races, but no further. As much as respect from my employers and my status in the peloton fulfilled my desire to be regarded as a real professional cyclist, the thing that had become increasingly important at that stage of my life was to earn good money, especially now that I had Camilla, and a home to pay for. In the tough days at De Nardi, while I had stood shivering on the start line of yet another Giro stage with my knee-warmers on, wondering if the rain was turning to snow on top of the Dolomites looming in front of us, I repeatedly told myself: 'This will pay off.'

I assumed that a big pay day would come along with a great team – that it would be a happy ending. As it turned out, money, indeed, doesn't equal happiness. Especially not in a cycling team.

* * *

Two days after arriving in Monaco and sneaking into my hotel room like a thief, I was readying myself to roll down the start ramp of the stage-one time trial. In 2007 the race had filled me with a creeping dread, and I was mentally tired after I'd already been under a lot of pressure at the Giro. But now the team was so relieved that I had dropped everything and come to the race that I was flavour of the month just for turning up. That relaxed me, and knowing that I would finally be recognised on the international stage provided great motivation. Cadel was in with a real chance of a Tour win, and so, unlike in 2007, I had a clear purpose.

For a brief moment, the eyes of the world looked to me at the start ramp. I started my Tour de France precisely one minute in front of Lance Armstrong in his comeback year from brief retirement. Everyone was swarming around Lance. I felt for the poor guy behind him, who would have problems getting to the start on time because of the sheer volume of press. Everywhere Lance went there was a tidal wave of reporters and cameramen literally falling over each other to get close to him. The Tour felt more in the spotlight than ever that year because of his return, and in a way Monaco itself was the perfect metaphor for what was going on all around: money, celebrity, glamour, all under the umbrella of the Tour. This was a world so far away from the reality of my life, but just for once I was going to enjoy it all. There was only one spanner in the works that I could think of, but quite a major one all the same.

I had known when Lotto had hired me that a big part of my remit would be to build a relationship with Cadel. Living so close to each other in Italy it made sense that we trained together and got to know each other. This would allow Cadel to trust in my help, and would build loyalty between us. In reality, though, I found this much more difficult than I'd imagined.

Shortly after I had signed my contract with Lotto Cadel invited Camilla and me to a restaurant for dinner with himself and his wife, Chiara. By this point in my career, after so many years in Italy, I had learnt to release my more gregarious side, and with Camilla I had re-learnt how to enjoy socialising, but that night was hard work. The whole experience was like a bad job interview; it was stressful and I couldn't relax for a moment, and I wasn't sure Cadel could either. I started to wonder if I was doing something terribly wrong, and it put me on edge. Conversation was difficult, and it started to become obvious that Cadel had some major issues with the team. It wasn't just me who felt uncomfortable, either. On the way home Camilla registered surprise that he had bothered to bring such a nice bottle of wine with him, put it on the table, and yet not open it before taking it home with him again! He may not have even realised he'd done it, but at the time it seemed an odd, and hardly inviting, gesture.

As we progressed through the year and the Tour approached, training with him proved just as difficult. He had a habit of continually getting lost between our two houses, which made finding him to even start training a challenge. Once over this erratic start, when we did get going Cadel seemed up and down; with so much on his mind, and working so hard to win the Tour, he questioned those around him. He never seemed convinced that the team was doing all they could. Perhaps they weren't quite doing enough, or didn't have the resources he needed, but I couldn't help but infer that he took it personally. In truth, my own attitude was changing and I no longer had the energy to tolerate behaviour that I couldn't understand. As a younger man I might have risen to the challenge, but instead I just became frustrated. Silence-Lotto may not have been the best team for a Tour contender at the time, but I thought they had done a lot for Cadel, and they had invested heavily in helping him win the Tour, yet Cadel seemed convinced that things weren't measuring up.

In the 2008 Tour Cadel had famously warned a journalist that he would 'cut his head off' if he touched his dog (which he had with him). The team thought that perhaps, seeing as Cadel could get a little stressed by the media throng at the Tour finishes, he might like help. So, for the 2009 race, they hired a bodyguard called 'Big Serg' to look after him. Cadel didn't see that the team were helping him, and instead complained about having a bodyguard follow him around. He seemed to *want* to take everything the wrong way.

Cadel wasn't on the Giro programme so our paths didn't cross for a number of weeks. But as soon as the Tour started he decided that, because of the risk of losing time through crashes in the first week, he wanted to be at the front all day. This isn't a bad suggestion in itself, but when Cadel said 'the front' he didn't mean he'd be happy being *close* to the front, he wanted us to be *literally* on the front. He couldn't accept that we could afford to sit on the wheels, even in 20th place, for a moment. Instead of relaxing and letting the race evolve around us and using other people to take us up to the front (and thereby saving our team's energy for the mountains, where he would really need us to be fresh), he ran the whole team ragged in the first week.

For me the biggest problem was that I felt Cadel simply wasn't a natural leader. There are men who are natural leaders, and there are men who have talent, but for whom leadership is something that they have to learn. In my experience Cadel simply did not have enough natural ability relating to the men he was supposed to inspire. As a *domestique* a big part of my job was to learn about my leader's character and allow him to get the best out of himself. Part of the job of a leader is to work out the characters of the men who sacrifice themselves for him, and for him to know how to get the very best out of them.

At Liquigas I had worked hard for Danilo Di Luca, not only because I was a professional and it was my job, but because every so often, when the chips had really been down, I had ridden beyond myself having been inspired by Di Luca to do so. There I had seen, first hand, how a natural leader behaved; for all his faults Danilo was a real leader and he knew how to stand up and be counted as one. If he didn't get the results he wanted, he continued to treat us with respect, and he shouldered the responsibility himself. For example, Danilo liked to ride at the back of the bunch for as long as possible so he could stay relaxed, and then focus when it mattered. On occasion the team manager, who could clearly see eight lime-green Liquigas jerseys at the back of the bunch, would go into a panic at the thought of the race happening without us and would start screaming down the radio that we had to move up. But Danilo knew exactly when he wanted to move up, and if we went any time before that it would be a wasted effort. While the team manager would be shouting himself hoarse, Danilo would just tell us, 'It's OK, *ragazzi*, wait with me, I'll say when.' The team manager could be going berserk, but we would stay with Danilo because we trusted that, *even if it all went wrong* and we messed up and got to the front too late, he would stand up after the race and say, 'That was my fault.' Danilo would never dream of going to the press after a stage and saying his team had let him down. He knew that the way to inspire eight exhausted bike riders wasn't to tell the world that they were all useless. Conversely, in 2009 it felt like this approach had become routine for Cadel.

It wasn't just when things went badly that the differences were so apparent. In 2007, after he'd had won the Giro and my contract had come up for renewal, Danilo came to see me in my hotel room and enquired how much I was getting paid. When I told him, he simply said, 'That is not enough.' He didn't say anything else, but he took it upon himself to see that I was offered a much bigger contract. Sure enough, by the end of the week I received a much better offer from the team. Danilo never said anything else about it and he never felt the need to make a big point of it. If I did well for Cadel, to be fair, he'd often thank me publicly, but in a way that, if I'm honest, lacked the simple, personal touch I needed to inspire me. In truth, it just wasn't working, and I was beginning to find it hard going.

● ● ●

I was due to be married later in the summer, and for the first time in my cycling career I finally felt like I had a happy and balanced home life. Now, when I was cast back into the strange world of professional cycling, I started to see cyclists and my profession in a different light. Ideally, like all cyclists, I needed to be trained and rested, like a racehorse, and anything else in life was an issue that would either have to be overlooked and sorted out later, or dealt with by someone else. I was a sportsman, so people saw this behaviour as dedication, something that throughout my life was seen as a credit to my character. Now that I had a partner whom I loved and wanted to spend time with, I realised that my character could really be quite difficult for others to deal with. The most important thing in my life was my physical condition. A realisation dawned: I was a self-obsessed, self-centred hypochondriac.

I started to see that being an athlete encouraged the most deplorable behaviour in people. Society's admiration for athletes is based entirely on the achievement of an ideal. People see a cyclist as someone who had a goal and, through hard work, attained it. The public loves to see someone who has managed to do something they didn't, and has reached the pinnacle of physical condition. To fans who pore over books and magazines about cycling, the notion of *sacrifice* is an honourable thing, but those things you start to sacrifice when you are a 30-year-old man really need to be reconsidered. I had to be prepared to make sacrifices in my relationship for cycling. Of course, I understood that sacrifice is necessary in everyone's lives, but in the real world a workaholic who ignored his family would be regarded as a piece of shit, and yet I saw that I was doing exactly the same thing while being revered by an adoring public, cheering by the roadside and queuing in the rain outside the team bus in order to tell us all how great we were.

But the paradox of cycling is that if you are riding well then you are kept from your failings as a human being. The morality of dedication required to achieve racing success is never once questioned, except, perhaps, by the more sensitive cyclists. In most cases, it is also in the team's interest to perpetuate the myth that a good rider is a good man, because, as long as he wins, personality is irrelevant.

The more I looked around me that year, the more I saw other people (and myself) in a new context, thanks to the perspective my home life was giving me. I started to think that we absolutely didn't deserve the credit and the applause that we were lauded with: we were a bunch of selfish arseholes who spent our lives trying to stand up as little as possible.

What would happen, I wondered, when I did start a family? While I was at work I would be a gleaming Lycra-clad gladiator who made up the Tour peloton, but when I was at home I would be a father who rolled back over when his children were crying in the night; a husband who would leave his wife at the drop of a hat to go away for weeks on end, only to return a grumpy shell of his former self; a grown man who wouldn't do the dishes at night because he didn't want to be on his feet for an extra ten minutes of the day. I could potentially miss the births of my children and great chunks of their lives in order to bask in the warmth of success in the eyes of people I didn't know. As I went through the motions of the race I could feel a question bubbling up from deep down within myself. What the hell I was I doing here?

. . .

In the end, the 2009 Tour wasn't all bad for me. It was still the biggest race on the planet, and that year I felt like my relationship with it matured. A few small things happened there that seemed to act as confirmation of what I had noticed in previous races, but hadn't yet truly understood. As a cyclist you are constantly trying to figure out where your place is in the class system of the peloton, where you stand in relation to others, and how that constantly changes. It is, as I have said many times before, nothing more than a giant multilingual schoolyard, and finding your place in it takes years. Even once you know your role as a rider, your social role is far more complicated. On the bike you want to be viewed in a certain way, and you want to be involved in the right circles when certain conversations are happening. I hadn't walked straight into my new school as a neo-pro and found myself instantly amongst the 'cool kids'. Instead, I had worked my way there, and by the 2009 Tour I felt that I had finally slipped into the upper echelons of the international peloton.

Having a good reputation made my job easier in many respects, and in some ways more interesting. There is no better measure of a rider's standing in the hierarchy of the world of cycling than that gleaned from informal chats while the peloton is rolling freely. During a mountain stage I overheard the Caisse D'Epargne rider Pablo Lastras talking to one of his teammates behind me. Lastras' young teammate asked him a question that, in the noise of the race, I missed. But Lastras' answer rang out as clear as a bell. 'Go and ask Charly, he'll know.'

Lastras was a rider whom I looked up to. The tall Spaniard was one of the most polite, professional and honourable riders in the bunch: he was a real gentleman to absolutely everyone. He won big races occasionally, but what I really admired in him was that he was so widely respected in the group. It had made me unimaginably proud that Lastras saw me as the person others would seek out for help or advice. Now *I* was the person other people would look to to get an idea what the weather was going to do, or the person to keep close to when the break was going to go. From the outside of the sport you would hardly have known, but inside it moved me. I had gone from being the rider who was desperately looking around for Erik Zabel at the Vuelta to know when I could get dropped, to becoming a reference point for other people in the group. It was a big moment. I had respect.

On the final stage of that 2009 Tour, as we reached the hairpin bend that the bunch U-turn around to shoot down the back straight of the Champs-Elysées, I finally caught up with my young Australian teammate, Matt Lloyd. As we rounded the bend and I moved up alongside him I could finally get my breath back and yell, 'Matt! Drink? Do you want one?'

I did not get the answer that I was expecting. Laughing, he shouted back: 'Fuck off, smart-arse!'

I was confused. Matt had a great sense of humour, but I couldn't see that this was in any way funny, or, more to the point, the time to be pissing around. I tried again: 'Seriously, Matt, do you want a drink?'

It was then he looked at me and clicked that it wasn't me who was joking: 'Charly, it's the last lap!'

The joke was on me. I had no idea that we were within a few kilometres of the finish of the race, and that the whole process of dragging my backside down the bunch to go and get bottles had been a complete waste of time. For a split second I thought about the team manager and mechanic who were probably laughing their arses off in their team car too, and, chuckling a little myself, I threw away the bottles and sprinted back into line in the bunch. It was typical of my mentality towards the end of that Tour; the whole thing seemed to be passing in a blur. Cadel had been off the pace throughout the Tour, and hinted throughout that the lack of support from his team was to blame. As the finish approached, the less mental space I gave to the racing, the more I seemed to be drawn to the deeper questions lingering in the darker recesses of my brain. My body was still doing the job but my mind had started to drift.

After the Tour I thought that my year of surprises was over. I went back to Finland in August and married Camilla in a ceremony with many friends who had come from Italy and the UK. I felt myself unwind; I was truly happy. Through Camilla I had begun to reconnect with Finland, and the things I loved to do there and the freedom I felt there became important to me again. We walked in the woods, swam in the lakes, and looked after Camilla's horses. We loved being in each other's company, and we both enjoyed the space and simplicity of Finland. We spent time with Camilla's friends and I loved getting to know people who had nothing at all to do with cycling. In Italy my entire social circle was formed of bike riders, or people I knew through being a bike rider, but in Finland it couldn't have been more different. We enjoyed being away from the chaos of our life in Italy. I didn't have to question myself because I was happy, and when I thought about my career I told myself that, overall, the year had gone well. With Dekker's positive and Cadel's disaopointing result, the Tour might have been a disaster for the team, but they were still so delighted that I had even turned up in the first place that I had held a kind of 'get out of jail free' card. I knew, too, that being in Finland put some much-needed distance between me and the job. I figured that a bit of time in Finland before a return to my usual end-of-season programme would recover my mental and physical strength, so that upon our return to Italy I would be ready to return to the swing of things.

But then, with some sort of inevitability, the phone rang again.

This time it was Hendrik Redant, one of the *directeurs sportifs*, who had drawn the short straw and had called to inform me that in nine days the team wanted me to go and start the Vuelta. Bitter, angry tears welled up in my eyes. I could not believe what I was hearing. I was still on my honeymoon and I was getting a call to tell me that because Cadel had done badly in the Tour he wanted to have a tilt at the Vuelta. I looked across the room at Camilla as I shook my head in disbelief. As much as it would be difficult and painful for me to be away for all that length of time – again – I knew Camilla would understand. But that didn't help the fact that I felt utterly powerless. It wasn't only my personal life that would suffer; it was a stupid move for me physically too. I was a rider who was used to my programme changing, but this was ludicrous. Riding all three Grand Tours in one year was hard enough for anyone, but starting two of them in a completely unplanned and unprepared fashion was just ridiculous. It is conceivable for riders to do all three Grand Tours in a year, but it takes an exceptional kind of athlete to do all three and then be good the following year. Even in terms of the investment the team had made in me, it made no sense. I couldn't understand why, when I was on a two-year contract, the team would want me to ride the Vuelta like this, and potentially ruin my following season.

I felt so dejected that I had to be honest: I told Hendrik that I would really rather not. Instead of listening he said, 'OK, I'll let you think about it then.' The decision had apparently been left to me but that didn't stop him calling me back five more times that day. The team knew exactly which buttons to push to get me to go, and the emotional blackmail began. Time after time he layered it on thick, telling me the team was *relying* on me, and that they *needed* me to do this. I wanted to ask him – wasn't it enough that I had already raced two Grand Tours that year, and that I had gone to one of them with six hours' notice after they had chosen to drop me from the race to punish me? But it didn't matter. I knew it wouldn't help. 'My' decision was made a lot simpler when the emotional blackmail gave way to being offered a simple choice: 'If you don't agree to do the Vuelta then I will send you to Belgium to ride one-day races for the same amount of days you would be in Spain anyway.'

I gave in. Two weeks later I duly took myself to the start of the Vuelta, in Holland of all places. But I knew that I didn't have the mental strength left in me to try to finish a three-week race. After the third stage I lay on my bed in my hotel room staring at the ceiling. I was still in the tracksuit I'd hastily changed into at the end of the stage, and my bag full of my dirty cycling kit was unpacked. My roommate Matt Lloyd was going about his post-race routine, unpacking his kit and sorting through his suitcase. I thought about getting up and doing the same, but I just couldn't. I realised that I just wasn't going to do it.

'I'm out, Matt. I'm going home.'

'Oh yeah? Shit. What are you going to tell 'em?'

'I don't know. I'll tell them I've got a knee injury... something, anything will do. They'll know it's bollocks no matter what I tell them, but I don't fucking care. This isn't fair. They can stick this bloody race up their arse.'

'Fair enough, mate. When you've gotta go ...'

I knew Matt would understand. It was our first year in a team together but we'd got along really well. He broke the mould in a lot of ways: he was atypical for an Australian cyclist because he was a pure climber; he was slight and small (whereas most of the Australian professionals came from track backgrounds and were generally sprinters). In my mind he was unique because he had wit –a devilishly quick mind that many didn't understand – and attitude. Matt Lloyd acted like he didn't give a fuck, and I *really* liked him for it. Matt's outlook was the antithesis of the subservient mentality that I had always thought a rider had to have to fit in; he wasn't difficult or hard to work with, he just didn't let the bastards grind him down, and he didn't take any shit. He was different to me because he was a winner, and that was significant. His was the attitude that I'd dreamed of having throughout my time in Europe, but my role as a *domestique* had condemned me to subservience. If ever there was someone who I thought might just understand the situation I was in, it was Matt. I was really glad he was there.

I started the stage the next day, but climbed off part-way through, telling Redant that I was just too fucked to keep up. He was unimpressed, there was no way that he believed me, but there was nothing he could physically do to keep me in the race and he knew it. Leaving a race under any circumstances is never nice. There was no feeling of relief, no secret satisfaction at sticking my fingers up at the team and the way I was being treated. Instead, there was just a bitter regret that doing the right thing for myself could be so hard, and feel so awfully wrong.

When I was finally away from the team, sitting in another featureless departure lounge in an airport that I didn't even know the name of, all the buried questions at the Tour resurfaced again. I thought of who I had been at the first Vuelta. I knew that if my younger self could see me now he would think that I had everything: respect, a big team, money, plenty of big performances under my belt. But now that I had everything I'd ever wanted out of my cycling career, I started to see what a narrow road I'd cycled down.

CHAPTER 14

One Tour Too Far

My parents-in-law (like many families in Finland) own a small lake house. Their wooden cottage sits in splendid isolation a few metres from the shore of one of Finland's many hundreds of small lakes, nestled in a forest of tall, silent pines. In winter, deep snow makes the small track from the road through the forest completely impassable. The weight of the snow makes the trees susceptible to falling down, and each spring, when my parents-in-law return, there is a great deal of path clearing to be done to be able to reach the house.

In summer, though, the house is a sanctuary. Then, the seemingly endless hours of daylight (which fade only into a prolonged twilight) pass by with blissful simplicity. I loved the house from the moment I first saw it. It was the place Camilla and I had chosen to spend our wedding night, and three wonderful days alone together in the summer of 2009. There was no mobile-phone signal, and once there there was no way that anyone in the world could get hold of me. I could live the simplest life I could imagine. I would chop wood to heat the sauna, swim in the lake, row out into the silence that hung over the middle of the water, and walk the dogs. My favourite thing of all, though, was to lie on the wooden decking on the veranda of the house, looking up at the sky, listening to the most beautiful silence imaginable.

This was exactly what I found myself doing on 17 July 2010; but it wasn't, however, what I was supposed to be doing. Two days previously I had been a part of the Tour de France peloton. But, in my fourteenth Grand Tour, things had gone very wrong. Now, as I lay there on the decking listening to the sound of the pines creaking and the lake lapping at the shore, I knew I was a sick and exhausted man. I was broken, but I could see that my abandon in the Tour was the inevitable conclusion – one Tour too far.

Ironically, I had actually gone into the 2010 Tour with hopes of having a good race. After the disappointments of 2009 with Cadel and Silence-Lotto I needed change to keep me hungry enough. With all the troubles of late selection, 2009 had been a struggle, and I had been forced to really start to question what I was doing. Marriage had changed me. After I had come home from the disastrous Vuelta I realised that I had spent the better part of my adult life with my head buried in the sand, simply doing what I was told. Meeting Camilla had made my life so much fuller and made me adopt a more objective view – of myself, and of my career choices.

For example, it had long ceased to occur to me that I could be a professional cyclist anywhere other than Italy. But when I looked at it in late 2009 I no longer rode for an Italian team, and I had teammates who lived all over Europe and flew in to races, so why on earth did I have to live in Italy? What had kept me there was the same desire to brand myself with legitimacy that had stopped me making the two-hour flight to England when I had time off in my early years. I'd felt that would be too easy, that I would be 'cheating'. But now my attitude had changed; now my priority was to make my life easier, not harder. Punishing myself no longer came into it. I had already branded myself as a cyclist deeply enough.

After that first disappointing year at Silence-Lotto, Camilla and I realised that we needed to make a change. We had been living together in Italy for three years and it was wearing us both down. The tiniest little things seemed to thwart me. No matter how well I grasped the culture and the language, I still didn't truly understand the place. It would take me an entire afternoon to get even the simplest errand done because things that I needed were never where I expected them to be, and every single business and bank in Italy seemed to have different opening hours. It didn't bother me so much when I was single because I never did anything. But when I started living with Camilla I really needed things to work. I had a different kind of life, and getting my head around all of Italy's idiosyncrasies became hard work all over again.

One day, in the winter of 2009, the axe just fell. As we were making coffee in the morning, I turned to Camilla and said, 'What do you think about selling this place and moving somewhere else?' I could see the same thought rushing through Camilla's mind: 'We no longer *have* to be here?' It was a tipping point; once I had vocalised the idea I knew there was no going back. I was tired of not being truly settled. In Italy I was still *bagai* – the boy. I didn't want to be 'the boy' any more. I wanted to be a man, and I wanted to live somewhere where I could be that man. We both wanted a home, and that was in Finland. Over the past few seasons we had been spending more and more time there, and I felt that was the place that I would find the life I had been craving.

The only way that I could really describe the feeling of being 'at home' was the feeling of being safe. It was a feeling that had been absent since my mother and I had turned up to the Vendée U training camp in France all those years before. In the meantime I had lived for so many years abroad, I'd mastered languages and tried to understand cultures. I had even become a homeowner in Italy. But I'd never felt safe. I had always felt exposed, on the line; my life felt like it was constructed on a temporary platform which at any moment could be pulled away from under me. The annual undercurrent of worry about whether or not I would have a decent contract for the following season, and what would happen to my mortgage if I crashed badly and could no longer earn the wage I was used to, rumbled within me, and I wanted to be rid of it all.

In some ways I felt like a person who'd been misdiagnosed by a doctor and wrongly condemned to suffering for their whole life. Suddenly I saw there was another way that I could go about life *without* the pain. But what I couldn't have known until I finally tried to alleviate these anxieties, pains and insecurities was that the discomfort of it all was the very thing that had been making me push myself so hard to achieve on my bike – and that the happier I was at home, the slower I would ride.

• • •

We rented our Italian house to Matt Lloyd while it was on the market and moved out of Italy for good. The 2010 season got underway and slowly, as we established our foundations in Helsinki, my thoughts once again began to stray from the comforts of home life, and back to my job of being a professional bike rider. Many things had changed in the interim: as well as the team being renamed Omega Pharma-Lotto, over the winter Cadel Evans had left. Despite my finding him difficult to work for, this wasn't in itself all wonderful news. Like him or not, Cadel was the man that I had been employed to help, and now that he had gone I was a spare part in a team that didn't really know what to do with me. Fortunately, my saving grace came that year in one of Omega Pharma-Lotto's new signings – Adam Blythe. Adam was a young British neo-pro, and his appearance in the team really breathed some life into me. In my ten years in the peloton I had come across countless young riders who had ascended through the Italian system and were simply spoilt brats, who felt they knew everything and had no time for a rider who was 'just' a *domestique*. Adam, however, was very different. I could tell instantly that he wanted to learn: he really made an effort to listen when I told him things. And, crucially, he was actually fun to be around.

Now that I had the 'old man' tag foisted upon me, I was keen to help Adam. Ten years worth of disappointment and hardship had formed a crust over how I viewed bike racing; I had forgotten why I even enjoyed cycling in the first place. As we went through the training camps and the early-season races I felt that Adam's enthusiasm was influencing me, encouraging me to embrace riding my bike again.

Adam's pleasure was infectious, but the flames of hope really began flickering with Matt Lloyd's performance at the Giro d'Italia. Matt had been with the team since 2007 and he really came of age that May.

Matt's breakthrough stage win on stage six, combined with some inspired riding to keep hold of the green jersey for best climber, took the whole team through the Giro. It was a buoyant performance and things really fell into place for us. The team clicked in the race and Matt took a stage and a small lead in the King of the Mountains competition – something we had great fun defending on the road to Milan. My own ride was positively influenced by the camaraderie and spirit amongst the group of riders in the team, and ironically, just before what came to be my last ever Grand Tour, I produced one of my best-ever performances in a three-week race. I finished 27th in the Giro, despite losing an enormous amount of time on stage seven when the race took in the *strade bianche* (gravel roads) in the pouring rain, that I simply didn't have the nerve to go tearing down.

The good feeling that bubbled up at that Giro did come as a surprise to me, given my internal struggle in the run-up. I left the race and came bounding back home on a high. It felt like I had rediscovered cycling, and I was coming home to tell Camilla about this really exciting new hobby that I'd started. It was one of the few times that I ever came home from a three-week race and retained the desire to ride my bike. After only a couple of days' rest I was back out on the road, first with some gentle recovery riding, and then soon into the full flow of training. The Tour was on my programme and I wanted to be good for it. I would be there with a big team again, but this time without the negative baggage. I leapt at the opportunity to go with the team to a training camp in Sierra Nevada and spent eight days at altitude, training hard and trying to capitalise on the momentum.

However, on my return home I started to feel unsettled. I was sleeping but I wasn't waking up in the mornings feeling rested. Something in me wasn't quite right. At first I told myself that it was the sudden return from altitude. As an athlete you can always find a reason to ignore the fact you are feeling a little off-colour. You spend your life thinking about nothing but your physical condition, to the point that you can always find *something* that is not 100 per cent right – a sore knee or an aching back. I knew that I usually felt a little odd in the weeks building up to a big race because I would break my routine to rest up for the event. I told myself that because I was doing so much resting I was probably over-thinking, and that when I joined up with the team things would improve.

But when I arrived at the team hotel in Rotterdam the Wednesday before the start, things didn't improve. On the Thursday morning we did the pre-race blood tests and the doctor told me in a very off-hand way that my body showed a sign of infection, but it was 'hardly life threatening'. I wanted to brush it off. Deep down I knew there was a lot was riding on this race, and I couldn't face going back now.

I gambled on things getting better, but they didn't. As soon as the racing began I knew I wasn't feeling well on the bike, and as the days passed I seemed to get worse and worse. I had been forced to abandon a Grand Tour through sickness only once before, and I remembered all too vividly the fever that hit me at the top of the Zoncolan, which had struck through me so quickly and so obviously that there was no time to suffer in the saddle. This time, though, things were different; this was a creeping illness that was building within me, and each day became more and more of a struggle.

I focused my mind on the intermediate target of making it to the first rest day. After an uncomfortable week I made it there, but I had slipped from being near the back of the race to right at the end of its ragged tail. There were times when I was in trouble even when other riders were casually rolling along and stopping to pee. I was still playing the usual athlete's game of denial, though; I told myself that if I had a day off to rest then I would be OK. I just wanted to keep going.

But after the rest day things worsened still. Even my sleep, the holy grail of a stage race, began to be aggravated and fitful. I woke in the morning of the ninth stage feeling even more tired than the night before, dreading the day to come and the pain that I knew was awaiting me. My (usually insatiable) appetite was gone. At breakfast it was all I could do just to sit and stare at my food while my stomach craved water. No matter how much I drank I couldn't rid myself of the hellish thirst that parched my lips and tormented me through the nights. There was no more room for denying that things were going very wrong.

Still, I tried to keep quiet. I had suffered in races before and I knew that suffering was something that I could certainly endure … to a point. Many times before I felt I had become so used to the pain that I had revelled in it, toyed with it, pushed its boundaries. But now pain was exacting its revenge on me. I felt so empty and weak that every little thing found a way to hurt me: every bump in the road, every gust of wind, even the road itself with its seemingly unending gradients. No matter how hard I tried I felt like I was never more than a pedal stroke away from being ejected out the back. I clung on out of desperation and sheer will, but at some stage it was all going to have to stop.

I went to bed early on the night of the tenth stage to Gap. I was completely drained, desperate for the embrace of restful, comforting sleep. My body ached and I slipped into the covers, but my over-sensitive skin was greeted not by the soft fresh sheets that I longed for, but the sandpaper-like linen of a cheap hotel, atop a mattress that might as well have been made of a slab of rusting iron. I couldn't find the strength to stretch out my body to feel the tingling comfort of blood flowing to my limbs, so I curled up tight and closed my eyes, hoping sleep would find me.

I started to sweat, and I felt a hotness grip my neck. It was still early, so there was time to get to sleep. The television flickered silently and the light made patterns inside my eyelids as Matt Lloyd casually went about his evening routine. As long as he was still up it was OK, because it was still early. I kept repeating these words – 'still early, still early' – to assuage my feverish panic. I forced my eyes closed tight against the low light, and felt sweat drip down the ridge of my nose. Then the lights went out and I heard the muffled sounds of Matt climbing into bed, beginning his night's rest. I rolled over in the dark. It was OK still, because if Matt had just gone to bed then it wasn't too late yet: he wasn't asleep either. There was still enough time to rest. Still early, still early … My head pounded so hard. Matt was asleep now, and time was slipping away. I tried to force my eyes closed but they sprang open. Darkness, not the soothing darkness that I loved but a lonely, hurried darkness, taunted me for being wide awake. My mind spun in furious circles, and I turned over in the bed, twisting the sheets into a damp corrugated mess beneath me. I flipped my pillow neither side was cool and dry, and the sound of Matt's slow, relaxed breathing enraged me. It felt like the whole race, the whole world was resting and recovering, getting ready to open fresh eyes the next day, and mine were being squeezed tight. I became stricken with panic and desperation as time danced away from me. It was fucked, I was fucked, everything felt fucked. My head was a bloated, burning mess of activity. I stared angrily across the room at the curtains, and then I saw it. As if it had just reached the top of the ladder it had been climbing all night to get to my window, the grinning light of dawn arrived at the curtains and crept across the room to me. The light yelled in my face: 'Better luck tomorrow!' I heard the sound of the mechanics opening the trucks and vans and beginning their work. I had been awake the entire night.

Matt was still happily dozing, oblivious to the torment I had been going through on the other side of the room. I knew there was nothing I could do now, so I stood up and walked to the bathroom. What I saw in the bathroom mirror shocked me to my core: there in front of me was a hollow-faced old man.

It was time to do something that I had never done before. I slowly dressed myself in my horrible team-issue black and red tracksuit and shuffled down the corridor to find Marc Sergeant, the team manager. I walked out of the hotel to the bus where I knew the staff would be having a coffee, and there he was. It was immediately obvious to everyone that something was very wrong. As soon as I saw him I blurted out that I simply couldn't go on. Marc looked at me and didn't even attempt to talk me out of it. He just said, 'If you really don't think you can do it, then you can't do it.' Once he had spoken those words I knew it was all over. I still went through the formality of talking to the doctor, but his response seemed so typical of the Belgian doctors that I had worked with: 'Can't you just *try* to race?' I had been trying my damnedest for nearly ten days of the Tour de France; there was no trying left in me.

Word gets around a team quickly when a rider is sick or quits. Suddenly no one really knew how to treat me. It was as if someone had died. After breakfast, the riders filed out towards the bus where I was hovering, wishing I could disappear. But I couldn't. I was stuck with the team until someone could take me to an airport, and that meant hanging around at the race. Some of the guys seemed genuinely sorry for me and offered me a kind word and a pat on the back, but others avoided me like the plague (I literally was). I understood them, I knew what they were thinking: they were worried that I would infect them, not only with my virus but with my failure. A sick cyclist becomes toxic in the eyes of his teammates so quickly that it dehumanises him immediately.

We arrived at the *départ* and my teammates stepped off the bus and began talking to the press and fans. The whole excited circus of the Tour was carrying on without me as if nothing had ever happened. I tried not to look out of the mirrored glass at a group of excited Australian fans, wrapped in flags and carrying inflatable kangaroos. I felt the weight of guilt and shame pushing down on my shoulders. Guilt suppressed my feelings of illness. I forgot the state I was in, and I started to question just how ill I really was. Perhaps the doctor was right? Perhaps I should have just tried harder? To me, in reality it didn't matter how sick I was. Leaving like this was a disgrace. I was a quitter, a failure, and a hoax. I wanted to crawl into a hole in the ground as far away from the Tour de France as possible.

* * *

By the time I made it back to Finland and found myself lying on my back watching the clouds pass over the tops of the trees that July afternoon, I could feel that things had changed permanently. As I lay there I felt like my body was telling me something that my mind had been hinting at for a while. I was tired of exploiting myself physically; I felt like my body was a planet and I'd gorged all the crude oil out of it. I had mined my resources dry. It wasn't just the sickness, or even the monumental effort of riding three-week races, but it was the day-to-day of being a cyclist that had finally caught up with me.

I knew then that the drive that had sustained my career had ebbed. Throughout the summer that followed, I felt nervous. The pressurised engine that had propelled me forward in the world of cycling was now slowly spluttering to an end. It was as if throughout my entire life there had been a clock ticking loudly in the back-ground: it drove me to go out training in the rain, it pushed me to do another interval on a climb because I knew I could squeeze one more effort out of myself; it ticked relentlessly while I suffered in training … suffered at home … suffered in Italy. And then, suddenly, it stopped. The silence was deafening.

Throughout that summer I would continually return to the lake house. I needed to rebuild myself and it was the only way I knew how. I saw doctors and specialists about why I was so tired all the time, and no one could diagnose a specific problem. It felt like a period of limbo. I was stopping and starting – never knowing if anything was really wrong. I was desperate to be fixed, but I couldn't see what needed fixing. My mood swung with the amount of optimism I could muster. My day-to-day life was so calm and relaxed that I could often forget about my problems and start to feel better. But as soon as I started to train, the clouds formed on the horizon in my mind, as if my body knew that if I got fit I would have to leave the sanctuary of home again. I tried to go training but it was impossible; my body simply wouldn't allow it. I had to take so much food and so many energy gels with me because my body just couldn't deal with exercising. Food felt like it went straight through me without a single kilojoule of energy being absorbed from it. While diagnosis of my actual physical problem wasn't forthcoming, I decided that I had to work on my mental health. Going to the lake house seemed to me the ideal fix; it was energising to feel so alone that no one could come and get me.

At races the problem with noise had been obvious: it interfered with my sleep. A tired bike rider needs sleep to recover and I cherished my precious hours of rest, but hotels are noisy places; rarely are they exclusively filled with bike riders and considerate hushed guests. There always seemed to be weddings going on, or nightclubs next door, or parties of drunk and rowdy masseurs and race officials yabbering away by the team vehicles out in the car park. In the mornings doors in the corridor would slam and soon the unmistakable sound of tyres being inflated by a compressor would mark the dawning of a new day, full of the sounds of cars, helicopters, sirens, klaxons, questions, cheering and shouting.

But even away from the racing I felt I couldn't escape the noise. Italians lived their lives at such a volume that, instead of being bothered by it and asking someone to quieten down, they would just throw their own noise in to drown out the other sounds. The whole country dealt with noise the same way that they went about conversation – they just got louder and louder. In recent years I had noticed that the noise levels around my apartment were off the scale. There were screaming neighbours, dogs, car alarms, babies and even a fucking turkey that seemed so delighted to have survived being eaten on several successive Easters that she felt the need to gobble her head off with joy day and night.

One summer's day in 2009 the noise made me crack. I had come home from the Tour in my usual fragile state of mind and body, and in my exhausted state I was trying to catch up with some sleep in the afternoon, only to be awoken from my slumber by the infuriating buzzing of a hedge trimmer. I looked at my watch and saw that it was just after 3 p.m. I pulled back the blinds to see who the culprit was. I recognised the neighbour, who kept three hunting dogs in his backyard that yapped incessantly through the night. It was too much. I stormed out on to the balcony in my underwear and yelled as loud as I could: '*PORCO DIO!*' My neighbour spun around to catch sight of an emaciated man, with strangely defined tan lines all over his body, glaring right at him. He was so taken aback that all he could think to say as he looked at me nervously was, 'Me?'

'Yeah. YOU!' I replied, before realising quite how strange I must have looked and abruptly turned to go back inside. For whatever reason the escaped-lunatic look must have worked, because he was really friendly to me after that, and while the noise pollution continued his personal contribution was significantly lower from then on.

In Finland, though, it was all very different. Outside the lake house I took great pleasure in lying there and counting the seconds until I heard the sound of another human being doing something. I could count seemingly for hours and not hear a single trace of human activity.

I knew it wasn't just Italy, or any geographical location, it was the whole cycling world. Cycling was a cacophonous noise to me: the noise of my own gnawing ambition, perhaps, and the confusion of the life that I was leading had seemed to manifest itself in this unending din. Finally, in Finland, and in my home with Camilla, I had found a way to make the noise stop.

* * *

In the autumn the team asked me to return to competition at the Trittico Lombardo, a series of three one-day races that I knew well and were close to my old home near Varese. After a month and a half away from competition I had started to feel better. I was eating a little more food, but I still possessed a tiredness in my bones. The trouble for an athlete who has reached that stage is, you often lose perspective and can't tell what tired *is* any more: I asked myself every morning how I felt, and I told myself I felt tired. Every day, the same response.

People who have been around cyclists and who know cycling intimately can tell within a second of looking at a rider if they are in form or not – from their gait, their complexion and the colour of the whites around their pupils. When I arrived back in Italy to race my eyes were two tiny empty holes bored into my head, and instead of moving with the latent power of a professional athlete I shuffled about like a homeless man. When I saw Damiani for the first time since the Tour he virtually recoiled at the sight of me. He peered at me and asked, aghast, 'What's *wrong* with you?'

I had no written diagnosis from a doctor but I knew what was wrong with me: ten years of fatigue had walloped me at once; my body wasn't just tired, it had nearly stopped functioning, and the worse my body felt, the worse my mental state was.

The last of the three races, the Coppa Bernocchi, used to be a local race for me. I had raced it what felt like countless times; I knew it inside out. I used to enjoy riding it, not least because I could be sat back on my couch by late afternoon – some kind of semblance of normality. But as I sat on the back of the bus and we drove through the small towns on the way to the start that August Sunday morning, I looked out of the window and saw a middle-aged man walking out of a newsagent's with a paper under his arm. As we passed I could see him look up at the bus, and a smile of recognition shot across his face. He may not have known anything about who we were exactly, but he recognised the gleaming team bus plastered in stickers and the job that we did. I wondered if, just for a second, he wanted to be on that bus, to break free of the shackles of the mundane life I imagined for him. I had no idea what he might give to be in my place, but I did know one thing: at that moment I would have given anything to be where he was.

The time that I'd had to reflect during my convalescence had shown me something. I was at my lowest ebb physically, and my career had (as a result of my bad Tour de France) started to take an ominously downward trajectory. But what was really important was that I realised it wasn't the end of the world. The ticking sound of my ambition hadn't returned, even when I had come back to Italy. Being happy and having made a real home in Finland with Camilla removed the manic need to push myself so hard. I didn't have a point to prove any more. I looked around at my fellow team-mates, the riders that made up the peloton. There was no sign of the good, clean, 'noble' desire to achieve sporting excellence that people seemed to imagine was the driving force behind athletes. These finely tuned sportsmen were more often than not just fucked up. They were lost sons looking for their fathers, or desperately seeking acceptance from themselves or elsewhere. It is quite normal to love cycling, and to love racing bikes as a pastime, but to do it for a living was something else. There is nothing normal about a professional cyclist.

It isn't just the dedication. In a very simple way the amount of pain that a professional cyclist goes through, even on a normal day, far exceeds what most people would experience in their entire lives. As a racing cyclist you learn to live with pain. It isn't the same pain that someone who rides a bike for fun or for sport would feel, it is much deeper and much more scarring than that. The pain of being a professional isn't just that of exercising; it is exercising for performance. It is a pain that is branded into you, and you learn to live with pushing yourself physically and mentally to your absolute limits.

In the case of foreigners who weren't from countries where cycling is a part of the culture, the question as to why was multiplied tenfold. It's like a Finnish person going to do judo in Japan – why would you do it if everything was OK at home? There is nothing balanced or normal about people who need to achieve at that level.

My bizarre behaviour reflected an erratic life lived on the road: a life filled with pain, discomfort and, what I now realised had long been a feeling of bitterness. I had once laughed at my teammates' obsessive-compulsive behaviour but now I was obsessed with the room being as comfortable and as close to my home environment as possible. I travelled to races with my own pillow, and a tool kit to make sure that I could make the room as dark as was humanly possible – I always carried with me an array of eye masks and a pair of scissors and electrical tape. The first thing I would do when I walked into a room was to cover every single blinking LED light, every digital alarm clock display or any tiny crack of light behind a curtain or a blind, or even under the door. I had no idea that I had turned into a lunatic. As always, it took Camilla to point out just how strange my behaviour really was. As I packed up my black-out kit to go away to a race one morning, she calmly noted, with a shake of the head, 'You know, darling … that is not normal.' I looked back at her and couldn't help but laugh. It wasn't normal, but then I didn't lead a normal life.

Looking out of the window, I saw the grinning man disappear back off into his life that Sunday morning. I turned my head and looked back into the bus. I knew what was going to happen next. We'd pull into a car park full of people and I would begin to dread, even more deeply, the inevitability of dragging my exhausted body through the race. I would look back through the window at a group of cycling fans practically masturbating at the sight of the gigantic bus that was advertising snoring medication, and I wished with all my might I could be anywhere but there.

It was a deep feeling that was compounded by the dreadful sense of guilt that I had towards the fans who came to watch races. I knew there wasn't a soul in that car park who I could take by the arm to a quiet spot around the corner and say, 'I really hate what

I am doing … oh, and everyone on that bus is a fucking lunatic!' There were grown men in that car park who had successful careers, happy wives and children, and who probably spent more on their cycling holidays than I earned in half a year. They would happily have swapped everything to be able to do what I was doing. How could I communicate how I felt to anybody? In a way, I felt sorry for them: I could shatter their dreams if I explained the truth. But at the same time I was angry and sorry for *myself* because once upon a time it had been my dream too, and the reality felt so different now. I was so confused that my blood would boil. Was it my responsibility to tell people how it really was? Or should I just keep smiling, keep selling the dream? There was no way these people would ever be in my position anyway. I felt totally and utterly helpless.

I knew too that there was no one in the cycling world I could confide in. As a cyclist you spend so long dressing yourself up in a virtual suit of armour to defend yourself against attacks from all sides that dropping your guard and showing weakness to your colleagues would be unthinkable madness. And then everyone else I knew outside of the sport had seen me work so hard to get to where I was that they didn't really believe my protestations. I was stuck in a nightmare, with a mob of well-wishers pushing me towards a cliff. The more I protested, the more they thought I was encouraging them to keep going.

My life no longer felt like my own. Instead, it had started to resemble one of those public-service adverts from fifties' America, where the impossibly happy family presented an unhealthy and unattainable level of perfection. As cyclists we were involved in an incredible amount of advertising; and everything we did promoted us as happy, smiling, shiny examples of human brilliance on two wheels. I knew that to someone outside of that bus I looked the way that Malcolm Elliott had looked to me in 1990. I had become one of those shiny people, but inside it felt nothing like I had imagined.

On days like that, the feelings of helplessness turned to anger, and I was entirely convinced that I hated cycling. I hated cycling because of the gaping disparity between the way the sport looked on the outside, and what I knew to be the truth of it on the inside. I hated it because I had given my youth to it – so much of myself – and the payback was so meagre and fleeting, especially compared to those who took big risks and ignored the consequences. I hated it because I was so tired all the time, so tired that, from the age of 18 onwards, I couldn't tell when I was sad or just exhausted. And I hated it because I wasn't sure if I could really live without it.

Cycling defined me as a man, so what could I do after my professional career was over? It is the same for so many sportspeople the world over. No matter the sport and no matter the person, finishing a professional sporting career is a kind of death. Like mortality itself, you see the end coming, after a dwindling demise, but you have no idea what the afterlife will hold. As much as I knew that I wanted to walk the dogs on the weekend and buy the paper, I knew too that I couldn't *just* do that. But I wasn't sure what else there was for me. Cycling had me in its grip; me and my bike still needed each other, and this intricate dependence made me hate the bike and all it symbolised even more. Becoming a professional and doing what I loved for a living had forced me to live with this inevitable and strange contradiction. As I was drawing closer to the end, the balance was tipping. I wasn't done yet, but I was getting there.

CHAPTER 15

Vuelta a Asturias, Stage Five

I didn't even know if there was anybody up the road when I attacked. But, as I pressed on the pedals and looked ahead into the freezing gloom, I noticed with an excited alarm that there was no one between the finish line and me. I was the first rider on the road. I was alone in front, racing towards the win. This was it.

The 2011 Vuelta a Asturias was a tough race. Smaller and less renowned events were always hard. In the absence of clear favourites everyone saw their opportunity to grab a win, and this five-day stage race in the north-western region of Spain was no exception. The racing had been savage and unpredictable up until then, and the inclement weather had made things even tougher.

The first 170 km of the fifth and final stage since setting off from Lugones that morning had been so hard that when we came to the final climb of Alto del Naranco the race had been whittled right down to the strongest and most determined riders in the field. Earlier in the week I had suffered food poisoning caused by a meal served at our appalling hotel – so dubious a dish that we were unsure if it was fish or turkey. But, despite this setback, my form was good. The tiredness in my bones was still there, but it had relaxed its hold over me. My United Healthcare teammate Christian Meier was well placed overall, holding eighth position. The stage, and the race, were only five kilometres from their conclusion, but it was far from over. A group of riders had escaped on the twisting, undulating roads heading to the climb, and I knew that if Christian was going to get back into the race there was work to do ...

And so it was that I found myself in the action in that small Spanish race, riding for an American team almost by accident. I had very nearly ended up not racing in 2011 at all. In the autumn of 2010 I found myself at the mercy of some frustrating contract negotiations that followed my difficult summer. Only two years previously when I had signed my contract with Silence-Lotto I was in demand from all sides, but it seemed that those twenty-four months with the Belgian team had changed things dramatically, and now teams who were once forthcoming and honest were difficult to contact and refused to make commitments.

Despite my feelings of doubt towards the sport, I knew that the shambolic and sporadic attempts at racing in the autumn were no way to finish a career. I wanted at least one more year to put things right and to finish the job on my terms. The cycling world is as cruel and fickle as a tabloid newspaper. Finishing up when you decide to, and not when you are forced to, is the only dignified exit for an athlete. It is something that every rider wants, but few really get. I felt like I had honoured my profession, and I wanted my profession to honour me this way.

At first, finding a contract for 2011 hadn't seemed like it would present too much of a problem: in the spring of 2010 I had interest from the most surprising of places. Bradley Wiggins had previously contacted me about a potential move to Team Sky, the new outfit that British Cycling were setting up. I believed in Brad, and I have the utmost respect for him, and I would have really enjoyed riding for him, despite whatever had happened in the past between me and British Cycling.

Marc Sergent told Alex at the Tour that Lotto wanted to keep me on the same money, and that everything was fine for me to continue there. So, thinking that I was OK either way, I was still quite relaxed. Even if Sky did go cold – which it ultimately did – then I was safe with Lotto, or so I thought.

I had completely forgotten about my early exit from the 2009 Vuelta, but the management at Lotto obviously hadn't. In September 2010 I received an email from Lotto that said the words I had never had to read before: 'We will no longer be requiring your services.'

Disappointment after disappointment followed. Teams acted interested, only to pull out or stall at the last minute. It ground me down to a point where I knew I had to make a decision. I wanted another year, and there was an offer on the table from a small American team – United Healthcare. UHC wanted an experienced road captain to help their young American riders adapt to life in Europe. After genuinely enjoying playing my small part in mentoring Adam Blythe the previous season, I was attracted to the idea of passing my knowledge on to young riders. After some deliberation I decided that I would go for it. It felt nothing like the satisfaction of my two previous contracts, but I knew my options were thin on the ground. On the day I signed with the team that November, after hardly speaking a word through dinner, I looked over at Camilla and said, 'At the end of the day this gives us nine months of paid time to think about what to do in the future.'

The end was coming now, and I had finally accepted it. I had a year of racing ahead of me that I knew would be my last. Knowing that I was nearly done seemed to have calming effect on me. It was like a burden had been lifted; the big show was over and I was like a band coming back on stage for an encore. Each day that I went out on my bike that winter I was besotted with the simple pleasure of training. Becoming race fit after a break is like a change of season in your body, and I loved feeling that. I could feel the familiar sensations of fitness rising through the fibres of my muscles as, day by day, I became stronger. I enjoyed the feeling of being able to ride faster, and watching my body change as it got into shape. I loved to watch my numbers too: the mathematics of my work. I knew the figures that I needed to be competitive, and it was those figures that kept me motivated. The figures didn't lie, they didn't hassle me and they didn't betray me. They cleared out the junk from the world of cycling that was cluttering up my mind. Clarity is something that you don't often have as a cyclist: decisions are clouded by the desire to perform, and then are lost in the fog of fatigue. I felt no pressure any more, and despite the fact that UHC turned out to be a small and shambolic team, my new-found freedom was about to be unleashed.

• • •

As we made our way towards the conclusion of that final stage of the Vuelta a Asturias I was faced with a scene that was all too familiar from ten years spent in the professional peloton: an uphill finish and a gap to close. I knew exactly what I had to do. As soon as we hit the lower slopes of the climb I was itching to get going. I ramped up the pace as the gradient steepened and plunged myself into that familiar zone of discomfort. I felt good, my legs pushed hard, but my hands were relaxed. I didn't need to grip and wrench the bike towards me with my arms like I did when I struggled to make the pace; instead, I pushed the bike away from me with my legs. I found my pain threshold and I kept nudging at the edges of it to allow me to find more, to go faster. I could hear in my mind the delightful sounds of the elastic snapping behind me as rider after rider gave in to their own limitations. The climb was fast; as I came out of each of the hairpin bends I kicked as hard as I could with Christian right on my wheel. With three and a half kilometres to go our time check came through: 23 seconds.

The game in my head began. It was one I had played so many times before. I had to close that gap before the line. No matter how fast the escapees were going I had to go faster. It was a game I played blindly, always telling myself that they were going faster, and demanded of myself that I push harder. With two and a half kilometres to go the next check came through: 19 seconds. I was winning, but not by enough. I had to push harder still. Whatever speed they were doing I had to better it.

With a little over two kilometres to go we shot out of the trees and the mountain rose up ahead of us. I could finally see my prey. The game would get easier now, but it wasn't over. I had to dig in and give more. I could sense that Christian was on his limit behind me. I glanced back to see him tucked on my wheel, with only one other rider keeping us company. My pace had detonated the race.

Sucking in deeper and deeper the cold air that thinned around me, I lifted the pace once more. I had to get Christian back to the race leader if he was going to have a chance to go for the win. I had to lay it on the line.

I clawed back the inches between us like a man dragging himself to safety. For the next 1,000 metres I squeezed out everything, every ounce of energy I had. I timed my effort to perfection. As we passed under the 1 km banner, it was done. We made the junction and for the first time since the climb began I found myself on the wheel of another rider.

I had been so focused on catching this group that when we caught them suddenly my mind went silent. I had done my job. I had succeeded in my own eyes and in the eyes of my team manager and teammates who relied on me to play my part. There was no failure left to fear that day.

But I wasn't done. With only half a pedal revolution to recover, and without a single thought forming in my mind, pure instinct took over. With 800 metres to go I stood up out of my saddle and attacked.

The gap between myself and the group opened up in what seemed like an instant. I looked over my shoulder once and the group already looked smaller; I looked over a second time and they seemed to have disappeared. The gap grew so quickly that I began to doubt that I had attacked for the win. Maybe there was someone in front of me, and I was racing for second? But as I looked forward I saw the TV motorbikes were all focused on me. There was no one in front. I was the head of the race. A feeling came over me that had been hidden so deeply inside that I thought I had learnt to deny its very existence. I felt that heart-stopping realisation that I was going for the win.

There were 600 metres between that uncrossed finish line and my front wheel. I could see the barriers that lined the final twists and turns towards that line. I was so close. I realised then that I wanted to win a professional bike race more than anything in the world.

My heart had been bursting out of my chest. Now it seemed to bury itself deep down into my stomach. I could see the metre boards as I passed them: 500 metres to go. I was inside the final barriers on the run-in to the line. I could no longer think of anyone else. I liked Christian Meier and I enjoyed working with him, but this was mine. This was for me. I didn't need to impress my manager at UHC, I didn't need to impress Damiani, or Amadio or Stanga or another manager who I hoped might want me in his team the next year.

I had been at the sharp end of a race before and I had missed out every time. At the Vuelta Pays Basque, at the Tour de Suisse and at the Giro I had been in winning situations where someone, somehow had got the better of me, had outraced me. I knew that it was a weak rider who would say he is cheated out of anything, but I had swallowed those failures in the only way that allowed me to deal with the constant defeat; I had pushed them far away. I had ingrained it into my racing psyche that winning didn't matter to me, that it wasn't my role. I made myself so sensible and clinical that I persuaded myself that I didn't give a fuck. I had found other things that I considered to be successes and I had gone after them instead, telling myself I was happy with closing a gap, or hurting people's legs, and that it was enough that I was a professional cyclist without having to win races too. I had been like a jilted lover who couldn't

face committing to anyone again. With 200 metres to the line I realised that what my head had been coldly telling me for so long was
bullshit. I wanted to win. I *had* to win, and I was prepared to give
my all for it. By now, as I pushed on towards the line, my body was
contorted with pain. I weighed each pedal stroke; there was no part
of me that wasn't committed to getting my bike across that line first
and just once, after eleven years raising my arms in the air.

I was so close now that a feeling rushed up from inside me that
I hadn't known for over ten years. It was like someone had dusted
down my youth and handed it back to me. I was going to win. I
knew it now, as I threw every part of my body into pedalling, all
my composure gone. My physique, which I kept so perfect and
still when I raced normally, was now bent over the bike – shoulders
slumping from side to side and mouth gaping. I didn't care what I
looked like, or how I did it. I was going to win.

With 100 agonising uphill metres to go I suddenly felt that
horrible chill of shock you feel just before the phone rings with bad
news. I felt the fear pulse through me: the other riders. They were
suddenly almost inexplicably there. I heard them first, and then I
saw them – Constantino Zaballa and Javier Moreno, the two riders
who'd been in the break and whom I'd caught a kilometre earlier.
They rode straight past without even looking at me. I couldn't
believe it. As soon as they passed me I stopped pedalling. It was
over. Now, for all I cared, I could finish 80th or climb off my bike
without even crossing the line. It had been all or nothing.

Those two riders fought out the win and I crossed the line in
third feeling like I had just had my heart wrenched out of my chest.
I didn't know where to look or what to do. I slumped over my

handlebars and began to weep. It was too much. I had admitted to myself that there was no pride for me any more in being the rider who'd had a long, distinguished career but who'd never won a race. That was gone for ever now. I had exposed myself to thoughts that I'd hidden from myself for so long. I *did* want to win, and it *did* matter, and now I had to face it all.

As my emotions overwhelmed me it felt like the stitches on a wound had been torn open and everything poured out of me. I thought if I could have just won then it would all make sense: my whole career rounded off with a nice win at the top of a famous climb. It would make sense of the shit that I'd eaten through the winter, being kicked around by teams; it would make sense of eleven years of races I'd started with no intention of working for myself; the countless races where I'd turned inside out to be there in the finale, only for my leader not to even need me; the days away from my wife, the time away from my family, and the life I'd had to live to be a professional cyclist. It would have made sense of a long career of servitude, because it would have been *mine*, my personal triumph. It would have been one photograph I could put in a frame: me crossing the line a winner; cycling's gift back to me. But it didn't happen. At that moment, as I sobbed into my hands and the tears mixed into the sweat and filth of the dirty roads that covered my face, I knew the truth about professional cycling: it's no fucking fairytale.

Acknowledgements

For all the help received during his career and for assistance with this book, Charly would like to thank:

Camilla and Emil

My mother and her poor 1 litre Bordeaux red Ford Fiesta

Aldo Sassi

Mapei Sport staff

Zanini family

Mike and Pat Taylor

Ken Matheson

John Herety

Tim Buckle and George Ellis

All the mechanics and soigneurs that ever ran around after me

Jonathan Vaughters and Slipstream sports

David Luxton

The fucking lawyers

For help with the writing of this book Tom would like to thank:

Georgie

My old man

Ma'

Basia Lewandowska Cummings (editor)

All those in the cycling world who helped out with memories, recollections and conversations to help this book get going

All those in the writing world who offered encouragement from the word go

Kilgore Trout

Jane Wegelius

Camilla

And most of all, Charly – thank you for your trust and patience . . . Also, sorry about breaking your sink and crashing your car . . .